HYPERWORLDS, UNDERWORLDS

JASON LOUV

ULTRACULTURE

Other Books by Jason Louv

QUEEN VALENTINE
MONSANTO VS. THE WORLD

(as Editor)

GENERATION HEX
ULTRACULTURE
THEE PSYCHICK BIBLE

© 2015 Ultraculture Incorporated.

Published by Ultraculture Incorporated
www.ultraculture.org
ultraculturegate@gmail.com

All rights reserved.

No part of this publication may be reproduced or transmitted in any form or by any means, electronic or mechanical, including photocopying, recording, or by any information storage and retrieval system, without permission in writing from the author. Reviewers may quote brief passages.

ISBN-13: 978-1503396999

10 9 8 7 6 5 4 3 2 1

Ultraculture is a trademark of Ultraculture Incorporated.

For Chelsea Manning

The symbols are not magic charms,
But new angles to know the self from.
There is no goal but to know self
Which is to be awake
But fall asleep
And you will see only the symbols
And lash out at those who bear different symbols
And such is the history of humanity
The asleep killing the asleep
Dreaming faces long forgotten.

Acknowledgements

Thank you to my parents, Devi Brule, R. U. Sirius, Kelly McKay, Gea Philes, Suzanne Baran, Shushana Djavaheri, Jon Graham, Roland Frauchiger, Carl Abrahamsson, Woody Evans, Vincent Baeza, Howard Bloom, Buzz Aldrin, Jude Evans, Lana Popovic, Brian Merchant, Season Cole, Denny Sargent, Marty Beckerman, Dennis Woo, Duncan Trussell, Mark Frauenfelder, KyHenderson, Andrei Burke, Vinay Gupta, Donald Michael Kraig, Alex Pasternack, Derek Mead, Thomas Negovan, Phil Eichenauer, and everybody who helped directly or indirectly in the writing of the many articles contained herein.

CONTENTS

Foreword by R. U. Sirius

Hail to the Broken-Tusked Elephant Lord
Introduction: The Upturned Rock of Western Civilization, and What I Found There

I. THE APOCALYPSE IS CANCELLED

The Three Keys to Species Survival
On Becoming a Conscious Creator of Reality: Mastering the Stages of Self-Determination
We Deserve a Future: Circumventing the Horrors of the 21st Century
Leave Earth to Save Earth: The Survival of Our Species Comes at the Cost of Our Illusions

II. THE SEXUAL DELIGHTS OF FASCISM

The Two Great Lies
Soft-Sell Slavery
Meet the Planet-Murdering Sociopaths Bankrolling Climate Denial
Zbigniew Brzezinski vs. Global Awakening
We the People are Tired and Cold
From Fast Apocalypse to Slow Apocalypse
A Federal Court Approved Chevron's Request for Activists' Data
When the CIA Got Busted Selling Crack
The NSA Has Set Up Shop at the US Embassy in Mexico
The Trans-Pacific Partnership Could 'Establish a War of All Against All'
Slave Children Used by Major Corporations to Make Chocolate
The Dalai Lama Will Not Return to Tibet (He Has Something Better in Mind)

Germany Condemns "Illegal Killings," Halts All Purchases of American Drones
Insanity: Female Inmates Forcibly Sterilized in California Prisons
The Long Tail of America's Eugenics Problem
When Monsanto Had Its Own Disneyland Exhibit
Mexico Just Won a Major Victory Against Monsanto
Why Neil deGrasse Tyson is Dead Wrong About GMOs
Every Person on Earth is Polluted With Hundreds of Human-Made Toxins
Scientist Threatened and Stalked for Findings on Syngenta Herbicide
Thanks to Dredging and Coal, the Great Barrier Reef Is More Threatened Than Ever

III. BEAUTIFUL OUTSIDERS

How America Interrupted Wilhelm Reich's Orgasmic Utopia
Paramahansa Yogananda, and the Legacy of India's Quest to Enlighten America
Buckminster Fuller's Vision of Enough for Everyone
Colin Wilson, Grandfather of the Occult, 1931-2013
Judee Sill, the Rosicrucian Folk Singer That Time Forgot
James Dallas Egbert III: The Dungeon Master
Robert Anton Wilson's Cosmic Trigger, and the Psychedelic Interstellar Future We Need
It's Aleister Crowley's Birthday
The Beast in Berlin
For Lady Jaye Breyer P-Orridge
Chelsea Manning is Dying for Our Sins

IV. LOST IN THE FILTH KALEIDOSCOPE

California Screaming: Los Angeles' Culty Weirdness
In Memoriam: Arthur Magazine, 2002-2011

Lost in the Filth Kaleidoscope
In the Valley of the Porn Witches
Lady Gaga and the Dead Planet Grotesque
Brooke Candy, 'Opulence,' and the Work of Integrating the Shadow
Die Antwoord's 'Pitbull Terrier' and Occult Social Control

V. TRANSHUMANISM AND OTHER BAD IDEAS

Imagine! The Metropolis of Tomorrow!
I Am a Mechanical Man: Robocops and Robowars
Get Up Make Love: 21st Sentury Space Sexploration
Dementing Augmented Reality: How Future Activists Will Break People Out of Their Digital Trances
The Headset Revolution Will Be a Blizzard of Conflicting Realities—If it Happens, That Is
Will Smart Drugs and Cybernetics Create a Superhuman Workforce?
Extraterrestrial Intelligence
Wal-Mart Mutants: Welcome to Aisle 23
There is No Singularity. Welcome to the Multiplicity.

VI. TRANSPERSONAL TACTICS

The Freedom of Imagination Act
On Compassion
11 Secrets for Witch House Kids
Looks Like All's Well in Ayahuasca-Land, Then
A Divine Invasion
Why Does ISIS Consider the Yazidi 'Devil Worshippers'?
The Man of Earth and the Lord of War
The 8 Circuits of Reality
The World is a War Between Competing Stories About You
The Chaos Matrix: Back in Thee Day
Sutras for Satyrs

The Fox
You Want to Watch What You Say
An Interview With Jason Louv

VII. INHUMAN RESOURCES

Letter to a Student on the Day of Enrollment in the Academy
Conjurations in the Element of Flesh
An Oneironaut's Guide to Lucid Dreams
The Wizard Way of Bro Science
How to Make an Orgone Accumulator Blanket
Brion Gysin's Dream Machine: Build Your Own Portal to Inner Visions
Commandeering the Inner Space Shuttle
On the 8 Limbs of Yoga
3 Books to Take With You on a Psychedelic Voyage
10 Ways to Protect Yourself From NLP Mind Control
9 NSA-Defying Tools for Anonymous Browsing
How to Be Your Own Media Gatekeeper
The Western Esoteric Tradition—The World's Most Misunderstood Spiritual Path
Start Your Own McMansion Empire
5 Ways to Get Inner Peace
Learning to Let Go

Foreword
By R. U. Sirius

Fellow Mutants and ever-loving mindblowers, this is your book for 2015. Jason Louv's *Hyperworlds, Underworlds* is *now*.

Louv situates himself in the current (in all senses of the word) and, with both unyielding clarity and far vision, brings us a series of important intelligence reports about how our material and neurological/spiritual crises and our humane posthuman potentialities challenge us to live and act with a cheerful and life-affirming integrity.

Having earned his bonafides in the surreal funhouse of chaos magick, Louv capably smuggles the wisdom of our Founding Fathers—Crowley, Burroughs, Gysin, Gurdjieff, Leary and Wilson—into our repressed and surveilled present, bringing along his own original and hard won insights and applying it all to our street level concerns about politics, the environment, the virtualization of everything and just what the hell Die Antwoord is trying to tell us.

With 360° vision and a well integrated combination of journalism and poetic prose, *Hyperworlds, Underworlds* looks out at the past, present and future. It takes on environmental/political/psychological collapse; the outsider wisdoms of countercultural forerunners like Wilhelm Reich and folksinger Judee Sill; the filthy kaleidoscopic online world of 4Chan; the dark (or perhaps, vacant) side of robotic transhumanism; the new upsurge of Virtual Reality; a hopeful rejuvenation of Timothy Leary's SMI^{2}LE (Space Migration, Intelligence Increase, Life Extension) platform for an expansive future and much more.

Complete with recommendations for techniques for remaining conscious and compassionate (one of those recommendations being not to get arrogant about how much more aware you are than *those* people), *Hyperworlds, Underworlds* is at once a playful and earnest bulletin from one of humanity's best mutant scouts on the frontiers of human experience. From Louv's vantage point, we can see how close to the gates of hell we are now lingering but also how close we are to exciting, adventurous and ecstatic transmutations of our human-transhuman condition.

All this and a prayer to Ganesha. As Wavy Gravy said at Woodstock in 1969, "I must be in heaven man!"

R. U. Sirius is a writer, editor, talk show host, musician and elder statesman of the counterculture. From 1989 to 1993, his legendary magazine Mondo 2000 played a major role in catalyzing the online revolution and pointed the way to a utopian, post-scarcity, post-human future. He has written for Wired, the San Francisco Examiner, Artforum International, Rolling Stone, Time and Esquire, and ran for president in 2000 under the banner of the Revolution Party. @stealthissingul

hail to the
broken-tusked
elephant lord

One-tusked alabaster god
Sat in resplendent fury
In the halls of the mind
Eternal incense smoldering
Pre-cyclopean and justified
I called you and you answered
You who wrote my bedtime story
Have rewritten it again and again
Each time I fall asleep
And then awaken
Destroy the monsters under the bed
Destroy bad magic and those who practice it
Destroy the obstacles I create for myself
Destroy my mistakes
Destroy my conditioning
May there be
No obstacles to consciousness
No obstacles to love
No obstacles to the body
No obstacles to the truth
God is Great
And there you have hung upon my wall through every incarnation
Unchanging and watching through every incarnation
Through every world and reality you are
Ganesha Lord of Obstacles
Lord of the Path
Scribe of Eternity
Elephant God
One-Tusked
Dutiful Son
Master of Paths
Keep my path lit and open
Behold his mighty form
Aum Gung.

Introduction: The Upturned Rock of Western Civilization, and What I Found There

This book collects the best of my online writing, primarily journalism, from the years 2005-2014, largely focusing on 2012-14.

Most of the material was either written for my own blog (*Ultraculture*) or for the various online outlets I was submitting work to—*Boing Boing, VICE News, Motherboard, Humanity Plus* and several others.

While assembling the material into one book, the unifying theme became clear: It's a record of the end of the world. And a record of the beginning of a new one, as well.

More specifically, the articles in this book relentlessly chronicle the fringes of Internet culture, as a way of getting an outsider's perspective on the final stages of the transition of America from a manufacturing hub and into a node in the corporate, globalized world, with the old models of democracy giving way to a new kind of feudalism—with multinational and technocratic interests firmly entrenched at the top of the pyramid.

This transition, which has been an ongoing shift for decades but which seemed to lock fully into place during the Obama presidency, consists of the following trends:

1. Late-stage globalization, and the irrevocable ascension of multinational corporations above nation states on the global totem pole;

2. The constant connection of the thoughts of the majority of human beings on Earth via broadband and mobile Internet, the increasing use of these networks for population monitoring and policing, and the tendency for individual citizens themselves to mirror this by policing each other;

3. The robotification of war;

4. The application of "Big Data" and the data-driven mindset to nearly every human endeavor, including the managing of populations;

5. The complete collapse of all established social models, and of the human personality itself, in the face of this electronic intermeshing and the shift from print to memetic media.

This is the future that was predicted by Zbigniew Brzezinski—the geostrategist behind Presidents Johnson, Carter and Obama—in *Between Two Ages: America's Role in the Technotronic Era*, published in 1970.

"The instantaneous electronic intermeshing of mankind will make for intense confrontation, strained social peace," the young Brzezinski wrote, before going on to help engineer such strategic moves as SALT II, normalizing relations with China and arming the mujahideen fighters that became the Taliban. "The technotronic era involves the gradual appearance of a more controlled society. Such a society would be dominated by an elite, unrestrained by traditional values. Soon it will be possible to assert almost continuous surveillance over every citizen and maintain up-to-date complete files containing even the most personal information about the citizen. These files will be subject to instantaneous retrieval by the authorities."

Brzezinski's prediction has become literal reality, as first suggested by Julian Assange and others and then fully confirmed in 2013 by Edward Snowden. We are now coping not just with the psychic shock of global electronic media, but the shock of how quickly state and corporate control have metastasized to utilize these systems.

Our modern, digitized, covertly controlled world resembles, perhaps, the Tower of Babel, written of in Genesis 11:1-9—a towering city in which all humans speak the same language, built to stretch to Heaven and challenge God himself. This Tower of "Babble" (or Tower of Google) is where we now find ourselves, lost and confused in the din.

Perhaps rarely among journalists, I have not kept my geopolitical research constrained to dry, materialistic coverage of politics, conflict and technological advance. These are only the visible manifestations of the forces that move our world. Beneath these lie the vast glaciers of belief and faith, territory which is generally ignored by working journalists and which subsequently leaves a blind spot in understanding geopolitics.

We've been using the Web for 20 years, personal computers for 30, oil and synthetic narcotics for 150—and a good deal of online journalistic copy relates directly or indirectly to these subjects, as they are the flashpoints for capitalism. However, human beings in all cultures have been constructing their lives and worldviews based on the yearning for the transcendental since the beginning of thought and language, and religious belief, examined or unexamined, still drives the majority of humanity, no matter how many Apple or Samsung gadgets we acquire. Because of this, I have found a gonzo approach to spirituality—deeply immersing myself in the spiritual traditions of as many world cultures as I've been able to—critical in formulating a more comprehensive geopolitical model.

Simply put: Religions are the scripts that cultures operate on. Just because the *de facto* religion of the media elite of the West is technology, materialistic science and progressivism doesn't mean that the rest of the world shares this view, and this leaves most media workers cloistered in their ivory towers when it comes to actually understanding people.

Around 2009, I came to a demarcation point in my personal spiritual journey, the early stages of which were chronicled in my edited anthologies *Generation Hex, Ultraculture Journal* and *Thee Psychick Bible*. An initial teenage and early 20s fascination with Hermeticism, Qabalah and Gnostic Christianity had transformed into a very deep and meaningful practice of first Sufism, and then esoteric Hinduism and Buddhism. In this, I recapitulated much of the spiritual progress of the Baby Boomer generation, but deep contact with Eastern societies led to an almost total disinterest in Western culture. I no longer particularly cared about the psychopathology of the West and its constant Babble, and the constant jockeying for Internet, literary or art world status I saw my peers and mentors engaged in. You cannot spend time watching children die of starvation in India, or sitting at the feet of enlightened Himalayan yogis, and continue to care about the mass media rat race. I don't necessarily credit any particular spiritual form with this: I think that deep and real practice of any spiritual path will turn you away from the material and towards the eternal.

I wanted only peace, to annihilate myself in meditation. Like those who left the West to follow the Hippie Trail in the 60s, I wanted an escape from my society and its sickness. I stopped being a writer, and became a spiritual seeker instead—a non-person, in simple white clothes, crying at the side of the Ganges.

But it was not to be—not forever. In 2009 I came down from the mountain, and was thrust back into the Babble. Rather than rarified meditation in shrines 13,000 feet up in the Himalayas, I set up shop in Los Angeles, one of the most inwardly filthy places on Planet Earth. Like the Hindu adepts who meditate in graveyards and cremation grounds, I began rebuilding my writing career in a burning ground of absolute ego pollution.

I now found myself consumed with a new game: Snapping the spine of fascism.

Like the journalistic protagonist of Iain Banks' *Complicity*, there I sat, for years, writing, loading myself with obscure chemicals, browsing 4Chan and RSS feeds, playing video games to distract myself from The Horror and constantly, constantly, constantly mapping and charting man's inhumanity to man.

Meanwhile, everything around me was crumbling. The economy, the publishing industry, journalism, the environment, the souls and minds and hearts of the masses. It's like the sign I held up at Occupy: "They poison our water, food, land, air, hearts, minds and dreams." And it's like the deep message of Buddhism: Everything dust.

The bulk of this book, then, represents my scan of the potential dystopian futures for Western civilization: Corporate feudalism, the implicit possibility of genocide in the face of overpopulation, transhumanism, mass exodus into virtual realities, mass adoption of vague and ultimately hollow "New Age" religions, electronic policing, drone warfare and several more. Each of these futures represents a rock I have found in the garden of the West and lifted up to inspect. Where necessary, I have pointed to each of the poisonous beetles and scorpions underneath these rocks, or even suggested how to crush them. In many places, I have suggested better, more utopian alternatives.

While the articles in this book cover a large number of seemingly contradictory subjects (juxtaposing articles on trade policy and technology, for instance, with ones on spiritual practice), they are united by this common impulse: The destabilization of totalitarianism and dehumanization, and the re-imposition of basic human dignity and freedom.

I have come to many conclusions, explored throughout this book. Broadly, they are:

1. Space expansion is critical to the long-term survival of the human race. If the human population hits the global carrying capacity of 10 billion without a route off-world, population-checking by genocide or pandemic is inevitable. This makes space funding more important than ever.

2. An Internet controlled by Facebook, Google and the NSA has been an absolute disaster for human intellectual freedom. Electronic media is becoming as centralized and monopolized as print media was in the 1990s, and this must be reversed or superseded. This makes true journalism more important than ever.

3. We are experiencing desertification on all planes, and the degradation of the imagination and spirit is as serious of an issue as the degradation of the environment. This makes true art more important than ever.

4. Humanity has an absolute need for a real spiritual connection to the world of eternal forms, cycles and structures. The increasing tendency to replace real spirituality, of whatever cultural form, with materialism, faddish occultism or vapid New Age-ism is a serious public health issue. This makes true spirituality more important than ever.

5. Western societies currently control their citizens with a permissive instead of an authoritarian model, misdirecting their constituents away from the serious issues by constantly accentuating their generosity in allowing token social freedoms. This has turned America, in particular, into a kind of mash-up of Disneyland and Auschwitz. Because I have consistently attacked this confusing double-approach, I have at times come across almost monstrously in public. What sane person would attack the wonderful social freedoms we're given, after all? Simple: The kind of person who sees the iron fist in the velvet glove.

Throughout this book you will find several approaches to these problems. None of them are meant as final answers or political screeds; they have all been formulated as commercial Web journalism or entertainment, rather than humorless manifestos.

It's my hope that this book forms a record not just of this transitional period in the history of consciousness but also of my own transitional period as a writer, as I rejected my early successes to consistently hack at my craft and begin digging for a deeper intellectual analysis than the occultural approach I took in my early books. This book represents a chunk of my "10,000 hours," a la Malcolm Gladwell, and as a result contains a wide spectrum of experimental work. I hope you find gems to inspire, inform or even provoke you to outrage if need be. Enjoy as you will!

Jason Louv, Los Angeles, October 2014

I
THE APOCALYPSE IS CANCELLED

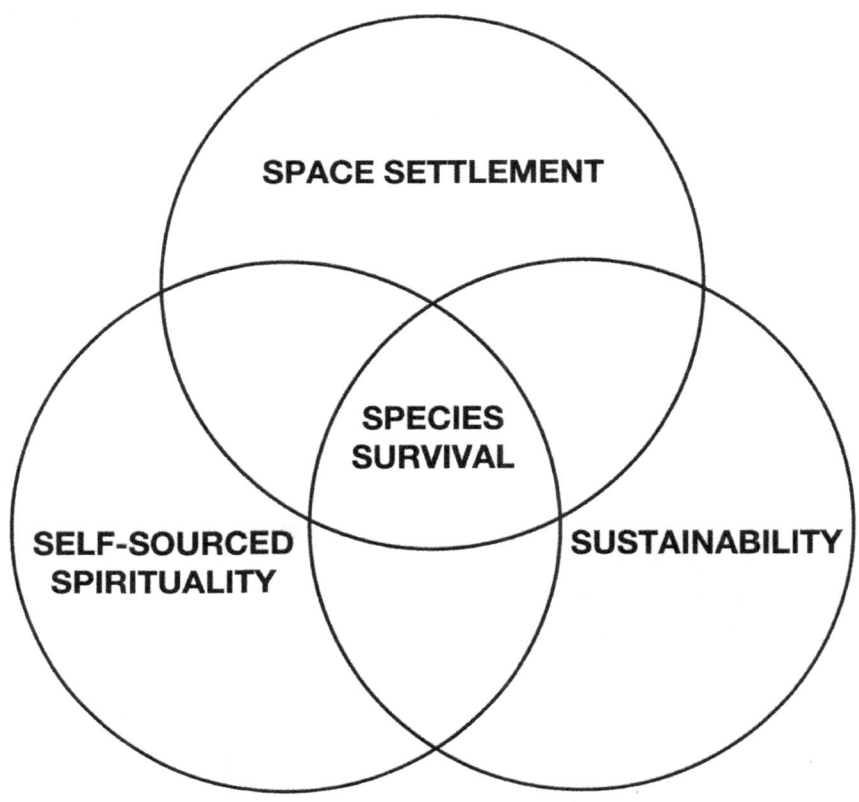

The Three Keys to Species Survival

I believe that life can work, and that life can be an adventure. And I want a participatory dialogue on how to get there.

I want a comprehensive vision of the future for a generation that's rejecting the unethical and unsustainable dreams of 20th century hypercapitalism, and looking to create a lifestyle that brings happiness instead of self-destruction. We want sustainable lives with the freedom to make our own meaning instead of being slaves to the machine, tied to credit and student loan debt. We want to take up the adventure of living instead of drowning in numb hypnosis.

I'm looking for backroads around the apocalypse, and I'm building neon signs to them. And as demonstrated in the diagram above, I believe that the three major keys to species survival are self-sourced spirituality, sustainability and space settlement.

To break that down:

Self-sourced spirituality sounds very loaded but, in its simplest form, is the belief that individuals should be able to learn about the universe and their place in it through self-directed study, discipline and logical experiment instead of being force-fed dogmatic imprints.

Sustainability goes beyond just environmentalism and is the effort to keep the biosphere—humans, animals and plants—not only alive, but healthy.

Space settlement is the funneling of efforts into public and private space efforts to make sure that the human race expands beyond the confines of Earth before it loses the resources to do so.

Put in another way, we need:

1. *The universal rights of humanity*. Human beings have the right to have their basic needs met. We have the means to do so for all on Earth; that we are not doing so is criminal. The ability to pursue and create truth is also a fundamental human right, as or perhaps more important even than basic survival needs. All must be free to pursue truth free of political, spiritual and sexual fascism.

2. *The sustainable existence of humanity*. Green and sustainable energy. This likely means that we will have to adjust our lifestyle, because there's no way we're going to keep our current rate of energy consumption going. But then again, many of the dehumanizing excesses of our culture are making us miserable anyway.

2. The ongoing expansion of humanity. Space travel. It's the only way we're going to get more resources and more living space for an expanding population. It's also a primary way we can re-instill pride and a sense of purpose in our species. Science fiction has been telling us this for over a hundred years, and first NASA and now private space firms have begun to make it a reality.

This is a start. I hope you'll help me continue to develop, learn and expand as I ask the question "where next?"

The following three essays will develop the above three ideas in greater depth.

I. Self-Sourced Spirituality

ON BECOMING A CONSCIOUS CREATOR OF REALITY:
Mastering the Stages of Self-Determination

Initiation is the process of ceasing to be a passive subject of reality and of becoming a conscious creator within that reality.

It is the hard path. The path less taken. The rewarding path. The often fatal path. The free path.

Here's how to self-will that process in five steps.

1. Start With the Body

Get and stay healthy. Exercise. Eat right. This is the step that so many skip, and which comes back to haunt them later. The body and mind are inseparable; don't make the mistake of dividing them.

The body is the cursor of your existence, the tip of the iceberg, and the easiest part to change. Positive changes made to the body have a compound effect on the rest of life. Start here. If you can change your physicality, you'll have a surplus of energy to use in the rest of your life and automatically open new doors. You'll be a more positive person. People will respond to you differently. This is true, lasting consciousness alteration.

Energy work, breath work and other modalities for changing the body can be excellent here but nothing short-cuts the basic, common-sense steps of exercise and diet. Yoga can be excellent for some, though not enough for others.

2. Meditate

Start an insight-based meditation practice. The varieties are endless, but simple is often best. Learn how to sit still. Learn how to breathe deeply and naturally. Sit and watch your thoughts without judgement or clinging. Let them pass through and waft away without grabbing for them. Start at ten minutes a day. Aim for an hour a day if you can. Half an hour is fine. But do it every day, like brushing your teeth. There is no single practice which will improve your life and outlook more.

3. *Learn How to Change the Story*

Who you are and what the world is are a series of carefully crafted and nested stories that were created long before you were born, will likely long outlive you, and which you will be a subject of as long as you don't consciously examine them. With the strong foundation you've built from exercise (self-directed change) and meditation, start looking at your life objectively. Ask yourself where you're complicit in other people's stories. If you like them, stay in those stories. If you don't, don't. You're not bound to any of it, though remember that if you want to get rid of the bad aspects of something you'll probably have to lose the good aspects, too.

The story of who you are, were, will be: you don't have to accept any of this. If you want, bypass selective editing and let the whole thing go. All of it. Stay on the blank page as long as you want; then write a new story if you like. Just remember that you'll have to write in roles for other people that they like if you want others to play along.

The more that you meditate, the more you let go of external determination, the more that you will keep coming back to yourself—your own simple presence, being, breath. Note that this would be why we started with step one.

But also note that "externally imposed" doesn't necessarily mean "bad." You may, in fact, already be living in the Best of All Possible Worlds. Your aim should simply be to bring every facet of your life into explicitly conscious awareness. More awareness = more freedom to choose what happens next.

4. *See the Others*

True initiation happens when you stop giving your power away to others—gods, masters, saviors, messiahs, groups, relationships, addictions, corporate ideas, media figures, mythologies, stories, ideologies—and give it back to yourself. There's a reason why you probably haven't been doing that: It's terrifying. It means taking responsibility for your own life and systems of meaning in the face of meaninglessness—but them's the breaks. It's called growing up. Put yourself on the spot.

Now take another look at the people around you, remembering that you are no different than anybody else. In fact, you are less than them in some ways now: you've shed some illusions and possibly some of the support that came along with them. If you want to leave your cave, you've got to deal with the woods.

The people around you are the same consciousness, the same will-to-power that you are. They're unconsciously moving within largely inherited behaviors and stories that they have consciously chosen because those keep them safe. Let go of that stuff, and you won't be safe—and people may well respond to you as something that is Not Safe. But you will be (more) free. Free to move as you will, join up with new stories as you will, create new stories as you will—with no guarantees. Leave the others be. Do not attempt to drag them with you. Do not attempt to divest them of their illusions, unless they ask. Respect them and the lives they are choosing to live with the same consciousness you are. Or they may make your life, quite literally, a living hell.

5. *Face the World*

The more self-determined you become, the more and stranger opportunities you will be given to take new paths. You can stay in the self-gratification loop, which is fine, or you can take a look at the world-as-it-is and ask yourself one simple question: How can I help?

It's probably not how you think you can. Or maybe it's exactly how you think you can. But, put simply, you can take off your fetters and kind of hang around loitering, or you can use your new freedom to walk to the place you know your efforts will assist other beings the most. Ask yourself "With the talents and tools I have, what is the optimal life I can lead to assist the greatest number of people?" Or, if you're more fatalistic, "What is the life I was meant to live?"

Good luck. The Final Secret of the Illuminati is this: Show up. There's no shortage of need for free pairs of hands to chop wood and carry water.

II. Sustainability

WE DESERVE A FUTURE: Circumventing the Horrors of the 21st Century

Overpopulation. Resource scarcity. These are the problems that underly all the wars, plagues, famine and, in many cases, disease. I believe that, ultimately, we will be faced with only two solutions to these problems: to get more resources and places for people to live, or to get less people. Space migration or genocide.

Encouraging the first, and averting the second, will require progress towards a more cohesive, unified world. The only way to function as a space-going race, or to circumvent the persistent "Othering" which allows for the dehumanization that makes genocide possible is, I believe, to function as a World Group. Our current divided system allows wheat to rot in the fields while millions starve. It allows the cosmic destiny of mankind to go untapped while government teams build billion-dollar parts for spacecraft which will never be assembled, simply to justify their funding. We can do better. We need a form of global cohesiveness that will work for individuals, not against them.

We need a One World Community. Not a one world government—which would imply fascist centralization of power—but a collaborative linking of global citizens increasingly able to see the world as a single system and work across the false political, racial and religious boundaries of the last millennium. Who are able to collaborate in maintaining a life-supporting world, in all senses of the word "life," in real time.

Theodore Roszak's Ecopsychology suggests that there can be no true assessment of the symptomology of a patient without seeing the patient as a microcosm, a holographic splinter of the world, and that the true healing of an individual can and must begin with a healing of the world that they live in; their larger, extended self. (From a more limited ideological perspective, we can see echoes of this in the SPK or Socialist Patients' Collective, the West German therapy group that, inspired by the 1968 student revolutions, declared that the REAL underlying psychological issue affecting the supposedly individual pathologies of patients was the inherent contradictions of late capitalism.)

Individuals able to think of the world as a single coherent system, and able to think beyond all false boundaries and dichotomies that, in truth, only exist as modularities within that system, are going to be increasingly needed. We are weighted with the outmoded dreams of dead men and dead systems, walking-corpse institutions and undead, blood-sucking ideologies long past their expiration date which yet haunt the planet, entrapping the joy of the living within the dead ribcage walls of their rotting, false order, and which direly need a stake through the heart simply because they are no longer relevant.

Yet as persistent as they can be, these old models are failing and falling all around us. We are called to create new ones, new models, new approaches to living that can make meaning from the world as it is, not as it was. We need new models for seeing the totality of the world system, for making sense of our growing exposure to information, for the ever-accelerating way in which we witness events happening in the world. We need new ways of assessing and utilizing our resources. We need new ways of co-existing with each other, of building community, of connecting and collaborating.

The alternative is to continue on the path we are already on, to the logical conclusion of globalization as it currently functions.

I have a persistent and troubling image of a potential future for our race that I can't quite seem to shake—as overpopulation increases and the dehumanizing abuses of the globalists continue, I can see a time in which human beings live in conditions not much different from the way we keep feed animals now. Imagine yourself growing up in a ten-by-ten pen, fed on sedatives and antibiotic drips to keep the sores now growing on your body due to close confinement from killing you, or to slow the spread of the pandemics sure to arise from such a situation. It's the condition we see fit to impose upon the mammals just below us on the tree of life and, after all, you are what you eat.

Imagine yourself growing up attached to a computer, farming data for your corporate overlords, lost in the pornographic virtual realities produced to keep you complacent just as prostitutes were kept on the payroll by companies to keep miners, railroad workers and other large-project manual laborers from revolting in the 19th and early 20th centuries.

Imagine being born into wide-scale camps little different from the corporate prisons that currently dot the landscape of the United States, but that nobody talks about—hells into which illegal immigrants and drug users are de facto disappeared and converted to slave labor for corporations like Sodexho-Marriott. Just under the surface veneer of America, this is what already lurks: factory farms; corporate prisons; the uncomfortable truth that slavery never ended, it just got sneakier. The uncomfortable truth, especially post-NDAA, that this may be what they have planned for all of us.

Such, I fear, is the dream of the elites: the ability to tag, sedate, transport, and utilize human beings as resources in much the same way that we currently use cattle. Watch how the corporate elite—Monsanto, for instance—treat crops and animals. You think they see human beings any differently? They've already begun to execute plans to cull the herd, to slowly weaken, poison and decimate our ranks with chemical additives and pesticides as surely as the native tribes were wiped away with smallpox blankets. The Codex Alimentarius, there for all to see. Or consider the voluntary surveillance system called Facebook, or the monthly bill you pay for the iPhone that slowly gives you brain cancer while it tracks your every movement. This is what they want: A mechanized planet with no humanity or compassion, only Production. A concentration camp world, slowed down so you don't notice what's happening to you; mashed up with Disneyland so you don't care.

Perhaps (one hopes) this is more of a persistent fear than an impending reality, a "monster under the bed," a shadow mythology that stands as a signpost marked "do not go here." Either way, we would do well to heed the signpost.

Our world is unifying. We have a choice of doing so with brute force, as is currently being done, or doing it with intelligence, wisdom and compassion. To begin to drop the shells we have built around ourselves and reach out to each other, or to further calcify in mutual fear and distrust to the point that our shells become prisons, quite literally. In the face of the Machine, of annihilation, we are tasked with re-centering our world on our humanity, our humane-ity.

We deserve a future. It is so easy to lose hope, to become entrenched in the self-loathing that can infect and corrode so quickly. Yes, we have done terrible things, all still fresh in our memory. Yes, we continue to do terrible things. But it is all too tempting to allow the will-to-annihilation to neutralize us. To, unconsciously or not-so-unconsciously, hold to the belief that, whatever horrors await us in the 21st century, we deserve them. That perhaps we should be wiped out as a species, since we cause nothing but pain to the world that bore and which bears us.

This is one of the greatest traps, the greatest deceptions. For all of our horrors, we are, at the end of it all, The Human Race, the ones who brought you such greatest hits as the Sistine Chapel and a man risking his life to push a homeless girl out of the way of a speeding bus. The moon landing and every sudden and unprompted moment of compassion you have experienced, and shown, in your life. Who brought you weird coffee shop art and freaky dances.

If it can be hard to see, but that doesn't mean it isn't there. That basic goodness.

The stars or the bomb: This is your choice.

III. Space Settlement

LEAVE EARTH TO SAVE EARTH
The Survival of Our Species Comes at the Cost of Our Illusions

I believe in a world that works for everybody. I believe in a solar system that works for everybody.

We live in a world of dwindling resources, caused by, let's be frank, a group of people who were technologically more advanced than the others killing the shit out of everybody else and stealing their resources. All of this in order to build joyless machine-cities filled with dead-eyed people whose only pleasure in life is watching the fucking *Wire* on DVD. But it's too late to fix that. Those battles have been fought already, by people better than us.

Now we are stuck with late-stage capitalism, and no real opposition to it. This is the best social machine mankind has managed to build, with generally far less internal friction than previous attempts at social order.

However, this system was built on one very crucial lie: that the unrestricted market would naturally correct all imbalances within capitalism. Ah, yes, but you forgot to factor that this equation requires raw resources, and raw resources are not infinite. Capitalism may fractal out in a perfect pattern, but only to the limits of the circle it is bounded within. That circle, or sphere, rather—our planet—is currently getting to the last of its shale oil. Oil goes into capitalism; modern civilization comes out, along with the carbon emissions that are slowly destroying that civilization. In a few short years, the oil will be gone, and by that time the icecaps will have melted (the Arctic is expected to be devoid of ice by 2030), adding the equivalent of 20 years' worth of carbon dioxide to the atmosphere.

So, here's the problem. We have a few decades left of oil, our most precious resource, which we can either use to make a solution, or continue to use to anesthetize ourselves until we burn alive.

I believe that, in the face of such a problem, most everything else simply ceases to matter. Our ideologies are revealed to be hopelessly outdated 18th or 19th century fantasies. Our celebrities are revealed to be leeches on individual human will. Our stories about what life is meant to be start to look like the self-serving Horatio Alger or Jane Austen daydreams that they are.

But I'm not here to make you feel bad. You've got our whole civilization to do that for you.

There are answers. In the last several years I've spent thinking about this, the best one I've honestly come up with is space expansion. First I considered this problem from the straight environmental angle, working to help change policy in corporations, where it matters most by dint of sheer scale. But after a round working with Buzz Aldrin on space-based solar power, I came to realize that the solution to running out of living space and resources may simply be to *get more*.

There are $1 trillion of raw resources in an asteroid (you know, the ones we should be making sure don't crash into us). Mars can be colonized, and has water. Saturn's moon Titan looks like a good fit for human habitation.

The space option has another greatly added benefit: it doesn't go against the current of human nature. It works with our natural propensity to expand, not counter to it, as environmental restrictions and cough "austerity measures" do, or the slow return to the dark ages promised by the world's competing religions. Our species hit a wall, ladies and gents. That wall is confinement to our terrestrial sphere; when we collided with it, I suggest, we began to contract and shrink back into ourselves, and we've seen the awful horror of what that produces since the end of the seventies.

Today the hope of space exploration is increasingly held by private firms like Elon Musk's SpaceX. I still believe in the work of anarchist collectives like the Association of Autonomous Astronauts to make space exploration a thing that you and I can at least start to think about for ourselves.

Resource lack is becoming critical; I'm doubtful that clean energy bandaids will remedy the problem. They may take off some of the harsh edges for those who can afford access to them, but they won't fix the problem. Either we get more resources or we collapse into a more manageable state. (Note that that second option is not nearly as happy and fluffy as it sounds.) It's likely we'll see some combination of both. But if we lose our chance at space travel, we lose out on our biological destiny. Done right, it may yet prove that the hell of the 20th and 21st centuries have merely been the launch blast of humanity into space, showing that we are, as Brion Gysin said, merely Here to Go. That, as William S. Burroughs said, Earth is just a space station. The first step in our journey, but not the last.

That's what I believe in. But to get there, we've got a lot of sand to pull our heads out of. The good thing about pulling your head out of the sand, though, is that you only have to do it once, and then you can see what you've been missing all along: the stars.

(March 2013)

II
THE
SEXUAL
DELIGHTS
OF
FASCISM

The Two Great Lies

Ignoring the abuse of the environment and the poor is corroding our culture from within

We live in the era of the self-congratulating lie.

I'm not talking about the lies of government or corporations—not even the secret mass surveillance conducted by the NSA. Those are all there, and are being revealed every day, and they're awful. But underneath those, in a putrid substratum, are the bigger lies: the ones perpetuated not by people in power, but by all of us.

Those lies all fall under one broad umbrella: "Everything is fine." While we discuss the finale of *Breaking Bad*, or plan for our futures, or try to do the best for the people around us in our own small way, we're doing the right thing—but unfortunately, the right thing rests on an illusion. The illusion that everything is fine.

Everything is not fine. Everything may be fine for a short time, for a privileged group of people. And when I say "privileged," I'm not talking about "white male privilege" or whatever else passes for advantage within an already privileged group—I'm talking about *first world privilege.*

For the first world privileged, "everything is fine" for two reasons:

The first reason is that we're artificially inflating the economy and greasing the cogs for just a little bit longer with hydraulic fracturing, stripping the last reserves of shale oil out of the planet to keep the party going.

The second is that the Age of Imperialism and Slavery never ended. It simply became corporatized and more refined. Now it takes the form of corporate abuse of third world resources, of sweatshops, of military occupation and drone policing. In the "Homeland," just under our noses, it takes the form of private prisons and incarceration of minorities for drug offenses—to be converted to legal slave labor for corporations. It takes the form of corporate rape of the environment and the dumping of toxic chemicals in poor, minority communities.

For the nominally free classes, the imperial disease takes the form of white-collar indentured servitude, enforced by criminal student loans, political disenfranchisement and shrinking opportunities for the young. It takes the form of an overpaid, militarized entertainment industry and "distraction-focused Internet" which stretches into every aspect of our lives, continually seeking to keep us small, powerless, afraid, scattered and numb.

Yet for the individual constituents of the System, life is still better than it ever has been, even if our freedom has been traded away. That quality of life depends on simply going along with the plan. Maybe individuals focus on a social issue here or there, or on the token frictions between Republicans and Democrats. But to question the overall plan—to discuss that our oh-so-advanced modern world is an abattoir, a meat machine—this is forbidden. To question the two great sins of our culture—that our quality of life depends on the destruction of the environment and the global poor—this is forbidden.

Even the indentured servants of the American middle class, as shackled as they are, stand on the shoulders of the slaves below them. The iPhones, computers and consumer goods come from sweatshops that drive their workers to suicide. The food comes from corporate plantations, abused migrant workers and tortured animals. The pharmaceuticals and cosmetics come from toxic, profit-driven black science and animal testing. The porn comes from an international system of human trafficking and institutionalized sexual abuse. (And I'm pro-sexuality, pro-sexual expression and not for the limiting of consensual adult sexuality in any way—but let's simply consider how many of the stars of porn, male and female, chose their career after experiencing childhood sexual abuse. Not all of them, but enough, certainly, that America's favorite pastime would collapse were child sexual abuse to stop. How could we fill the constant need for new porn performers then? Is not porn, then, economically dependent on the prevalence of child abuse or, failing that, the economic marginalization and economic disenfranchisement of the young people who turn to the sex industry for sustenance? Uncomfortable, no?)

And speaking of institutionalized sexual abuse, let's not get started on the religions meant to cleanse the guilty consciences of the cogs in the system.

Sweeping the abuse of the environment under the carpet and the abuse of the poor under the carpet—these are the *two great lies*. They run through our entire culture and corrupt everything they touch. And, as far as I can see, there is no easy escape. They are a manifestation of nature in its purest form: vicious, brutal, red in tooth in claw. Non-egalitarian, non-democratic, non-compassionate. Concerned only with who eats who. Like an eagle who snatches a lizard in the desert and tears into it on a rock. This is reality and this is nature unveiled. The great advance of Western Civilization is not that we have overcome our base nature but that we have learned to keep our nails clean and our smiles bright, to pretend it isn't happening, to pay others to keep it out of our consciences.

To pay others to slaughter and prepare our food. To pay others to fight our wars for energy and then to take the blame when we get angry at them for serving our interests, keeping our consciences pure by pretending it was Bush or Cheney or Obama who did the dirty deeds when they were just fulfilling *our* needs. To pay others to enact the sexualities we're afraid of exploring ourselves. To pay others to entertain us and keep us numb with pharmaceutical concoctions, to stave off the demon of self-awareness.

"What keeps mankind alive?" asked Kurt Weill. "The fact that millions are daily tortured, stifled, punished, silenced and oppressed… Mankind can keep alive thanks to its brilliance in keeping its humanity repressed. And for once you must try not to shrink the facts… Mankind is kept alive by bestial acts."

It's not them. It's us. And the way out is to acknowledge it.

Not to revel in it. Not to become overwhelmed by it. But to see it. See the lies. Don't get guilty, don't get fucked up about it, but see and acknowledge what's happening. Sit with it. Understand that no single person can change it, but that minor acts of resistance and choosing higher paths when confronted with the ability to make those choices can, cumulatively, change everything.

Mankind raised itself out of the darkness of prehistory, has overcome diseases, overcome some of the more outwardly brutal forms of oppression. The Middle Ages weren't that long ago, and consider how far we've come since. The Western ideas of egalitarianism and human rights are only a few centuries old. How much further can we go? New advances in science are occurring at a rate too fast to keep up with. Can we not maintain that catastrophic rate of advancement in the field of human dignity and human freedom? We not only can, but we must—or, as many have told us before, our capacity for technological wizardry will be our demise if not coupled with the wisdom and focus on basic humanity that will allow us to use our new toys properly. I do not wish to see a world in which the human is discarded for the transhuman. Not Ever Nope Never.

This is my non-distracting statement to a distracted world. May all beings in all realms attain to peace, freedom and happiness.

(October 1, 2013)

Soft-Sell Slavery

Going on a Facebook Tear About Global Inequality and the Evils of Mass Culture, Two Weeks Before 12/22/2012

>Future historians will see this age as the APEX of human slavery and they will puzzle and puzzle over how everybody could turn a blind eye. They will ask how masses become evil, how casual genocide and torture can be ignored by whole cultures. And they will come to no conclusions.

>I am not worried that this present world will end in two weeks. I'm worried that it won't.

>So let's be real for a second. Mass media and electronic media have one function and it is NOT to keep plutocrats in power over you. It is to hide the blood on YOUR HANDS from YOUR exercise of power.

>The planet is dying. The third world slowly starves to death. Drones terrorize the poor. There are more black men in America incarcerated now than in 1850. The economy runs on physical and sexual slavery and the electronics you herald as creating a "new utopia" are made by shackled children. Your religions lie to you that salvation is coming while you destroy Eden Itself, keeping you enslaved with threats of damnation in the next world and nuclear weapons and death camps in this one. This Is Not How It Should Be and You Are Doing It To Yourself.

>I laugh at the Western idea of progress. I fucking laugh at it. It is a fucking lie. I've seen more happiness in the eyes of Nepali children with NOTHING but the dirt on their faces than I've ever seen in the eyes of a Westerner.

>The "progress" of Western Civilization is the progress away from the Garden of Eden. The Fall.

>Your face when you realize slavery never ended, the whole shit is rigged and we might as well live in Ancient Egypt except that all the crap we make is digital so there won't even be any sweet ass pyramids left to tell our tale

>We Know Enough to Know Better

>Embracing the things your culture has rejected (i.e. the occult, trash culture, otaku shit, etc.) can be a profound gesture of alienation from that culture, but when said society is killing the planet, what then? Reassimilation into the fold might be seen as collusion in mass murder at that point. But is it enough to embody a kind of permanent opposition to modernity? Most of what I've been saying in one way or another in my career is, no, it's not. Dwelling on the fringes can give you perspective and clarity on the sins of your culture like nothing else, but we must remember that this is also the position from which the insights and experiments that can change the course of culture happen.

>Our current mass culture is one of the most sophisticated weapons ever developed. Human sacrifice pyramids of celebrity exist solely to sell you the products that pacify, weaken and slowly kill you. How well they have learned from the horrors of the ancient world and how well they have perfected soft-sell slavery.

>But the real horror is that the Spectacle doesn't exist merely to "keep us down." Yes, it does that. But it also fulfills the role that confessionals and religious theatre used to. It distracts us from ourselves, from seeing the blood on our hands, from seeing that the lifestyle it sells us and that we demand is raping the world, the animals and the poor.

>It's all too easy to claim you are being kept down. Far harder to see those you are keeping down. Especially when we are so invested in keeping our society's slaves invisible, faceless, voiceless, held in for-profit prisons or behind sweatshop tables.

>You think slavery ended just because we stopped importing labor from colonized countries? No. We simply became advanced enough to run the countries, keep the labor there, and ship the goods to us, "as if by magic," out of sight and out of mind.

>Our dreams are to become famous, to be recognized, to be powerful, to be successful and we cry and cry when we don't get what we want… their dreams are to eat, to not have to watch their children starve to death, to live free of disease, to have any hope at all… and we do not see them in the slightest.

>We go on about token "freedoms" like gay marriage and marijuana legalization that amount to little but privileges for a privileged class, the shuffling of blood money, while we systematically destroy and enslave cultures wholesale, a silent and persistent holocaust far greater than anything Hitler could have imagined or accomplished. And for what? The "freedom" to choose between a range of consumer items. A way of life that is making you sick and, believe you me, will make our children even sicker.

>It's feel-bad week on my Facebook. Something to offend everybody.

>Number of people killed in Holocaust over a six-year period: 11-17 million. Number of people who die of poverty-related causes every year: 8 million, i.e. 48 million per six years, with no end in sight. Cost to end global poverty over a twenty-year period: estimated $175 billion a year, less than 1% of the combined income of the richest countries on the planet. You do the math.

>Whole countries turned into concentration camps. Hitler did not lose. He was merely replaced. Improved upon. The blame bureaucratized and shared so consciences could stay clean and the Plan could not end with any one man.

>Yes. It is real. Yes. This is happening.

(December 12, 2012)

Meet the Planet-Murdering Sociopaths Bankrolling Climate Denial

Sociologist maps the conservative foundations and think-tanks dropping ungodly amounts of money to push climate denial and let their Earth-murdering oil company buddies run wild

Drexel University environmental sociologist Robert J. Brulle, PhD, just completed the first ever peer-reviewed analysis of the sources of funding for climate denialism. Brulle was able to identify the massive foundations that bankroll the "countermovement"—the largest ones being Donors Trust, Scaife Affiliated, the Lynde and Harry Bradley Foundation and (no surprise—though they've scaled back donations in recent years) the Koch Brothers.

He also discovered that a massive amount—a total of 75%—of contributions are so-called "dark money," meaning that it passes through foundations that keep contributors' identities completely anonymous and their contributions untraceable, like the aforementioned Donors Trust. Guilt and shame much? Or did they just freak out after seeing *The East*?

Many of the funding sources maintain links to conservative media and politicans. (The Lynde and Harry Bradley Foundation, for instance, was instrumental in funding the Project for a New American Century; the Koch Brothers were major funders of Mitt Romney and the Tea Party.) Several of them were founded specifically to push "free market" ideology.

The top four contributors are:

1. Donors Trust/Donors Capital Fund, $78.8 million, 14%

Donors Trust, established in 1999, is a 501(c)(3) donor advised fund that throws money at conservative causes and specifically climate change denial; it keeps its own donors completely anonymous, and assures them that their contributions will never go to support liberal causes. It has distributed over $400 million to 1,000+ conservative and libertarian groups.

2. *Scaife Affiliated Foundations, $39.6 million, 7%*

A collection of four foundations based out of Pittsburgh, including the Carthage and Sarah Scaife Foundations, which focus on pushing domestic and international policy (to what end they neglect to mention on their website). The other two—the Allegheny and Scaife Family Foundations—focus on improving Pennsylvania and the welfare of families, women, children and animals respectively.

3. *The Lynde and Harry Bradley Foundation, $29.5 million, 5%*

A massively loaded (to the tune of billions) foundation located in Milwaukee that drops over $30 million a year on conservative causes, including federal institutes and education. The foundation is "devoted to strengthening American democratic capitalism and the institutions, principles and values that sustain and nurture it." For them, this means smaller government (big surprise); the Foundation also helped bankroll the smear campaign against Bill Clinton and later helped fund the Neoconservatives' Project for a New American Century, with a focus on the push to invade Iraq as far back as the late 1990s. Charming.

4. *Koch Affiliated Foundations, $25.3 million, 5%*

The *bêtes noire* of the American political and media landscape, the Koch brothers are a walking "libertarian" horror show that bankrolled the Tea Party, the efforts against Obamacare, California Prop 23 (which would have overturned anti-global warming regulation), the campaign against Obama's re-election, Mitt Romney, Scott Walker's campaign for governor of Wisconsin, anti-union groups, keeping young members of the Democratic Party from voting and more. They've also paid for a lot of bunk anti-global warming science and massively pushed the Supreme Court on rolling back the EPA's regulations on greenhouse gas emissions. *Los Angeles Times* reporter Margot Roosevelt called the twosome "the nation's most prominent funders of efforts to prevent curbs on fossil-fuel burning." (The Koch Brothers subsequently tried to buy the *Times*.)

Other funders include the Howard Charitable Foundation, John William Pope Foundation, Searle Freedom Trust, John Templeton Foundation, Dunn's Foundation for the Advancement of Right Thinking, Smith Richardson Foundation Inc., Vanguard Charitable Endowment Program, Kovner Foundation, Annenberg Foundation, Lily Endowment Inc., Richard and Helen DeVos Foundation, ExxonMobil Foundation, Brady Education Foundation, Samuel Roberts Noble Foundation Inc., Coors Affiliated Foundations, Lakeside Foundation, Herrick Foundation, and 118 others whose donations made up less than 1% of total funding each.

Brulle's next project will be to examine funding for the climate movement, after which he will compare funding sources for both.

(December 21, 2013)

Zbigniew Brzezinski vs. Global Awakening

Zbigniew Brzezinski "Admits" That the Internet Has Foiled Hopes for 21st Century American Hegemony

Zbigniew Brzezinski is a clever, clever man. One of the cleverest.

The former US National Security Advisor under Jimmy Carter, Brezezinski is a Henry Kissinger-level behind-the-scenes state manipulator. The type of man who gets real power, wields it from the shadows, and never lets it go — that is, the kind of man who has a hand in actually running things.

While serving as Carter's vizier, Brzezinski engineered the training of the Afghani mujahideen to fight back against the Soviets. That would be the mujahideen who later became the Taliban and executed one of the biggest incidences of blowback ever. And those would be the same mujahideen that his new protege, Barack Obama, is currently droning into oblivion in Afghanistan now that we've decided they're our enemies.

Brzezinski is a big thinker, and a big actor. *The Grand Chessboard*, the title of his most famous book, neatly summarizes how he sees the world.

Brzezinski has now stated that a new American century has become impossible thanks to the global "awakening" that electronic communications have created, and that widescale political consciousness and awareness are too deeply entrenched in the masses for any country to maintain the type of stranglehold they did during the Age of Empires.

Now, when a man like Brzezinski states something as an outright truth, it's a fair bet that he's already thought about a dozen layers down... at least. Why would such a man come out and say something as seemingly concessive as "the Internet is beating us big bad guys"?

After all, isn't this the same Zbigniew Brzezinski who said, while under Carter, "The instantaneous electronic intermeshing of mankind will make for intense confrontation, strained social peace"?

Well, what Brzezinski predicted, Mark Zuckerberg and the *Innocence of Muslims* director prove. I don't think these people are afraid of the Internet at all. If anything, I think they see the Internet as a distraction and method of populace sedation that the television networks could only dream of. Because no matter what your grudge is, no matter what your angle is, there's a place in the Filth Kaleidoscope (as I call the Internet) for you, a place to distract you, a place for you to run in circles and burn off steam. The Brzezinskis of the world must laugh at the actions of "cyber terrorists" like Anonymous, who largely achieve nothing but toothless agitprop, or even Julian Assange, who, despite the bombast of his personal drama, didn't actually leak anything that posed any real threat to the State.

I could even see how it might be of great interest to men like Brzezinski to encourage and play into the "global awakening" he discusses here. WHAT, I ask, do people think they're waking up into? Some kind of New Age paradise, a completely new layer of distraction? Surely not the realization that men like this protect us from the true horrors of the world, and prop up the presidents we think rule us to whisper comforting lullabies and enact illusions and shadow-plays of power so that we will not go mad from seeing the awful chaos of the world-as-it-is? No, how quickly they would put themselves back to sleep if they saw THAT reality…

Here's a few more quotes from Z.B., from 1982:

"We have a large public that is very ignorant about public affairs and very susceptible to simplistic slogans by candidates who appear out of nowhere, have no track record, but mouth appealing slogans…

"The technotronic era involves the gradual appearance of a more controlled society. Such a society would be dominated by an elite, unrestrained by traditional values. Soon it will be possible to assert almost continuous surveillance over every citizen and maintain up-

to-date complete files containing even the most personal information about the citizen. These files will be subject to instantaneous retrieval by the authorities."
  – *Between Two Ages: America's Role in the Technetronic Era*

"In the technotronic society the trend would seem to be towards the aggregation of the individual support of millions of uncoordinated citizens, easily within the reach of magnetic and attractive personalities exploiting the latest communications techniques to manipulate emotions and control reason."
  – Ibid.

Think about that next time you're cut-and-pasting one of those privacy notices on Facebook.

These are the people that engineer the lives you think are your own, who actually wield power—and those behind them, who you will never hear or read of. This is not conspiracy; it is simply how power operates.

So who are you, Zbigniew Brzezinski? What happens inside that mind and behind those calculating eyes? What is the world you see? What is the history you feel?

(November 1, 2013)

We the People are Tired and Cold

Why I Don't Care About Mitt Romney's Carnival of Hate

Right now the airwaves and the Internet are on fire dissecting the speeches at the RNC—Mitt Romney, Paul Ryan, Clint Eastwood. They're pointing out the hypocrisies and lies, or expressing adulation, or going on about Ron Paul, that anti-environmentalist, if their dissent has been commodified in that way.

I'm sitting here up late on Thursday night listening to the crickets and this weird LA rain and I'm tired. I'm tired of watching people surrender themselves to leaders, whoever those leaders are, and I'm tired of this TV show.

Listening to public radio discuss the RNC, I flashed on an image of it as a tent revival. I imagined seeing a tent filled with people way out on the edge of a dead cornfield, shining with light from generators, while those inside whipped themselves into a frenzy with invocations of Reagan and nukes and religion and the free market and lynched Obama in effigy. A meaningless sideshow out in a very cold and very unforgiving night.

And beyond that tent, way out in the town beyond the field, I saw Tired People. Hungry people, with no health care, in the dust and cold, their houses falling apart or already taken from them, unfilled prescriptions, crushed under the weight of reality. Like medieval peasants doing the dance of death. And underneath them, on geological time, a planet exhausted of fossil fuels and preparing to make a few more fossils.

What's been done in this country is criminal. Our country's had its future stolen, and those who've done it expect us to treat them as our saviors and, like good vampires who always ask permission, invite them back for more. And we do. Stockholm syndrome.

I don't care enough about these people to dissect their every word. I don't care enough to treat them like "the sports team you love to hate" and Tweet or Facebook about their every move to somehow prove how different and better I am. I don't even care enough to complain about the controlled media or the Great Digital Trance anymore. I hate the players and I hate the game. I'm tired of it.

The lives of the people in this country mean something. Their health means something, their future means something, their kids' future means something. The soccer trophies mean something and their beliefs mean something and their jobs mean something. And here they go again, preparing to get fleeced of all of that by another wolf who will turn it into one thing: War.

It's time to end this story. It's time to stop putting our trust in Great Men, hoping they'll save us, and it's time to stop wringing our hands and crying out into that uncaring night about how we've been wronged. Americans have a lot of blood on their hands. They've also seen a lot of misery recently. And I still believe in them and what we were and are and will be, not as some kind of special people with some leftover Puritan City on a Hill mandate horseshit, but as Just People. The people that I grew up with, and who right now I feel like I'm watching choose to die instead of fight.

Nobody will save you from the uncaring night. Not the tent revival of hate. Not Obama. Not another war or some last minute technological miracle.

That power lies only with you.

(August 31, 2012)

From Fast Apocalypse to Slow Apocalypse

Updating and Reorienting for Obama's Second Term

Since Obama's re-election, I've gone a bit quiet. Some of the pressure is off, along with some of the sense of impending doom that came along with the idea of a Romney win. I'm slowly trying to get re-oriented to a country that looks like it's probably going to be OK for a while yet.

I came to term as a writer during the Bush Jr. years. My reality was defined by terror and the crushing weight of America's actions post-9/11. Living in squalor in Queens, New York and working at a company mongering conspiracy theories (Disinformation) did not help. My life was a blur and the country was spinning down the drain, every passing day announcing a new affront to decency. Guantanamo, the invasion of Iraq, the Patriot Act. The people who stood up to that got hammered hard.

That experience has permanently marked me, and those who were awake during that period of time, in a way I think possibly more profound than the Kennedy assassination or Watergate did the people who lived through those events. It's one thing to have your faith in feudal god-kings shattered by having one offed and the other steal some files. But, really, how can that compare with a fascist takeover of the country followed by "OK, so, we're just going to torture the shit out of people now. You cool with that?" Seeing images of children covered with napalm in Vietnam is deep trauma, but compare a moment's fire to images of children mutated by uranium bullets in the Middle East, bullets with a half-life of 0.24 million years?

Obama has, if anything, refined and even expanded this savagery. He has made Bush's damage to civil liberties permanent—even Bush didn't pull stunts like passing the NDAA, and we can now look forward to a century of mechanized warfare that completely removes soldiers from the ethical realities of choosing to kill.

But for all that, it bears remembering that Romney very likely would have led us into a nuclear exchange in the Middle East. That's not an option that's off the table—our world is so schizoid now that state tensions are erupting over YouTube videos—but in many ways I feel like the pressure has been lifted and, despite all of America's failures and flaws, economic and military, we're off the rocket ride to Fast Apocalypse.

Which means it's time to get back to work on the far less glamorous task of circumventing Slow Apocalypse, and taking the consistent, non-dramatic, daily efforts required to route out creeping problems like Peak Oil.

We need clean energy, something Obama is thankfully stepping up to plate on.

We need to restore the damage done to the US Constitution by the last twelve years and, if necessary, re-establish a new charter of individual rights, one updated for the globalist world we live in and which offers protections not just from the state but from the rampant abuses of corporations.

We need to continue to fight back on the effort to clamp down on Internet freedom. It's an increasingly shrinking window of free speech, generally the last one we have left, and one we need to protect.

We need to push back against a state defined by surveillance and drone warfare. (What is this, *The Prisoner?*)

And we need to re-establish America on more secure economic footing. My generation is completely useless for any task except self-promotion and getting likes on Facebook, raised by the children of the Sixties to believe that everybody can be famous, everybody can be cool and everybody can be the center of attention, an attitude of extreme privilege which has ultimately defanged us. We need to re-connect with the challenges of the physical world.

Let's see what shakes out of reality by the end of the year, and get ready to face the challenges of the new term.

(November 14, 2012)

A Federal Court Approved Chevron's Request for Activists' Data

It's not just the NSA collecting your data. Now corporations are getting in on the game as well.

Oil giant Chevron just subpoenaed Google, Yahoo and Microsoft for the metadata of over 100 journalists, activists and lawyers who have been critical of the company, claiming their targets had formed a criminal conspiracy. And a federal judge not only upheld the subpoena—he also ruled that because the journalists and activists were anonymously named, they had no recourse to First Amendment rights, and could not even be counted as US citizens.

Chevron's ire was first invoked when the company lost a $18.2 billion lawsuit in Ecuador over environmental contamination, in which the multinational was sued over dumping toxic waste into Amazonian rivers, causing massive damage to the rainforest and poisoning the local indigenous people's drinking water.

The company's response to its court loss in Ecuador? Chevron filed a new lawsuit in the United States against more than a hundred journalists, activists and lawyers that the company is alleging were directly or indirectly involved in the Ecuador suit, or who have been critical of the company—claiming that the plaintiffs were conspiring to defraud them. (Chevron brought suit against the plaintiffs under the Racketeer Influenced and Corrupt Organizations or RICO Act, used to try criminal conspiracies.) As part of the lawsuit, it's subpoenaed Google, Yahoo and Microsoft for all of the metadata associated with their targets' e-mail addresses.

Despite pushback from the Electronic Freedom Foundation and EarthRights International, the enforceability of the subpoena was approved by US District Judge Lewis A. Kaplan in New York—meaning that Chevron would be given, according to Kaplan:

"…the IP address associated with every login for every account over a nine-year period. Chevron could identify the countries, states, or even cities where the users logged into accounts, and perhaps, in some instances, could determine the actual building addresses.

"Chevron would not learn who logged into the accounts. That is to say that Chevron would know who created (or purported to create) the email accounts but would not know if there was a single user or multiple users for each account. Nevertheless, the subpoenaed information might allow Chevron to infer the movements of the users over the relevant period (at a high level of generality) and might permit Chevron to make inferences about some of the users' professional and personal relationships."

Here's the kicker: Because the activists and journalists targeted by Chevron were proceeding anonymously, and presumably because the original lawsuit was in Ecuador, Kaplan assumed they were not US citizens—and therefore not entitled to First Amendment protection. In fact, Kaplan may have approved the subpoena because those named had not shown themselves to be US citizens.

So now we have the terror of dealing with corporations vindictively culling data—possibly even more frightening than NSA spying, as there's a certain comforting miasma of bureaucratic incompetence and red tape associated with the federal government that corporations simply don't have.

But even more disturbing is the potential legal precedent that anonymity can deprive an individual of not only First Amendment rights, but even treatment as a citizen of the country they're being tried in.

Anonymous may want to reconsider its approach right about now.

(July 11, 2013)

When the CIA Got Busted Selling Crack

In mid-January, the Mexican newspaper *El Universal* alleged that the US DEA allowed the notorious Sinaloa cartel, considered Mexico's most powerful drug traffickers, to operate with impunity in exchange for informing on rival cartels—smuggling billions of dollars of drugs without interference, previously including nearly 200 tons of cocaine and heroin between 1990 and 2008.

El Universal also alleged that Operation Fast and Furious—in which Arizona ATF agents allowed arms sales to cartel members in order to track them—was part of a larger scheme to arm and finance the cartel in exchange for information on rival cartels.

The DEA's strategy with Sinaloa is one that America has also allegedly used in Colombia, Cambodia, Thailand and Afghanistan. And while *El Universal*'s revelations were barely touched upon by the mainstream media, for those who have followed drug war policy, they come as no surprise.

Gary Webb: The Man Who Knew Too Much

Let's rewind the clock to August 1996.

Gary Webb is a reporter at the *San Jose Mercury News*. He's 41, and he's been writing for the paper since 1988. He's made his way to California after dropping out of journalism school to write for local papers in Cleveland and Kentucky. He's already begun to make a name for himself as an investigative reporter, exposing computer issues at the California DMV and freeway retrofitting issues that surfaced during the 1989 Loma Prieta earthquake.

But that's small stuff compared to what Webb is about to deliver to his bosses, and the public: he has a new three-part, 20,000 word investigation called "Dark Alliance." For those paying attention, it will radically shock the foundations of what we think of as American politics. It will also effectively end Webb's promising career—and soon enough, his life.

Here's what he reveals: During the 1980s, Nicaraguan cartels were freely selling crack in Los Angeles. The funds they were raising from distributing this most ruinous of drugs were directly funneled back to the Contras in Nicaragua—the Contras that the Reagan administration and CIA were covertly supporting, even though aid had been explicitly banned by Congress. According to Webb, the CIA was well aware of what was happening, and allowed shipments of cocaine into the US; he also alleges that White House personnel, including Oliver North, are involved. North had previously arranged for the clandestine sale of arms to Iran and the funneling of the proceeds back to the Contras (he currently has his own show on Fox News). None of these people informed the DEA about any of these actions.

The article causes immense scandal—it also pushes 1.3 million hits a day back to the *San Jose Mercury News* website... and this is 1996. That kind of traffic would break many sites' Web hosting now, in Internet-ubiquitous 2014. But this is when most Americans are still on AOL, if online at all.

The spin doctors immediately leap into action, and Webb comes under attack from the big dogs: the *Washington Post, Los Angeles Times* and *New York Times* all rush to debunk his findings, often attacking Webb directly. (Sound Snowden/Assange/Manning-esque?) The *Los Angeles Times* plays the race card, claiming that Webb alleged the CIA was trying to addict African Americans to crack, which he did not. Webb claims that the DC, New York and LA papers are acting as mouthpieces for the government (much as Glenn Greenwald has done throughout the Snowden scandal). But they can't hold the story back: it's one of the first times the Internet undermines the power of the mainstream media in allowing a story to spread.

Under heavy fire, the *Mercury News* hangs Webb out to dry. His editors aren't contacting him about the story by January 1997; the paper's executive editor writes an editorial criticizing Webb's work in May. Webb is reassigned to a suburban wing of the paper that's 150 miles away from where he lives. Unable to handle six hours of commute a day, he quits the *Mercury* in December 1997. His career in journalism is effectively over: he never gets a job at a daily newspaper again, and though he keeps writing, he can't support his family. He goes to work for the California Assembly Speaker's Office of Member Services; after being laid off in 2003, he finally gets a job writing again, at the *Sacramento News and Review*. But he still can't keep his family afloat, and loses his home.

Then, in December 10, 2004, he turns up dead. It's ruled a suicide, due to years of depression from being economically marginalized. The coroner finds a suicide note, and additional notes mailed to his family members.

Oddly enough, however, he's got two gunshot wounds to the head. Be that what it may.

He Who Shines With the Brightest Light Will Cast the Darkest Shadow

Though an initial investigation into the CIA/Contra link by the Los Angeles County Sheriff failed to substantiate Webb's findings, later investigations did, including a CIA internal investigation. A 1982 letter between the CIA and the Justice Department, revealed by Representative Maxine Waters in 1998, showed that the CIA had been legally freed from the responsibility of reporting drug smuggling by its assets (including the Contras and the Afghan rebels who would later become Al Qaeda).

A 1998 Justice Department report also revealed that the Reagan administration did nothing to stop Contra drug trafficking, and that the CIA shared nothing of its activities with other law enforcement agencies. Further CIA investigations revealed that the Reagan/Bush White House protected 50+ Contras and drug traffickers, with the CIA preventing information on drug crimes from going to the Justice

Department, Congress or factions in the CIA likely to be concerned. CIA internal reporting even found that the pyramid of drug trafficking and money laundering went all the way to the National Security Council under Oliver North, and that this had been routinely covered up.

Even though all of this was validated by 1998, it was already too late for Webb, the shot messenger. Before his death, however, he succeeded in publishing a book expanding his reporting—*Dark Alliance: The CIA, the Contras, and the Crack Cocaine Explosion*.

After his death—only after his death—the mainstream media began to change its assessment of Webb and how he had been treated. The *LA Times* claimed "Gary got too much blame" and called him a "great investigative reporter" in 2006, despite having rushed to hammer in the nails ten years earlier. A movie about Gary Webb and the "Dark Alliance" story, entitled *Kill the Messenger*, is scheduled for release this year, starring Jeremy Renner as Webb.

So clearly, the Webb scandal is a relic of a darker time, of the long shadow of Reagan, Bush, Oliver North and the Cold War, and we can put this behind us, right?

Not quite, as we see from this month's revelations about the Sinaloa cartel. If anything, the connection between federal law enforcement and drug trafficking appears to have gotten worse. And as we've seen from the treatment of whistleblowers like Edward Snowden, Chelsea Manning and Julian Assange, the US government is still no fan of messengers. In fact, the Obama administration has aggressively prosecuted journalists and brought more whistleblowers to trial than any other administration in United States history.

Perhaps the Jeremy Renner movie will go some way towards alerting the American public to what has been done—and continues to be done—in their name. But until the time when the same outrage erupts over covert intelligence agency activities like CIA and DEA drug trafficking that has erupted, say, over NSA spying (and to say that the American public is angry over NSA spying is *highly* generous), the Dark Alliance continues.

(January 23, 2014)

The NSA Has Set Up Shop at the US Embassy in Mexico

When Edward Snowden's leaks revealed what the NSA had been up to in Mexico, Mexicans were understandably outraged. The National Security Agency had spied on Mexican presidents Enrique Peña Nieto and Felipe Calderón, on Caledrón's cabinet, and on multiple governmental agencies as part of an operation dubbed Flatliquid. An August 2009 NSA operation in Mexico, somewhat insensitively code-named Whitetamale, included a wide-scale hack of Mexico's Public Security Secretariat, the body that polices the trafficking of drugs and people. And Mexican phone calls and texts were collected as part of operation Eveningeasel.

The operations netted the NSA info not only on drug cartels but also on diplomatic talking points that, according to *Der Spiegel*, "allowed US politicians to conduct successful talks on political issues and to plan international investments." Operations Whitetamale, Flatliquid and Eveningeasel—it's unclear how many NSA guys high-fived each other after coming up with the names—were conducted from the NSA office in San Antonio. But other Snowden documents showed that the NSA captured and analyzed internet traffic from a US diplomatic post in Mexico City, and that the US embassy hosted agents from the joint NSA/CIA Special Collection Service, a black-budget program dedicated to bugging foreign embassies and government installations.

But it took a separate, recently declassified memo to confirm that the NSA maintained a secret office inside the US Embassy in Mexico City.

That office is a so-called fusion center. The existence of fusion centers in the United States is no secret; they were established in the wake of the glaring 9/11 intelligence failures to promote information sharing between US intelligence agencies, the military, and state and local governments. The centers were primarily a creation of the George W. Bush administration; at least 72 had been established by 2009.

The secret fusion center in Mexico City, however, was only confirmed by a 2010 Department of Defense memorandum requested by George Washington University's National Security Archive project under the Freedom of Information Act. The document also revealed a network of joint US/Mexican intelligence centers open to staff from both countries—but Mexican personnel weren't allowed access to the one in the embassy. Support was given to the fusion center by the Department of Defense's office for Counternarcotics and Global Threats, and was largely channeled through US Northern Command (NORTHCOM), which is charged with protecting US interests in North America.

Despite the existence of the memorandum, the NSA is backing away from any admission that the Mexico center exists, and is refusing requests for further information. According to *Unredacted*, the National Security Archive's blog, the NSA has given a Glomar response to further FOIA requests—in other words, they're saying that they can neither confirm nor deny the existence of more documents. (This despite the fact that *Unredacted* has already published the memo.) NORTHCOM has also refused additional FOIA requests, stating that the material is classified.

Why is everyone refusing to discuss something thats existence has already been established? It's because the center is broadly concerned with "high-value targets" (HVTs), or what the DoD calls "a target the enemy commander requires for the successful completion of the mission." HVTs are typically understood to be terrorist leaders. But the fusion center at the US Embassy in Mexico appears to have a somewhat broader definition.

"Reading the document, we know that the Mexico fusion center is focused on high-value targeting, but it's not clear at first glance who or what those targets are," Michael Evans, director of the National Security Archive's Mexico project, told me. "In Mexico, one might logically assume that high value targets are the leaders of criminal organizations—drug traffickers, human smugglers, etc."

But as Evans points out, we now know—thanks to Snowden—that the National Security Agency applied the HVT label to Peña Nieto, along with other world leaders who were the targets of US snooping. "Given that this is a top secret, US-only facility," Evans said, "my guess is that the Mexico fusion center probably takes an 'all of the above' approach, targeting both criminal organizations and Mexico's political leadership."

The memo revealing the existence of the center was written by William Wechsler, who at the time was the head of Counternarcotics and Global Threats at the DOD. It's addressed to then-Assistant Secretary of Defense Mike Vickers, and calls for multiple interagency centers throughout Mexico, to be kept separate from the US-exclusive fusion center in the embassy.

The United States and Mexico have worked closely to police narcotrafficking since the 2006 inauguration of Calderon, who reached out to George W. Bush for aid against the cartels during Bush's second term. Among the targets of a $1.9 billion American aid package, according to the *Washington Post*, were the cartels' brutal death squads. In order to help the government, the US began employing Predator drones in Mexican airspace for reconnaissance by mid-2009.

"It's important to remember that it was only a few years ago that Mexico and the United States were touting the establishment of the joint-intelligence fusion centers, in which both countries worked side-by-side against the drug cartels and other shared threats," Evans said. "But we now know that the US has been pursuing a two-track policy: One, a network of joint-intelligence centers staffed by personnel from both countries. The other, a secret facility to which the Mexicans were not invited."

After the initial disclosures, Mexican legislators demanded the country's attorney general investigate the secret facility and any espionage being conducted by the United States.

So Mexico is mad, but was it worth it? A two-year bipartisan investigation into domestic fusion centers by the US Senate Permanent Subcommittee on Investigations, released in 2012, found that the centers' intelligence reports were largely worthless, that they violated civil liberties and privacy, and that the data gathered often had little to do with terrorism. The subcommittee report also found that between $289 million and $1.4 billion of taxpayer money had been spent on the centers, including line items like $75,000 spent on 55 flat-screen TVs for the San Diego Fusion Center to conduct "open-source monitoring."

That, no joke, is essentially how they refer to "watching the news."

The National Security Archive is fighting to overcome the NSA's Glomar response and NORTHCOM's denials in order to uncover more information about the NSA's secret office in the US Embassy. Meanwhile, earlier this month, US Ambassador to Mexico Tony Wayne witnessed the signing of a new data-sharing agreement between the US and Mexico.

(February 24, 2014)

The Trans-Pacific Partnership Could 'Establish a War of All Against All'

The Trans-Pacific Partnership (TPP) is coming, and it could give multinational corporations even more influence over global policy.

That's what critics of the trade deal between 12 countries along the Pacific Rim (Australia, Brunei, Canada, Chile, Japan, Malaysia, Mexico, New Zealand, Peru, Singapore, the United States and Vietnam) are saying. It's not helping that the contents of the agreement have largely been kept secret, even though the TPP is the biggest trade deal since the creation of the World Trade Organization in 1995.

The TPP partner countries are currently conducting their 20th round of talks, scheduled to last until July 12, in Ottawa, Canada. The venue was moved from Vancouver at the last minute, which critics of the agreement are saying was a calculated move to avoid protests. (Canadian Prime Minister Stephen Harper's government has stated that the event was moved solely to save more than $150,000 in hosting costs.)

Both President Barack Obama and Japanese negotiator Koji Tsuruoka have stated that the Canadian meetings will be a crucial step toward a planned November finish for the talks, which largely hinge on negotiations between the US and Japan.

What's known about the TPP's 29 chapters—of which only five cover trade, and only three have been leaked—has sent chills through activists on both ends of the political spectrum. Here's a breakdown of the five biggest issues the TPP presents:

It's Being Kept Secret From the World

Thanks to leaks published by Citizens Trade Campaign and

WikiLeaks, we've seen draft chapters of the environmental, investment and intellectual property sections of the TPP. But the rest is a mystery, and mainstream media coverage has been scant.

Obama himself has remarked that "objections, protest, rumors" and "conspiracy theories" around the TPP are inevitable, reflecting a "lack of knowledge of what is going on in the negotiations."

That "lack of knowledge" isn't elective, however. Though TPP stakeholders, including 600 corporations and multiple labor unions, including the AFL-CIO, are allowed access to the draft, the public is not. Even Congress is being kept on a short leash—while a few Congress members have been allowed to read draft text of the trade agreement, they've also been sworn to secrecy about what they've seen.

"I read some sections of a draft of the TPP that identified sections that were still being negotiated, that did not identify what positions were being taken by which countries," Florida Representative Alan Grayson told me. "I was the first member [of the House] to read it; since then, other members have read it. Aides were excluded on all counts, and I was told I couldn't discuss it or shouldn't discuss it with aides.

"A number of staffers from the Trade Representative's office came, brought the document with them, and insisted on staying in the room and looking at me as I read the document."

His general take on what he read, even if he can't reveal the details? "It would be a punch in the face to the middle class of America. But I can't tell you why."

It Will Extend the Ability of Corporations to Sue Governments

The investor-state dispute settlement provision (ISDS) of the TPP would allow foreign investors to sue governments over domestic policy that might diminish their profits.

Hypothetically, for instance, an agribusiness company could sue a country that bans GMOs in order to recoup lost profits. This has already been possible, to some extent, under NAFTA—as in the cases "Eli Lilly v. Canada" and "Metalclad v. Mexico"—yet these rules do not apply to countries governed by the WTO. The TPP would extend NAFTA-style ISDS to the 12 participating countries.

Lori Wallach, the director of Public Citizen's Global Trade Watch, told me that the ISDS "would formalize the elevation of individual corporations and investors to equal status with nation states."

"It makes a public treaty between two countries privately enforceable by any private investor or corporation... a foreign investor could challenge any government policy or action in an extrajudicial tribunal outside the domestic courts, outside the domestic law, and drag governments to face a kangaroo court staffed by three corporate private sector attorneys."

It Will Put a Stranglehold on Intellectual Property Law

The TPP would potentially make it criminal to break Digital Rights Management restrictions (whether you know it's a crime or not), would extend the length of time companies can hold copyright for, expand the statutory damages for copyright infringement, and even backdoor in a version of SOPA.

Maira Sutton, global policy analyst at the Electronic Frontier Foundation, told me that such measures could create a "censorship by copyright" situation in which we'd have "YouTubes, links on search results, academic papers, and posts on Reddit disappearing because rights holders allege it's copyrighted content. And we'd have people being afraid to link to things or share things."

The TPP may also extend patent protection on pharmaceuticals —potentially meaning that crucial, life-saving medicines could be kept out of the price range of the developing world, with generics delayed or blocked from coming to market.

It Will Allow Open Season on the Environment

The TPP's environment chapter isn't disturbing as much for what it contains as what it doesn't contain. Though the Obama administration previously took a hard line on environmental protections, those measures have become a casualty of the TPP negotiation process, as partner countries have protested that environmental protections would limit economic growth.

As such, only suggestions for environmental protection are included in the TPP—no binding obligations or enforcement policies.

It Will Allow Multinationals to Brutalize the Partner Countries

It's not hard to extrapolate how the global situation might shift if what we've seen of the TPP were fully exploited by multinationals. Tight controls on pharmaceutical patents could potentially lead to a resurgence of HIV/AIDS and other diseases in developing TPP countries.

The ability of the internet to bring information and education to developing countries could be shuttered. The environment of the partner states could be destroyed without remorse or recourse. And due to fear of economic assault under the investor-state dispute settlement provision, national governments would likely be unable to effectively fight back against multinational rule.

Domestically, the US could also be flooded by dangerously substandard products, lose more jobs to offshoring, lose "Buy American" procurement policies, and face the rollback of climate and financial protections.

Grayson is ferociously clear about what the effect will be: "The TPP would destroy our ability to govern ourselves. In large part, what you'd see is something between corporate rule and anarchy... It establishes a Hobbesian war of all against all."

(July 11, 2014)

Slave Children Used by Major Corporations to Make Chocolate

Lawsuit alleging that Nestlé, ADM and Cargill benefit from child slavery in their cocoa supply chain in back in court, throwing new light on decades-old concern that the chocolate industry is built on the backs of slave children

Swiss multinational Nestlé, the largest food company on the planet—and anybody who consumes their products—has a chocolate problem.

More specifically, they have a child slavery problem.

Since the late 1990s, allegations have continually surfaced that the company benefits from slave children in its supply chain, and that slave children are used in its cocoa production in West Africa.

The allegations—including reports from UNICEF and the US State Department—brought enough attention and heat, including coverage from the BBC, that Nestlé's CEO Bradley Alford signed an international agreement to end cocoa child labor in 2001, but by 2005 had not met the agreement's deadline for eliminating the worst child labor offenses from the company's supply chain.

In the same year, the International Labor Rights Fund filed a class action lawsuit on the behalf of three children from Mali who claimed that between 1994 and 2000 they had been lured into Côte d'Ivoire by child traffickers promising them easy work for good pay, subsequently enslaved on a cocoa plantation and regularly beaten. The lawsuit was later amended to name three companies as complicit in the chocolate-production slave trade: Archer Daniels Midland, Cargill and Nestlé itself.

According to the children's lawyers, "Plaintiffs, aged 12 to 14 when first forced to work as child slaves, had to work 12 to 14 hour days with no pay. They often worked with guns pointed at them, and were given only the bare minimum of food scraps… Plaintiffs were locked in small rooms at night with other child slaves so they could not escape the plantations. They were whipped and beaten by the guards and overseers when the guards felt the were not working quickly or adequately."

One of the three children (now adults) testified that "I tried to run away but I was caught… as punishment they cut my feet and I had to work for weeks while my wounds healed."

In September 2010, the lawsuit was thrown out by the US District Court for the Central District of California—not because the claims were found invalid, but because the court determined that corporations could not be held liable for violations of international law. (Despite the fact that courts in Côte d'Ivoire are so deeply corrupt that a trial in those countries would be a joke.)

However, after the US Supreme Court ruled that international corporate abuses could be tried in US courts, the plaintiffs have won the ability to show that ADM, Nestlé and Cargill aided and abetted child trafficking under the "actus reus" standard.

Whether any of the corporations named as defendants will be penalized, or will effectively end the use of child labor in their supply chains, remains to be seen. Nestlé has planned new monitoring programs after the Fair Labor Association found lax overview of human rights abuses in its internal reporting. A press release on Nestlé's own Web site states that "Nestlé and its partners will involve communities in Côte d'Ivoire in a new effort to prevent the use of child labour in cocoa-growing areas by raising awareness and training people to identify children at risk, and to intervene where there is a problem."

Notably, this puts the responsibility on local growers instead of Nestlé itself.

José Lopez, Nestlé's Executive Vice President for Operations, states that "The use of child labour in our cocoa supply chain goes against everything we stand for. As the FLA report makes clear, no company sourcing cocoa from Côte d'Ivoire can guarantee that it doesn't happen, but what we can say is that tackling child labour is a top priority for our company."

Nestlé purchases 1/10th of the cocoa produced around the world; 1/3 of that comes from slavery-rife Côte d'Ivoire.

While the first world regularly congratulates itself for eliminating slavery, using this as a marker of civilizational progress, the data shows a different story: It's simply been outsourced by multinationals, the slavery kept in developing world countries where we don't have to see it up close.

(June 17, 2014)

The Dalai Lama Will Not Return to Lead Tibet (He Has Something Better in Mind)

The Dalai Lama set off a firestorm last month by announcing that he will no longer reincarnate in a political role, effectively ending his centuries-old political lineage.

It's the latest in a series of controversial statements about the future of his role—including a hint that his next incarnation may be born outside of Tibet, and may be a woman. And it's another indicator of a sea change in how the Tibetan diaspora is adapting and revising its traditions for life outside of occupied Tibet. Though the Dalai Lama's statement was hastily reported in the media as meaning that he will not reincarnate at all, what he's saying is much more layered: he's looking to reincarnate as a spiritual leader only, and transition the Tibetan government-in-exile from needing him as a central authority, and towards a democratically-elected committee.

"We had a Dalai Lama for almost five centuries," the Dalai Lama told the German newspaper *Welt am Sonntag* in September. "The 14th Dalai Lama now is very popular. Let us then finish with a popular Dalai Lama… If a weak Dalai Lama comes along, then it will just disgrace the Dalai Lama."

"Tibetan Buddhism is not dependent on one individual," he added. "We have a very good organizational structure with highly trained monks and scholars."

While the Dalai Lama officially devolved his political role in 2011 (the head of the Tibetan government-in-exile is currently Harvard-educated legal scholar Dr. Lobsang Sangay), this statement further underlines his desire to democratize the Tibetan government—which he has been pushing for since the 1960s.

"He has been very happy since 2011, when he resigned from any political role," Dr. Robert Thurman told me (Thurman is a Professor of Indo-Tibetan Buddhist Studies at Columbia University, and is one of the Dalai Lama's primary interfaces with Western media and academia). "He also changed the constitution and made the final implementation of a change that no lama will be head of state in any future government that Tibetans approve of."

While that change may further endear the Dalai Lama and Tibetan diaspora to broadly supportive Western governments, China is not pleased—though the People's Republic considers Tibetan Buddhism another "opium of the people," it quite likes the idea of central authority—especially if it controls that authority's next incarnation.

Bodhisattvas of Compassion

As it is in many religions, reincarnation is an article of faith in Tibetan Buddhism—a process that has been studied, mapped and analyzed in detail by meditating lamas as if it were a subject akin to astrophysics, and described in texts like the *Bardo Thödol*. It's also considered to work differently for different individuals, depending on their level of Buddhist practice and attainment.

The Dalai Lama is considered to be a Bodhisattva—a practitioner who has reached the highest levels of attainment, but who has delayed their own final realization, swearing instead to continue reincarnating until all sentient beings are freed from delusion and attain to enlightenment. He's also considered to be the human incarnation of the deity Avalokiteśvara, the embodiment of absolute and universal compassion. Both a sequentially incarnating human and the temporal manifestation of a divine being—not minor stuff.

His human journey began in 1391, when Gendun Drup—who would become the first Dalai Lama—was born in a cowshed in central Tibet. After becoming a monk, he studied under Tsongkhapa, the legendary founder of the Gelug school of Tibetan Buddhism (which would become the most prominent and organized branch of Tibet's many sects and sub-sects, somewhat akin to the Catholic Church in the West). Drup became one of the most celebrated lamas in the country, occupying a critical spiritual role in the growing Gelug sect. At Lhamo La-tso lake, he was granted a vision of the fearsome blue-skinned, red-haired, blood-drinking female guardian spirit Palden Lhamo, who promised to protect his reincarnation lineage. Since that time, Gelug lamas have meditated at Lhamo La-tso for guidance in finding each successive incarnation of the Dalai Lama.

The role of the Dalai Lama was officially codified in his second incarnation, but it wasn't until several lifetimes later that he came into his own—as Ngawang Lobsang Gyatso, the Fifth Dalai Lama, one of the most critical figures in Tibetan history. Not only did the Fifth firmly establish the Dalai Lama office as a political role, he also unified Tibet, ending centuries of civil war by brutally crushing the rebel factions (with Mongolian aid) and uniting the country under himself.

The office of Dalai Lama subsequently became an embattled political role, with several incarnations likely murdered by political rivals or Chinese infiltrators. It was Thubten Gyatso, the 13th Dalai Lama, who declared Tibet politically independent from China in the early 20th century, exiled Chinese citizens from the country, and began to modernize the still-feudal nation.

Which brings us to Tenzin Gyatso, the 14th and current Dalai Lama, enthroned in 1950, in the middle of Communist China's invasion of Tibet. Only one year later, he would be forced to accept Tibet's formal re-incorporation into the PRC; in 1959, he would flee for his life to India, where he has ruled the Tibetan government-in-exile since.

While the 5th Dalai Lama faced the political burden of unifying Tibet, the 14th has been forced to preside over its destruction— witnessing the ongoing genocide of the Tibetan people and their cultural traditions within Tibet's borders, all the while struggling to re-assemble and ensure the survival of those traditions in India and the West.

I saw the Dalai Lama speak in New York in 2007. Though

cheerful, he was also flatly realist. He underlined that his singular goal is to ensure the survival of the Tibetan people, and chuckled at the tendency of Westerners to see him as a magically-powered, spiritual Santa Claus. When asked about the future of Tibet, and if it would survive the PRC's mass murder, religious suppression, strip-mining and strip-malling, his answer was sobering and succinct:

"I don't know," he said. "I don't know."

The Geopolitics of Reincarnation

Reincarnation isn't just a matter of faith or history. It's also a flashpoint in Tibetan-Chinese political relations. And only days after the Dalai Lama's announcement that he was ending his political incarnations, China hit back.

"China follows a policy of freedom of religion and belief, and this naturally includes having to respect and protect the ways of passing on Tibetan Buddhism," Chinese Foreign Ministry spokeswoman Hua Chunying told a daily news briefing. "The title of Dalai Lama is conferred by the central government, which has hundreds of years of history. The 14th Dalai Lama has ulterior motives, and is seeking to distort and negate history, which is damaging to the normal order of Tibetan Buddhism."

Earlier, in 2011, the Chinese foreign ministry issued a public statement that only Beijing can appoint the next Dalai Lama, and that any attempt to do so by Tibetan-recognized reincarnation would violate Chinese law. In 2007, the PRC stated that reincarnations of lamas can only be recognized after an applications process to the State Council.

The Tibetan government-in-exile has rejected this; the Dalai Lama has ruled that "apart from the reincarnation recognized through legitimate methods, no recognition or acceptance should be given to a candidate chosen for political ends by anyone, including those in the People's Republic of China." By ending his political incarnations, the Dalai Lama may well be hedging against a future in which China attempts to appoint its own Dalai Lama, claiming they have found his next incarnation and using their puppet to manipulate Tibet.

It's not like there isn't precedent for such a move. In May 1995, the Dalai Lama recognized six-year-old Gedhun Choekyi Nyima as the new incarnation of the Panchen Lama, the second most powerful figure in the Gelugpa school after himself. Shortly thereafter, the Chinese government disappeared Nyima, and appointed their own Panchen Lama. Nyima has not been seen since.

"[China] passed a law in 2007 that they control all reincarnations, and it's likely that they will go ahead and try to appoint their own Dalai Lama," Dr. Robert Barnett, Director of the Modern Tibet Studies Program at Columbia, explained to me. "There is some indication that they've set up committees to handle this, and may be planning to do this, but we can't be sure. Chinese leaders unquestionably have a vital need for a religious leader working on their behalf as an intermediary in Tibet, but they've obviously had problems finding a credible person to do that."

Tibet's Uncertain Future

Leading a diaspora both politically and spiritually while its home country is being destroyed is an unimaginable burden. Add to that the pressures of celebrity and the Western media, and dealing with the projected Orientalist fantasies of a West that has come to see the Dalai Lama as a kind of New Age Pope, without much actual understanding of Tibetan Buddhism, and it's no wonder that the Dalai Lama—now 79—is urging democratized rule.

While the decision not to return as a political leader is final, the Dalai Lama has publicly stated that he will not make the ultimate decision on whether he will return as a spiritual leader until he is 90 (in 2025). According to Dr. Barnett, reincarnation is not determined by individual lamas, but is urged by religious adherents through petition and prayer, making it highly unlikely that the Dalai Lama will not declare that he will return in a spiritual capacity. Because of this, according to Dr. Barnett, the Dalai Lama's comments to *Welt am Sonntag* are "not a categorical statement that there will not be a Dalai Lama in the future."

The uncertainty about both the future of the Dalai Lama role and the remaining lifespan of the Dalai Lama himself may be contributing to anxiety in Tibet, where a wave of self-immolations has accelerated since 2009 in response to the brutality of the Chinese occupation.

"If people did feel that he was he was expecting to die or definitely not coming back, that would have an effect," said Barnett. "People inside Tibet are becoming apprehensive of the potential loss of a leader and spokesman. There are signs that this has made people in Tibet tense about the future. Some people think that [the immolations were] related to insecurities as a result of his decision to retire, but we don't know that for sure. There's very little doubt that there's huge support for him in Tibet and that people would be dramatically affected if they felt he was about to die."

Dr. Thurman feels otherwise:

"[The Dalai Lama] doesn't consider that his decision has caused turmoil," he stated. "The immolation activity stems from the time of the Beijing Olympics, when the Tibetans had a plateau-wide nonviolent revolution, and the Chinese made an incredible crackdown, putting armored police and vehicles everywhere. Thousands of people were arrested and tortured, monks were not left to peacefully pursue their activities, and were forced to pledge allegiance to the PRC, just like in the Cultural Revolution. Monks and laypeople had no room to breathe, and probably felt like carrying out some sort of attack against the Chinese, but instead they immolated themselves to maintain non-violence. This was also found by a Chinese human rights commission, who reported that the immolations were caused by the hardline activities of the secret police and not the Dalai Lama; the report was then rejected by the top people in China, and the lawyers have been put away."

Despite the grim outlook in Tibet, the next generation of Tibetan political leaders remains hopeful about the future of the Tibetan people and resistance movement:

"The fact that the Dalai Lama devolved his leadership shows the incredible trust that he has placed in our people in regards to leading our movement and struggle, especially today, when there is an ongoing crisis with self-immolations," Tenzin Dolkar, executive director of Students for a Free Tibet told me. "His Holiness is our spiritual leader and will continue to be. We have faith and deep trust in His Holiness and his advisors to make the best decisions in regards to the next phase."

(October 24, 2014)

Germany Condemns "Illegal Killings," Halts All Purchases of American Drones

Germany may be leading the world in the rejection of drone policing, as a draft of a new coalition agreement revealed that the government will likely cease purchasing new drones for the next four years. The news is somewhat surprising in a European Union beset by US intervention.

Following her September 22 victory, German Chancellor Angela Merkel is forming a new government coalition to guide the country through the next four years—and a draft of the coalition agreement between the country's conservative Christian Democratic Union and Social Democrats is putting the brakes on finances for drones:

"We categorically reject illegal killings by drones. Germany will support the use of unmanned weapons systems for the purposes of international disarmament and arms control... Before acquiring a qualitatively new arms system, we will thoroughly investigate all associated civil and constitutional guidelines and ethical questions."

Germany had previously been in talks with American and Israeli arms manufacturers to buy sixteen Predator and Heron drones within the coming years.

Both Germany's Social Democrats and the Bavarian Christian Socialist Union have supported delaying the purchase of the drones. Their next move is to come up with alternatives to a proposal from the CDU that would allow the Bundeswehr (German military) to deploy without parliamentary approval if their military actions fit within the EU's legal framework.

When it comes to drones, however, Germany isn't exactly a totally innocent party. According to information released by Pakistani intelligence, Merkel's government worked with the United States to conduct drone strikes in Pakistan by releasing intelligence data on drone targets—including the targets' mobile phone numbers. The German branch of Amnesty International has described the attacks (many of which hit children and seniors) as "war crimes," and called the drone strike program "a license to kill, which completely ignores human rights standards and international law."

And Germany's delay of drone purchases may have as much to do with the financial bottom line as any ethical one. A single Predator drone cost $4.03 million as of 2010; Israeli Herons run around $10 million. Earlier this year, German Defense Minister Thomas de Maizière, a member of Merkel's Christian Democratic Union party, cancelled the Euro Hawk surveillance drone program after it failed the requirements for certification to fly in German airspace, and the terminated program cost the government more than 500 million euros (around $650 million).

It's been a strained time for German-US relations. Last month, German Chancellor Angela Merkel told the world that "spying on friends is not on at all" after it was revealed that the NSA had tapped her mobile phone and conducted massive spying operations in France and Spain. The relations between the two countries have been so damaged that even John McCain has called for NSA chief General Alexander's resignation.

Sea changes are occurring in European and American relations, post-Snowden—and it remains to be seen what new international order will emerge from the fray. But for now, it seems that American-style NSA/drone totalitarianism is anything but certain.

(November 15, 2013)

Insanity: Female Inmates Forcibly Sterilized in California Prisons

Between 2006 and 2010, at least 148 female inmates were sterilized by doctors under contract with the California Department of Corrections and Rehabilitation, according to a report by the Center for Investigative Reporting.

Though there was no official state approval for the tubal ligations—commonly known as having one's "tubes tied," a procedure in which the fallopian tubes are blocked or cut, permanently sterilizing the individual—the state is recorded as having paid doctors $147,460 to perform ligations between 1997 and 2010.

According to inmates and prisoner advocates, women who underwent the surgery (while incarcerated at the California Institution for Women in Corona or the Valley State Prison for Women in Chowchilla) were coerced into agreeing to tubal ligation. The women were signed up for the procedure while they were pregnant—inmates who had served multiple prison sentences or had several children were suggested for the operations.

Though state funds for tubal ligations have been restricted since 1994—requiring approval from a health care committee and investigation into each individual case—doctors continued to perform the ligations under the assumption that they didn't need permission. Officials claimed that the operations were performed to benefit the health of women who had undergone multiple C-sections; women were told that the ligations would be empowering, putting them on equal footing as women on the outside.

However, women who underwent the ligations stated that they had only had one C-section, were repeatedly pressured into agreeing to surgery and were not told why the surgeries were considered necessary. One inmate was pushed by a doctor to agree to ligation while sedated and strapped to a surgical table. Though in an altered state of consciousness, she successfully resisted—records show that doctors had tried talking her into ligation twice previously, without providing any reason or justification. Other ligations were pressured for while women were undergoing labor—which would be illegal in a federal prison, and has been ruled coercive, as the trauma of labor can impair a woman's decision-making process.

Corey G. Johnson—the reporter who broke the ligations story for the Center for Investigative Reporting—told me that interviewing the women who had undergone the ligations was an at-times grueling process due to the suffering they had withstood.

"The women have expressed sadness, mostly, with dashes of anger and reluctance," he explained. "Prison is not a happy place, and many of the women I spoke with experienced various traumas while on the inside. It hasn't been easy reliving those moments."

Questioned about the ligations by Johnson, officials claimed that the $147,460 the state spent on the procedures was minimal "compared to what you save in welfare paying for these unwanted children—as they procreated more."

Johnson relayed that the public and governmental reaction to the story has been massive:

"The public's response has been overwhelming. Strong outrage for the most part—with some counter voices of support for the doctors involved. The interest has crossed gender, religious, political and geographic lines… Reaction from governmental actors has been what I expected. Lawmakers called for investigations. The federal office in charge of prison healthcare told me they thought the story was fair. They're now responding to legislative questioning. And the state correction department—where these surgeries sprung from—has been quiet and virtually non-responsive."

Forced sterilizations of prisoners, the poor and the mentally ill were only officially banned in California in 1979. From 1909 to 1964, California was the United States' top sterilizer, forcing surgery on over 20,000 men and women under a statewide eugenics program so successful that even the Nazis asked for California's advice in the 1930s.

Much like the justifications given by the Valley State officials above, the reasoning behind California's early eugenics program was to save the state money by reducing welfare and relief. But California was by no means the only state running a eugenics program on its citizens—32 states in the US passed laws allowing forcible sterilization in the early part of the 20th century, beginning with Indiana in 1907; by 1979 over 60,000 Americans had been sterilized.

The dark history of America's eugenics programs is only now being publicly re-assessed. 2003 saw California's then-Governor Gray Davis issue a formal apology for the program. Some states, like North Carolina, are considering reparations.
With the old wounds of California's history freshly re-opened, the state is calling for an open investigation of what happened at the California Institution for Women and Valley State. But for the women who underwent ligation, the damage is already permanent.

(July 18, 2013)

The Long Tail of America's Eugenics Problem

Eugenics—the idea that the reproduction of human beings can be artificially managed to select for desired genetic traits—is one of the great shames of modern history. And while the concept is commonly attributed to Nazi Germany's obsession with racial purity, recent events in California stand as a reminder that the United States has a long history of eugenics programs as well.

After Darwin broke new ground with the theory of natural selection, it was only a matter of time before somebody misapplied the idea to human beings. The resultant "social Darwinism" and its applied branch, eugenics, were virulent memes in the late 19th and early 20th century—achieving their murderous apex in the Second World War.

The US's own eugenics obsession predated Hitler's rise to power by decades. From 1907 to 1979, in a dark history that is only recently being assessed, America forcibly sterilized an estimated 60,000 people. While compulsory sterilization programs—which attempted to keep the poor and undesirables from passing on their genes, and were clearly the product of eugenics—no longer officially exist in any of the 50 states (Oregon performed the last one in 1981), forcible sterilization is still happening, as evidenced by recent revelations in California prisons.

Beginning in the late 19th century, America's national eugenics program received funding from many of the country's largest corporate concerns, including from the Carnegie Institution, Rockefeller Foundation, J. H. Kellogg, Proctor and Gamble, Hanes and the Harriman railroad fortune. Proponents of eugenics (including Alexander Graham Bell and Luther Burbank) concluded that individuals with higher social standing were inherently genetically superior, and pushed not only for forced sterilization of the poor, disabled and "immoral" but also immigration restriction and anti-miscegenation laws. Even alcoholism was a trait targeted for elimination via eugenics.

From 1909 to 1964, California was the United States' top sterilizer, forcing surgery on over 20,000 men and women under a statewide eugenics program so successful that even the Nazis asked for California's advice in the 1930s. The state's early eugenics program was justified as a way to save money by reducing welfare and relief.

Forced sterilizations of prisoners, the poor and the mentally ill were only officially banned in California in 1979. A report published earlier this month by the Center for Investigative Reporting revealed that, at least in California, sterilization continued sporadically with female prison inmates up to 2010.

But California was by no means the only state severing the reproductive systems of its own citizens—32 states in the US passed laws allowing forcible sterilization in the early part of the 20th century, beginning with Indiana in 1907. North Carolina was a particularly egregious case: the state is recorded as having sterilized 1,110 men and 6,418 women between 1929 and 1974. 40% of those operated on were people of color, and 60% were white; a third of the women sterilized were under the age of 18, all the way down to the age of 9.

Widespread academic support for eugenics meant there were 376 university courses offered on the subject by 1928 among the country's top schools, with more than 20,000 students enrolled. Feminist and women's associations were also staunch proponents of eugenics.

The US even partnered with Puerto Rico to sterilize more than a third of the island's women between 1930 and 1970—Puerto Ricans referred to sterilization, which was given to women for free upon entering the workforce, as "La Operacion."

The program was conducted as a response to a slow economy and high population rate, targeting working-class women the government felt were too stupid to use contraception.

US pharmaceutical corporations also conducted early trials of the birth control pill in Puerto Rico in the 1950s before achieving

FDA approval, leading to three casualties. (Margaret Sanger, a primary American champion of birth control and founder of Planned Parenthood, was a major proponent of sterilization, believing it would prevent unplanned children from being born into poverty, as well as preventing the spread of disease and disabilities.)

Jane Lawrence, writing in *American Indian Quarterly*, alleged that the Indian Health Service sterilized over 25 percent of Native American women between the ages of 15-44 in the 1960s and 70s. The sterilizations were conducted, according to Lawrence, not just for population control but also to give doctors practice in performing gynecological surgery.

The history of America's eugenics programs has resurfaced in the public spotlight in recent years. 2003 saw California's then-Governor Gray Davis issue a formal apology for the program. Some states, like North Carolina, are considering reparations, although action has been slow coming.

For those who've lived their lives on the right side of the American dream, the sterilization programs may come as a shock, a corrosive instance of "it can't happen here" that did happen here. But for those who've already seen how ugly and brutal America's dark side can be, it may come as no surprise at all. And reparations or no, for those who underwent sterilization—many of which are still alive—the damage is permanent.

(July 29, 2013)

When Monsanto Had Its Own Disneyland Exhibit

Remembering the Monsanto-sponsored exhibit that touted Better Living Through Chemistry to a generation of American children, 1955-1966

Pliant, malleable, innocent, so trusting: This is the American mass mind, the clay that corporations and advertisers manipulate every day. This is the stuff from which the 20th century's greatest empire was built; it is America's greatest natural resource. In the name of harnessing that resource, every successive generation of Americans since World War II has been immersed in a liquid lattice of increasingly sophisticated electronic propaganda, aimed at embedding the will of corporations into every available mind.

There is perhaps no better example of the American way of propaganda than Disneyland—which might, from one angle, be seen as a massive factory for imprinting children with corporate values. A mechanized, corporatized colonization of the imaginal space of childhood—a space colonized and then bent to the will of the occupying force. That force being, of course, whoever happens to be footing the bill.

Between 1955 and 1966, the Monsanto corporation sponsored Disneyland's "Hall of Chemistry," a Tomorrowland exhibit that touted the benefits of Better Living Through Chemistry—specifically, the kind of chemistry that Monsanto (at that point still a chemical company, having yet to make the transition into agribusiness) specialized in.

The exhibit featured highlights like the "Chematron," displaying eight huge tubes of common materials found in nature—which the exhibit explained could be used to develop over 500 Monsanto chemicals. These chemicals, the exhibit cried aloud, would "promise to build a new and easier way of life for you, your children, and generations to come."

An advertisement in the *Los Angeles Times*, dated July 15, 1955, read:

MONSANTO… in Tomorrowland… shows you the romance of chemistry, how chemically-made products benefit your life, how they can make a new and startling world tomorrow. Your food, clothing, housing, health, and transportation all depend on chemistry… and the future holds some exciting, wonderful things in store for you.

The "Hall of Chemistry" would be only the first Monsanto-sponsored exhibit at Disneyland. Others would include the Monsanto "House of the Future," which opened in 1957, and "Fashions and Fabrics Through the Ages," in 1965; finally, in August 1967, came "Adventure Thru Inner Space," in which Disneyland attendees were shrunk to microscopic size for a magical mystery tour through the world of molecules and atoms.

"The problem with science is that it can be perverted."
– *The Prisoner*

But 1967 was not as innocent as 1955. As American children were being awed by Monsanto's new microscopic fantasia, their drafted older brothers were hard at work spraying the Monsanto-produced defoliant Agent Orange over the jungles of Laos, Cambodia and Vietnam, destroying 17.8% of the Vietnamese environment, affecting between 3-4.8 million Vietnamese, causing a reported 400,000 deaths and leading to an estimated 150-500,000 Vietnamese children being born with birth defects that would have made Lovecraft flinch.

While impressionable, trusting American children were being lead through Disneyland's mass-hypnosis chambers, inculcated with trust in Monsanto's Great Chemical Promise, Vietnamese mothers were being sprayed like livestock with chemicals that would lead to them giving birth to monstrous children—chemicals manufactured by the exact same company. To this day, Monsanto maintains that there is no causal scientific link between those tragedies and Agent Orange.

When America and the multinational corporations it raised are a memory, the effects of the empire's chemical, nuclear and biological weapons will linger. The genetically-modified crops; the atomic testing; the depleted uranium bullets. Their effects will stay. And of the propaganda and the delusions—weapons in their own way, though with no such half-life—there will be no trace.

(April 2, 2014)

Mexico Just Won a Major Victory Against Monsanto

Mexico just won a major victory against Monsanto: A group of beekeepers just blocked the agribusiness giant from planting genetically modified soybeans.

A district judge in Yucatán just threw out a permit given to Monsanto by the Mexican ministry of agriculture that would have allowed the company to plant over 625,000 acres of GMO soybeans throughout seven states in Mexico. This comes on the heels of protests by Mayan farmers and beekeepers, Greenpeace, the Mexican National Commission for the Knowledge and Use of Biodiversity, the National Commission of Natural Protected Areas and the National Institute of Ecology.

The judge was persuaded that Monsanto's GMO crops, and its Roundup pesticide, would pose not only a massive threat to human health, but would also devastate the soil, water and bee colonies. The alleged effect of glyphosate on bee colonies was enough to convince the judge that allowing Monsanto free reign could well have destroyed the state's income from export of bee products—European Union convention restricts the importation of honey derived from GM products ruled unfit for human consumption. It also mandates that any honey that contains more than 0.9% genetically modified pollen must be labelled as GM and non-organic, likely meaning that Mexican exports would be dead on the shelves.

(It's the fear of such sales drops occurring in the United States, due to consumers expressing suspicion or rejecting GMO products, that has lead the agribusiness industry to ensure that GMO products aren't labelled in the country, via lobbying and throwing funds against state initiatives focused on GMO labeling.)

Monsanto's soybeans are genetically modified to be resistant to the company's own Roundup pesticide. That means that a giant crop of Monsanto soybeans can be planted in a field and then sprayed with Roundup, and the pesticide will only kill the weeds in the field, leaving the Roundup-resistant soybeans intact—and meaning that the final consumer of the product not only gets a genetically modified crop, but one that's also been saturated with Roundup. Contrary to the questionable, potentially paid claims of "experts" like Neil deGrasse Tyson, this transgenic technology has nothing to do with the crop cross-breeding techniques that humanity has been using for over 7,500 years—transgenics have only been in development since the 1980s.

The ruling hinges on the Mexican constitution, which ensures that the government must consult with indigenous communities before making decisions that may affect them. Analysts have suggested that the ruling will set a precedent making it easier for indigenous communities to fight further pushes for GMO soy and corn—indigenous people in Mexico are currently forced to fight in courts simply to uphold those rights.

It's worth noting that while NAFTA makes it increasingly difficult for national governments to fight corporations, the upcoming Trans-Pacific Partnership may make it nigh-on impossible—allowing multinational corporations to sue local governments over lost profits from decisions like this one. Since the legal fees both for fighting and losing to multinationals could potentially severely penalize or even bankrupt national governments, instances like this of countries successfully standing up to corporations may become increasingly few and far between.

(August 19, 2014)

Why Neil deGrasse Tyson is Dead Wrong About GMOs

Neil deGrasse Tyson claims that genetically modified food is nothing to worry about, because human beings have been doing it for thousands of years. Here's why that's an utter, bald-faced lie.

Yesterday, a clip surfaced on YouTube of Neil deGrasse Tyson being asked about the fear surrounding genetically modified food. Tyson responded, emphatically, that there's no such thing as food that's not genetically modified, stating:

"Practically every food you buy in a store for consumption by humans is genetically modified food. There are no wild, seedless watermelons. There's no wild cows... You list all the fruit, and all the vegetables, and ask yourself, is there a wild counterpart to this? If there is, it's not as large, it's not as sweet, it's not as juicy, and it has way more seeds in it. We have systematically genetically modified all the foods, the vegetables and animals that we have eaten ever since we cultivated them. It's called artificial selection. That's how we genetically modify them."

He then, in most objective scientific fashion, angrily tears in to the person asking the question by stating:

"So now we can do it in a lab, all the sudden you're going to complain? If you're the complainer type, go back and eat the apples that grow wild... they're something that's this big" [mimes tiny area with hands] "and they're tart... they're not sweet like red delicious apples. We manufacture those. That's a genetic modification. Do you realize silk cannot be produced in the wild? The silk worm as we cultivate it has no wild counterpart, because it would die in the wild. So there's not even any silk anymore. So we are creating and modifying the biology of the world to serve our needs. I don't have a problem with that, because we've been doing that for tens of thousands of years. So chill out." [Audience laughter.]

Here's the problem: Not only did Tyson not actually answer the question, he actually spun the discussion in a completely unrelated direction, and then used his perceived authority and crowd support to shut down the questioner.

Go back to the beginning of the clip: The questioner doesn't ask about genetically modified food. He asks about transgenics.

The genetic modification that Tyson is discussing is plant breeding and hybridization. And yes, plant breeding dates back thousands of years—about 7,500, not the 10,000 that Tyson claims—to when farmers in Mexico created maize by planting the earlier crop *teosinte* and selecting for desirable genetic traits over the course of centuries. More recently—for instance, in the case of Norman Borlaug's world-changing dwarf wheat—scientists have achieved laudable successes with hybridization. This is what Tyson is rightly claiming success for.

But that's not what the millions of people around the world concerned about genetically modified organisms are worried about. And it's NOT what the questioner asked Tyson. He asked about *transgenesis*, a process put into use in the 1980s by big agribusiness firms like Monsanto.

Transgenesis, specifically, is the introduction of foreign genetic material into a living organism. Monsanto has most often achieved it by ballistic DNA injection or "gene gun," which blasts genetic material into undifferentiated plant cells in a petri dish—this destroys most of the cells, but usually leaves some that have successfully merged. Transgenesis can also be achieved using liposomes, plasmid vectors, viral vectors, pronuclear injection and protoplast fusion. Monsanto's current preferred method of transgenesis is using the bacteria *Agrobacterium tumefaciens* to infect plants with desired DNA traits. Transgenesis can even be used to insert genes that code for pharmaceuticals into living organisms.

Monsanto currently uses transgenesis technology to produce its highly successful Bt and Roundup Ready crops—in the case of Bt corn, for instance, Monsanto uses a gene gun to blast soil bacteria into corn DNA so that, in the field, the corn produces its own bacterial insecticide to burst the stomachs of the insects that eat it. This, of course, is claimed to be completely safe for the humans who end up consuming the corn (but then, big agribusiness tend to be the ones funding the studies—and big agribusinesses like Syngenta have allegedly stalked and even threatened the families of scientists who uncover data they don't want to hear about).

Other genetically modified products, like Monsanto's Roundup Ready seeds, are modified so that they can be sprayed with pesticide and live while the weeds around them die. The pesticide glyphosate then remains on the plant.

Or goats engineered to produce spider silk in their milk. Seems pretty natural.

A man of Tyson's intelligence and stature should surely know the difference between transgenic crops and hybridized ones. But that probably doesn't matter, because whoever pays him has him reciting the same talking points on GMOs that are always used to shut down dissent.

In using these talking points, he echoes both Tony Blair and even George W. Bush, who declared in 2001 that "for thousands of years, man has been utilizing and modifying biological processes to improve man's quality of life" (from the Federal Register). As Bush Jr. was reiterating the same talking points that Tyson parrots above, Donald Rumsfeld, John Ashcroft and Bush Sr., all of whom maintained high-level ties to Monsanto, were preparing to invade Iraq, where they would issue the post-war document Order 81, forcing Iraqi farmers to *only* buy registered seeds, primarily from Monsanto. Such is total war.

Neil deGrasse Tyson is not your friend—he's just another shill for the Apocalypse Machine. Shame on him. To appoint yourself not just a public educator but a culture's arbiter of reason, the one who decides what is real and what is not for the public mind, and then to vomit up corporate lies—this is treason to the science he claims to uphold.

tips fedora

(July 31, 2014)

Every Person on Earth Is Polluted With Hundreds of Human-Made Toxins

Every person on Earth is polluted—even newborns.

That's according to Dr. James Siow, of Australia's National Institute of Integrative Medicine. He claims that global pollution is now so bad, every human being on the planet is contaminated with hundreds of human-made toxins—and neither the world's governments nor its health care providers are doing enough about it.

Even infants come into the world tainted with 232 potentially fatal industrial chemicals and pollutants, said Siow, citing the Environmental Working Group. And that body pollution can be carried forward three generations, he says.

These pollutants come from consumer products like cosmetics, food, packaging, cleaning agents, pesticides, even bedding. The 275 worst global pollutants are listed here—the top three are arsenic, lead, and mercury.

The conclusion that environmental toxicity can have negative health effects isn't controversial. Siow is reiterating data from a series of studies, including ones from the *Lancet*, the University of Washington and President Obama's Cancer Panel. What *is* controversial, according to Siow, is that nobody has taken action, even though governments and the scientific community have known about the problem since the 1980s.

I got in touch with Siow to discuss what this toxicity is doing to us, why no action has been taken, and what people can do to minimize the effects of living on a poison planet.

JL: *Hello, Dr. Siow. You've suggested that everybody on Earth is polluted. Where's this pollution coming from?*

Siow: Mainly from superfund sites, which are leftover waste sites of their respective industries. It also comes from industries that put out air pollution; the US... has not ratified the Kyoto Protocol that deals with the gradual reduction from these industries.

Who are the main offenders?

Industries involving power generation from fossil fuel—coal, oil and natural gas. Any industries that have an industrial exhaust silo.

What are the long term ramifications of this toxicity going to be? And what diseases and disorders are we seeing now—or are going to see in the future—that are directly caused by or aggravated by these toxins?

The accumulation of toxicity will lead to a toxic body burden from combined exposures. This concept has been addressed through the World Health Organization, the International Program on Chemical Safety (IPCS) Harmonization Project, the EPA and the Council of the European Union, so there is general consensus on the severity of the problem.

For example, diseases related to air pollutants are diabetes, cardiac failure and cardiac ischemic events, lung cancer, and asthma. There are many studies currently assessing the effects of pollutants on human diseases.

Are doctors trained to look for the symptoms of chemical poisoning?

The study of clinical toxicology is a post-graduate medical course. The training is still available from specific post-graduate organizations. However, the training takes around three years, and isn't as popular as other post-graduate courses. Undergraduate medical courses will be lip service at best, as most undergraduate curriculum is already quite condensed as it is.

How persistent are the toxins?

It's dependent on the type of toxins; some radioactive substances like uranium have different long half-lives depending on the isotope.

Another factor in humans is the ability to clear the toxins from the body; there are large genetic variations in the ability to clear toxins depending on the effectiveness of the metallothionein system in each individual. The nutritional factors that contribute to this clearance are also dependent on the how healthy a diet the person adopts.

Toxins can access the human body via three main routes: What we eat, drink and breathe. Other exposures depend on specific circumstances. For example, if a worker is exposed to a specific toxin at work and keeps getting re-exposed on a daily basis, then the body burden and persistence will be high. For example, in the past, when many miners were exposed to asbestos, the long term accumulation led to asbestosis many decades down the line, and some [miners] went on to develop mesothelioma, a form of cancer affecting the lining of the lung. But the delay between the exposure and onset was separated by many decades, and it took a while to decipher the cause-and-effect relationship.

Today, we have evidence of newborns having some 200-plus chemical toxins in their cord blood; these can only come from the persistence of these chemicals from the mother, and through the placental circulation over the nine month in utero period.

I truly believe that this persistency will cause epigenetic issues and affect health adversely. Not every chemical will be removed from this baby in its lifetime, especially if awareness is not forthcoming. The persistence of these toxins in the environment has been extensively studied.

What evidence do you have that the toxins can persist for three generations?

The data comes mainly from epigenetic and genomic studies about trans-generational toxic effects.

A brief analogy: If you consider the cord blood study, you can appreciate that the 200-plus chemical toxins in the cord blood can only be contributed by the mother via placenta blood circulation—hence two generations. Now what are the chances that all of these toxins will be cleared by all ten babies before they become parents? (Another generation.) Now think where the toxins of the mother that gave birth to the tested baby may come from? (Her own mother would be a likely contributing source—another generation.)

You've called the lack of action on this issue "inexplicable." But what do you think is going on? Why have governments and health care professionals been slow to act on this? Is it just incompetence, or are there wider issues?

In one word: funding. There is truly a lack of funding and appreciation of global pollutants affecting diseases. Most funding has been directed towards remediation of polluted sites and environmental research by scientists, not clinicians.

The key issue that has contributed to the lack of action or understanding in the past has been the time lag between the cause and effect of specific toxins. The Agency for Toxic Substances and Disease Registry (ATSDR) has mentioned delays of around 10 to 40 years for the onset of diseases.

In the current age, however, there is really no excuse for not being aware of the issues of toxicity and the contributions these have to diseases. Unfortunately, most undergraduates and post-graduates in medicine have never been taught about these matters, and as such are quite alienated from the available data. Many chronic diseases in our current society are not satisfactorily managed, and addressing the issues of toxic burden together with currently known factors will certainly contribute to better standards of management.

At the national and global level, the US EPA and the WHO do recognize the importance of toxic chemicals and their impact on diseases. However, this knowledge has been slow in adoption into clinical practice. I guess I'm in favor of giving the benefit of the doubt to patients in circumstances where the question of toxicity arises, and chronic diseases have not responded to routine measures, because of my qualifications and awareness of these issues. However, in routine practices, I feel many cases are missed on a daily basis, and in the light of our current knowledge and understanding of health impacts due to pollutants, this is most unfortunate.

What action would we need to take to begin reversing the situation?

Managing the body's toxic burden is a preventative medicine issue in the main. Of course, there are cases of acute and chronic toxicity that are managed in emergency situations and in clinical practices as well.

All humans from birth to tomb have some degree of pollutants in their internal environment, and are also exposed to pollutants in the external environment. Christopher Wild has proposed the concept of the Exposome. This is the sum of exposures from all sources.

(October 11, 2013)

Scientist Threatened and Stalked for Findings on Syngenta Herbicide

Tyrone Hayes, a scientist at the University of California, Berkeley, was hired by agribusiness giant Syngenta to study the herbicide atrazine, which is used on half the corn crops in the US, as well as Christmas tree farms and golf courses. What Hayes found was exactly what Syngenta didn't want to hear: in studying atrazine's effects on frogs, he discovered that the pesticide has a disruptive effect on the endocrine system.

Ready for this? According to Hayes, it apparently interferes with male development, causes males to switch gender to female and develop ovaries and eggs, drops testosterone production, "chemically castrates" male frogs and later leads to development of homosexual behavior as the gender-altered frogs begin to prefer same-sex mating.

Hayes' research suggests that atrazine has the same effects on humans—however, before a thousand headlines like "Shocker: Corn Makes You Gay" are launched into the blogosphere, I'll note that while researchers can often switch sexual orientation in animals by altering hormone levels, there aren't significant differences in hormone levels between gay and straight humans. (In fact, gay men often have higher testosterone levels than straight men, not lower.) Yet I'll also note that a 2007 study found that testosterone levels have massively dropped in American males since the early twentieth century, for reasons unknown. Chemical and pesticide tampering with the food supply would be an obvious place to begin experimental inquiry.

Also according to Hayes, Syngenta was allegedly so displeased with the results that they began asking him to change or misrepresent data, eventually telling him not to publish his findings. They also hired new scientists to discredit the data, attempted to discredit Hayes and, according to the Berkeley scientist, began stalking him and making threats of violence, including threats of lynching (Hayes is black), sexual violence and even threats of sexual violence against his wife and children. Also according to Hayes, the University of California, Berkeley offered little aid or protection, expressing far more concern about the financial bottom line than any kind of truth or responsibility to its academics.

Another key takeaway is that atrazine induces overproduction of estrogen, potentially leading to breast cancer. Concurrent to its marketing of atrazine, Syngenta (previously known as Novartis) was marketing a treatment for breast cancer that functioned by blocking estrogen through the exact opposite mechanism as atrazine—making money, one might extrapolate, by both inducing and then offering to aid the problem they may have helped create.

Syngenta is a Swiss chemical company in the seeds-and-pesticides business; they reported $14.2 billion in revenue in 2012. Syngenta is a major "competitor" of Monsanto, though Syngenta has largely managed to stay out of the limelight and avoid the massive public outroar that its sister company Monsanto has faced. (The world's top four biotech companies are Syngenta, Monsanto, Bayer and DuPont.)

(February 21, 2014)

Thanks to Dredging and Coal, the Great Barrier Reef Is More Threatened Than Ever

On December 10, the Australian government approved the expansion of a coal port at Abbot Point in Northern Queensland. A victory for Australia's booming coal economy, it may also massively wound the nearby Great Barrier Reef.

That decision, however, has proved so incredibly controversial that the Great Barrier Reef Marine Park Authority has now delayed its decision on whether to grant permits to dump the dredge spoil in the Great Barrier Reef Marine Park until January 31.

Expansion of the coal port will entail dredging 3 million cubic meters of mud from the site, which will then be dumped into land infill projects. Australia's environment minister Greg Hunt told Reuters that the current agreement was reduced from 38 million cubic meters of dredging to protect the environment, while Greenpeace countered that any dredging on this scale will have disastrous effects on the reef. Adding to the environmental toll is the 120 million tonnes of added coal shipping capacity the port's four new terminals will provide.

Abbot Point will handle exports from the Galilee Basin, a geological depression that boasts massive coal reserves, but which up to now has lacked export infrastructure. The project will also create a coal-shipping highway directly through the Great Barrier Reef for thousands of ships to export coal to energy-hungry Asia. According to the Christian Science Monitor, Australia's coal exports, already the largest in the world, have increased by 30 percent within the last year alone.

Indian firm Adani Group, seeking resources for the subcontinent's similarly massive energy demands, will helm the Abbot Point project. Greenpeace estimates that the number of ships passing through the reef will increase from 1,700 a year to 10,150 by 2020. An $18 billion liquid gas facility and pipeline will also be built at nearby Curtis Island.

Construction of the Abbot Point coal port reached provisional approval directly following the election of Prime Minister Tony Abbott—a climate denier—whose conservative Liberal-National coalition took power in September amid promises of mining and gas industry expansion. Hunt approved the construction of the coal port along with the proviso that it will be built with the "strictest conditions in Australian history."

Despite those assurances, both environmentalists and the Australian tourism industry were enraged by the December 11 decision. According to a report from the reef's government authority, the Great Barrier Reef boosted the Australian economy by $5.68 billion from 2011-2012, and created 69,000 full-time jobs, mostly in tourism. Those numbers, however, are dwarfed by the $20 billion a year in tax revenues paid by Australia's coal industry into federal and state budgets.

If the dumping permits are granted, it's just the latest blow to the Great Barrier Reef. The world's largest structure constructed by living beings, the reef stretches 1,400 miles along the east coast of Australia, and can be seen from space. It's also a Unesco World Heritage Site. The Great Barrier Reef, and coral reefs like it, are among the world's most diverse ecosystems, playing host to about a quarter of marine life, despite only covering 0.2 percent of the ocean's total area.

While the dredging problem will likely remain relatively localized, the Great Barrier Reef has already been hit hard by climate change, and massive growth in the Australian coal industry will only make the problem worse. The reef's coral cover has declined by 50 percent over the last three decades due to pollution, ocean acidification, floods, cyclones and the epidemic spread of the crown-of-thorns starfish, which eats coral. Atmospheric carbon dioxide has also made it increasingly difficult for marine animals, including corals, to produce shells. That's on top of nearly a century of reef-killing agricultural runoff and development. Charlie Veron, chief scientist of the Australian Institute of Marine Science, has predicted that the Great Barrier Reef has no more than 20 years left.

(December 24, 2013)

III
BEAUTIFUL OUTSIDERS

How America Interrupted Wilhelm Reich's Orgasmic Utopia

It was the greatest incidence of scientific persecution in American history.

Dr. Wilhelm Reich—a brilliant but troubling psychoanalyst who had once been considered Freud's most promising student, who had enraged not only the Nazis and Stalinists but also the psychoanalytic, medical and scientific communities, who had survived two World Wars and fled to the US—was now under the thumb of the FDA, on suspicion of being a medical fraud engaged in a "sex racket."

Reich had taken Freud's theories far. Very far. Too far, according to the FDA. Starting with Freud's connection of sexual repression to neurosis, Reich had theorized that it was the physical inability to surrender to orgasm that underlay neurosis, and turned people to fascism and authoritarianism. He moved from Freud's simple talking cure to character analysis, a therapy designed to help his patients overcome the physical and respiratory blocks that prevented them from experiencing pleasure. And finally—and most dangerously—he claimed that the orgasm was an expression of orgone, the force of life itself, and that with devices called orgone accumulators he could harness this force to cure neurosis, disease and even affect the weather and help crops grow.

For these lines of inquiry, the FDA demanded Reich appear in court to defend himself. He refused, stating that claims of scientific truth should be settled by experiment, not in court. The court responded by issuing an injunction against the sale or transportation of his devices across state lines, and proceeded to systematically burn his books and journals—not just Reich's writing, but any written material that contained the word "orgone" was fair game for destruction. FDA agents also began destroying his devices and laboratory with axes. The book-burning campaign would continue up to 1970.

When one of Reich's associates broke the injunction against Reich's wishes, and transported an orgone accumulator across state lines, Reich was arrested on contempt of court and sentenced to two years in prison. He died of heart failure in the federal penitentiary in Lewisberg, Pennsylvania in 1957, ten years after the FDA had launched its investigation.

Instead of simply disproving his theories by experiment, the FDA had effectively burned Reich at the stake.

But who was Wilhelm Reich? What was it about this man and his theories that invoked the wrath of nearly every political and scientific faction of his time? What provoked a systematic campaign of attacks hardly suggestive of a sane and rational America that had just won the war against the book-burning Nazis—and more reminiscent of the Inquistion, the incineration of Giordiano Bruno, or the ending of *Frankenstein*, in which angry villagers with torches and pitchforks burn down the mad scientist's castle?

Fury on Earth

Reich was born on March 24, 1897 in Galicia, Austria-Hungary (now Ukraine). He grew up in a farm environment, and embraced sexuality early, first with family servants and, in late adolescence, in daily visits to brothels. At the age of 12, Reich discovered his mother having sex with one of his tutors. When he told his father, the man repeatedly beat Reich's mother until she committed suicide. Reich blamed himself.

Sent into the Army during WWI, Reich saw "man's inhumanity to man" first-hand at the Italian front. Afterwards he studied medicine at the University of Vienna, where he became dissatisfied with what he considered the "mechanistic" approach to life he saw in the students' cold dissection of corpses, and began a quest for the creative energy he felt must underlie life. It was then, in 1919, that he met Sigmund Freud. Welcomed into the burgeoning psychoanalytic movement, Freud allowed Reich to begin seeing patients at the age of 22—he was soon earmarked as Freud's star pupil, perhaps even destined for leadership.

Freud had identified the root of neurosis in repressed sexuality, and the driving force of life to be the libido—stating that "no neurosis is possible with a normal vita sexualis." His two greatest students, Jung and Reich, were to take his theory farther. But while Jung would move into the realm of mythology, symbolism and the occult, Reich would venture in a completely different direction: into the body.

Moving beyond the realm of psychic repression, Reich postulated that trauma was also repressed physically. A child who was abused, for instance, and who lacked the emotional development to process such an event, would "store" the trauma as muscular tension, which could become chronic pains in later life and form the individual's general physicality and character, their approach to life. Reich believed that the fascist character was created by early trauma and a repressive or abusive attitude towards sexuality that would manifest as physical and emotional "rigidity" in later life.

Reich's approach to therapy would therefore go beyond the simple talking cure: Reich would also use deep and often extremely painful tissue massage on the patient's areas of muscular tension to release the buried trauma, and work with clients to deepen their constricted breathing and express buried emotions, even repressed anger and rage. It was this approach, combined with Reich's pro-sexuality attitude, that scandalized the public and put his career on a rocket to nowhere. (He would later even have patients partially or totally undress, breaking analytic neutrality totally.)

Yet Reich soon found that working through blocks in both the psyche and musculature would create immense emotional release in his patients, even feelings of bodily elation and bliss. (Reich called these physical sensations "orgonotic streamings.") As his practice continued, he came to theorize that underneath the layers of muscular repression lay what he called "orgiastic potency," and that what his patients were armoring themselves against was the loss of ego in full orgasmic release. He codified his theory in his major work, *The*

Function of the Orgasm, in which he stated that the orgasm exists not only as a reproductive function but as a way for the body to regulate tension and achieve emotional release. Full orgasmic release—in which the individual holds nothing back and does not seek to repress the function psychically or physically—was seen by Reich as a key to mental health. As he wrote in the book, "Psychic illnesses are the result of a disturbance of the natural capacity for love."

Freud was ambivalent. Though he wrote of *The Function of the Orgasm* that "I am in no way opposed to your attempt to solve the problem of neurasthenia by explaining it on the basis of the absence of genital primacy," he withheld support for Reich's more extreme theories within the broader psychoanalytic community, perhaps with one eye on preserving his own hard-won cultural victories on the issue of sexuality. Without Freud's support, the psychoanalytic community quickly washed their hands of the young analyst.

Things began to take a turn for the worse for Reich. Struggling with the reaction against him, he asked to be psychoanalyzed by Freud. His mentor and father figure turned down his request for help—Reich was deeply hurt. Soon afterwards his brother died of tuberculosis; Reich also contracted it and spent a year in a sanatorium. Shocked by the sequence of events, he became radicalized and soon joined the Communist Party. Witnessing first-hand the police indiscriminately shoot and kill 84 workers and injure 600 in the July Revolt of 1927 in Vienna further convinced Reich that something was very wrong with the world. Watching from the sidelines, he noted not that the police were brutal but that they were robotic, as if in a trance—armored.

Working in the streets, Reich now connected sexual repression with the economic repression he saw all around him. He opened a series of clinics throughout Vienna, offering analysis as well as sexual education and contraceptives to working-class people. (At the time, liberals advocated contraception only for the married.)

Reich moved to Berlin just in time to witness the rise of the Nazis—the apex of character armoring. But though he continued to develop his theories and write, even the Communists delayed on publishing his material, and soon his contract with the International Psychoanalytic Publishers was cancelled, after he began advocating sexual education and contraceptives for teenagers instead of abstinence—and even suggesting that healthy, demystified sexual expression by children might be crucial to raising healthy adults, and that their questions should be answered frankly. His opponents took his statements to mean that children should be able to watch parental intercourse—not Reich's stance. He also spoke out against monogamy, advocating "lasting love relationships" which were not enforced, or held together by law instead of love, which would instead lead to "sexual dulling." He lashed out at the economically dependent status of women that kept them trapped in enforced marriages. Most radically of all, he suggested that children should be raised by an extended community, thereby freeing them from the neuroses of their biological parents. (These attitudes were to some extent influenced by similar social experiments occurring in the Soviet Union.)

Reich was entering taboo territory that few dared—or have dared since—to enter. His radicalization and experimentation left him a changed man, for better or worse. When he met with Freud again in 1930, his view of his former mentor was now diminished—he saw Freud as a "caged animal."

In 1933, the Nazis came down on Reich hard for his sexual stance, and Reich and his mistress escaped for Denmark—only to be thrown out of the Danish Communist Party. Heading now for Sweden, Reich was placed under surveillance; after the police saw a string of patients coming and going from his hotel they became convinced he was a pimp, and denied him a longer stay. By 1934, he was asked to resign from the International Psychoanalytical Association. (Reich had allegedly shown up at the conference to protest, camping in a tent outside the hall and walking around in a rage with a knife in his belt.)

He was a man disgraced.

I Got an Orgone Accumulator—And It Makes Me Feel Greater

It was in Norway, where he settled for the next five years, that Reich developed a new theory: he came to believe that orgasm carried an actual energy, which he termed orgone, that was expressed not only by the orgasm response but was, in fact, the energy of life itself. This energy, in his view, permeated nature and the cosmos, expressing itself in atmospheric phenomenon like the aurora borealis. (Freud had actually posited a similar theory in the 1890s, but scrapped it.) Reich further stated that the orgone could be observed objectively, and that it was composed of blue-colored particles called bions that he had seen under a microscope.

Having enraged the psychoanalysts, communists and fascists, Reich now came under direct attack by the scientific community. Norwegian scientists waged war against him in the liberal press, rejecting his research out of hand (but also refusing to submit it to a detailed control study), and seeking to deport him. The Norwegian government, which had just taken PR flack for deporting Trotsky, compromised and allowed him to stay, but arranged that he be unable to practice psychoanalysis.

When World War II erupted, Reich fled to America, taking up residence in Flushing, Queens and experimenting on injecting cancerous mice with bions. But fresh indignity waited: after being confused with another Wilhelm Reich, who ran a communist bookstore in New Jersey, Reich was jailed by the FBI on Ellis Island for three weeks. (They acknowledged their mistake in 1943.)

He soon began to attempt to harness and concentrate orgone with Faraday cages he called orgone accumulators, which he believed could heal mental and physical disturbances—potentially even cancer. Reich brought the devices to Einstein, who tested them enthusiastically, noting that the accumulators created a rise in heat. But when one of his assistants suggested that the orgone accumulator was producing heat simply because of the temperature gradient in the room, as it was elevated off the floor, Einstein rejected the boxes and refused completely to admit them to further experiment. It was a bitter echo of his rejection by Freud, by another father figure and gatekeeper of respectability.

Reich purchased land upstate and created his "Organon" institute, where he would continue research—now identifying DOR, "Deadly Orgone Radiation," a kind of orgasmic anti-matter present in (and responsible for) environmental degradation, which he believed blanketed the world. He soon came to see his work as standing in direct opposition to what the US government had done at Hiroshima and Nagasaki: he was in an arms race for life energy, not death energy. He began to build massive orgone guns called "cloudbusters" that he claimed could reverse desertification and create rain. (Farmers began paying him to produce rain for their crops—reportedly with success.)

It was soon thereafter that the FDA descended on Reich, burning his books and imprisoning him, where he was finally reduced to nothing, known by other prisoners as the "sex box man." He died in prison in 1957, just days before his parole. His work merited only a paragraph obituary in *Time* and a retrospective in a few anarchist newspapers; not a single psychiatric or scientific journal covered his passing.

I Still Dream of Organon

Reich is a troubling figure, who challenged or broke nearly every taboo of Western civilization in his quest, and angered almost every establishment force of the time, and who was killed for it—yet his influence may be far greater than he is generally given credit for.

While Reich languished in prison, the world was starting to change. Elvis made his television debut in 1956, shaking his hips in a decidedly orgasmic way, demonstrating the type of freedom from character armor that Reich might have wanted for his patients. By the mid-sixties, and the release of the birth control pill, the sexual revolution was in full swing. ("Sexual revolution," by the way, is a phrase Reich coined.) Students in the 1968 revolutions in Paris and Berlin threw copies of Reich's *Mass Psychology of Fascism* at police. Jack Kerouac and Allen Ginsberg embraced Reich's theories; William S. Burroughs investigated the orgone accumulators for years and wrote about them extensively in his work—he even constructed his own accumulator box, and would sit in it to write while smoking kif. Saul Bellow, J. D. Salinger, Michel Foucault and Norman Mailer also dug on Reich—like Burroughs, Mailer also built his own accumulators and went on an epic quest to free himself via an "apocalyptic orgasm." Even Sean Connery was soaking up orgone in his own accumulator while filming his Bond movies. *The New York Times*, in a 1971 review of *The Mass Psychology of Fascism*, called for a serious reappraisal of his work. Reich's work soon became so fashionable with intellectuals that Woody Allen parodied the orgone accumulator as the "Orgasmatron" in his film *Sleeper*.

Reich's ideas have never been reassessed by the scientific community—nor by psychoanalysts, who still consider him a black mark on their history. Yet his therapeutic ideas did filter out into the wider psychoanalytic community and took new form under different names, contributing to body psychology, ego psychology, Fritz Perls' Gestalt therapy and Janov's primal scream therapy. In many ways, nowhere can Reich's influence be detected more than in the vast array of "feel good" body therapies and even the mass popularity of massage and yoga. Reich's idea that man is caught in the "trap" of his own character armoring found a ready home there, as well. Today, only fifty years after the sexual revolution that Reich foresaw, we live in a hypersexualized society—constantly barraged by the opposite of the sexual repression. Everything around us seems to be hard at work accumulating our orgone—advertising, pop stars, television, magazines, Internet porn. (Reich probably would have seen this as just a new form of "running" from surrender to loving release.)

Though Reich was seemingly rejected by the gatekeepers of Western civilization, consider him from the eyes of the outsider to that civilization: The mass shooter Anders Behring Breivik, who delineated his view of the "liberal corruption" that he saw as weakening the West against Islam in his tl;dr manifesto "2083: A European Declaration of Independence," targets Reich as one of the key architects of said decadence, stating that "Wilhelm Reich's theory, when coupled with Georg Lukacs' sex education in Hungary, can be seen as the source for the American education cartel's insistence on sex education from kindergarten onwards and its complete negation of the paternal family, external authority, and the traditional character structure," and lashes out at Reich's assertion that, in Breivik's words, "Revolutionary sexual politics would mean the complete collapse of authoritarian ideology."

While 21st century humanity hunches over at computers and sweatshop benches, armors itself from life, trades connection with the physical for connection to a smartphone—and produces more and more Anders Breiviks—perhaps we owe Reich a second look.

(July 15, 2013)

Paramahansa Yogananda, and the Legacy of India's Mission to Enlighten America

When Steve Jobs departed the world, he had One Last Thing for those who attended his memorial service—a copy of *Autobiography of Yogi* by the Hindu guru Paramhansa Yogananda, the man who introduced America to yoga and meditation.

It wasn't as paradoxical of a gift as it might have seemed to some. Before becoming a business giant, Jobs had been a spiritual seeker, experimenting with LSD and Zen Buddhism; even travelling to India to find a guru. Jobs had deeply immersed himself in the spirituality of India, but it was his choice to do positive work for the world, karma yoga, by applying himself to invention and business—rather than monastic meditation—that would change the planet.

"That was the message: Actualize yourself," Salesforce CEO Marc Benioff, who was at the memorial service, said of Jobs and his chosen gift. "If you look back at the history of Steve and that early trip to India... he had this incredible realization that his intuition was his greatest gift. He needed to look at [the] world from [the] inside out... his message was to look inside yourself and realize yourself."

Autobiography of Yogi would be Jobs' way of passing on that message. The book recounts the spiritual training of Yogananda, a Bengali boy who became a self-realized meditator, and then came to America in the 1920s to introduce the West to Hindu meditation techniques. It's now considered a spiritual classic, having sold over 4 million copies. Among those deeply influenced by Yogananda and his book were Elvis Presley, George Harrison, Mariel Hemingway, Russell Simmons, the botanist Luther Burbank and Mahatma Gandhi—in many ways, it helped lay the groundwork for the explosion of interest in Eastern spirituality that was to come in the 1960s. Yogananda stood at the transition point between the millennia-old Vedic spirituality of

India and the New Age fusion that would emerge from the collision of Hindu, English and American religious ideas. And while much of the New Age backwash that was to come is easy to dismiss, Yogananda's influence is not so easy to brush off—the hem of his robe touched a few of the biggest cultural movers and shakers of the 20th century.

But who was Yogananda—and what was it about one simple meditator that created such a global impact?

The Blissful Devotee and His Cosmic Romance

Mukunda Lal Ghosh, the boy who would become Yogananda, was born into the *kshatriya* or military caste in Gorakhpur, northeast India. His father was a vice president in the Bengal-Nagpur Railway; both of his parents were disciples of the guru Lahiri Mahasaya.

Mahasaya initiated Ghosh and his parents into kriya yoga, a meditative practice that involves intense concentration on various points along the spinal column, which turns the mind inward on itself and finally empties it. This is the practice that the adult Yogananda would bring to America. It was at the age of 17, however, that Ghosh met the man who would complete his spiritual training: Swami Sri Yukteswar, a ferocious, lion-like kriya master who would spend the next five years transforming Ghosh the child into Yogananda the man. Spiritual discipleship in this context involves not just meditation but the ruthless and unflinching rooting out and destruction of the student's ego and delusions by the master, an utterly terrifying process.

But Yogananda won through. He recounts his enlightenment thusly:

"An oceanic joy broke upon calm endless shores of my soul. The Spirit of God, I realized, is exhaustless Bliss; His body is countless tissues of light. A swelling glory within me began to envelop towns, continents, the earth, solar and stellar systems, tenuous nebulae, and floating universes. The entire cosmos, gently luminous, like a city seen afar at night, glimmered within the infinitude of my being... The creative voice of God I heard resounding as Aum, the vibration of the Cosmic Motor.

"Suddenly the breath returned to my lungs. With a disappointment almost unbearable, I realized that my infinite immensity was lost. Once more I was limited to the humiliating cage of a body, not easily accommodative to the Spirit. Like a prodigal child, I had run away from my macrocosmic home and imprisoned myself in a narrow microcosm. My guru was standing motionless before me; I started to drop at his holy feet in gratitude for the experience in cosmic consciousness which I had long passionately sought. He held me upright, and spoke calmly, unpretentiously.

"'You must not get overdrunk with ecstasy. Much work yet remains for you in the world. Come; let us sweep the balcony floor; then we shall walk by the Ganges.'"

Yogananda was next tasked with running a school for boys in Ranchi, where he combined traditional education with instruction in kriya yoga. But after a few years of practice, his guru sent him on the most frightening errand he could imagine: Bring the teachings to America.

A Mission From God

Leaving behind everything, Yogananda arrived in the US in 1920—the first Hindu guru to openly teach Westerners. While Swami Vivekananda had come before him, bringing an intellectual outline of yogic mysticism to the Parliament of the World's Religions in Chicago in 1893, he had taught no techniques. Yogananda would change that, quickly booking speaking engagements across the country, offering instruction in kriya yoga and founding his Self-Realization Fellowship, a series of centers that he would wisely model on the Church, complete with pews and images of Jesus on the central altars, rather than the traditional Indian ashram setup, to decrease the cognitive dissonance he was facing in importing foreign teachings.

After middling reception on the East Coast, he relocated to Los Angeles—which he would describe in his *Autobiography* as the spiritual nexus of America. LA not only has a perfect climate for practicing yoga year-round, the entertainment industry creates an environment full of people seeking for something better than reality.

Though Yogananda's teachings and centers quickly became entrenched in Southern California, winning the adoration of the public, the backlash was soon to follow. The tabloid media began to label Yogananda's headquarters (on top of Mt. Washington) a "love cult" and allege that improper sexual relations were occurring; in tandem with the press assault, Yogananda's trusted friend and colleague Dhirananda departed the group. Though the allegations that Yogananda had (consensual) sexual relations with some of his disciples led to lawsuits, nothing was substantiated.

Weathering the storm, Yogananda travelled abroad in South America and India, where he once again met with his guru Sri Yukteswar, and with Mahatma Gandhi. But it was when Yogananda returned to America that he would devote himself to securing his legacy—his writings at the time reveal a very real fear that civilization would simply cease to exist, and a pressing need to create some kind of vessel to preserve the essence of right living. This meant crystallizing his message in written works and by further establishing his network of Self-Realization Fellowship centers. Writing became, for him, a way to reach more people than he could in person—the success of *Autobiography of a Yogi* would prove him right. His talks from the time stress the need for creating intentional communities, and for people to begin planting their own vegetable gardens—a prescient notion, and one which deeply took hold both in the 1960s commune wave and following the 2008 recession.

Yogananda may have been rushing particularly fast to preserve his message because his days were numbered. At a March 7, 1952 dinner for a visiting Indian ambassador in Los Angeles, he mounted the stage to urge co-operation between India and America—before collapsing from heart failure. He is now interred at the Forest Lawn Memorial Park Cemetery in Glendale; *Time* reported that the cemetery's mortuary director wrote in a notarized letter that

Yogananda's body remained in a perfectly preserved state, without decay, for twenty days after his death... take that for what you will.

The Legacy of the Guru Institution in America

So: What exactly was Yogananda doing?

Yoga and meditation are seen by the public as methods to exercise and relax, respectively. However, these are side-benefits of their actual purpose, which is to (over the course of many, many years) destroy an individual's attachment to their own limited body and mind, and allow a more infinite and cosmic view of reality to take its place—"enlightenment." For those who seek to take it all the way, this process is beautiful, profound and triumphantly awakening, but it is not light and fluffy, as it involves the stripping away of the individual ego and its attachments. There comes a time in the human maturation process, for some, where you start to figure out that your small-s self is blocking the view. Meditation, *yoga*, is a way of demolishing it. It's not self-help—it's self-annihilation.

None of this is considered to be possible to do DIY: All Hindu and Tibetan yogic texts stress that yoga is impossible without direct instruction from a guru. A guru, however, is much more than just a yoga-teacher-slash-therapist—and it's important to put the guru/disciple relationship in context here, as it has vastly different connotations in India than it does in the West, where the phrase has come to mean, simply, "somebody who's good at something and is also pretentious about it," a la "social media guru."

As opposed to a *pandit*, who is simply a teacher or expounder of spiritual doctrine, a *guru* is a kind of super-parent, whose job it is to carry the karma and responsibility for whole social groups. The guru teaches some form of meditation and Vedic philosophy, and acts as a guide for both solitary, renunciate seekers and whole families that seek to practice meditation more slowly and sustainably while maintaining their worldly duties. It's by-and-large the job of the guru (who may teach huge crowds or just a few people) to guide their disciples on the spiritual path, make sure they don't kill each other as they work out their group karma, and keep their egos and shadows from sabotaging their lives by continually whacking them with the proverbial zen stick. And it's by and large the job of the disciples to support the guru so that she or he can keep teaching.

This arrangement deeply troubles the Western mind, which is founded on the idea of self-reliance and independence—especially after decades of abusive guru scandals, from many spiritual backgrounds. The pattern is, however, hard-wired into Hindu culture—the guru-disciple relationship can in many cases be an extension of the family unit—and because that pattern largely relies on the context of Indian culture to work, it's been nearly impossible to export to the West. Instead, Hindu (and Buddhist) teachers in the West have largely had to make do with people who have already dropped out of their own culture—i.e. hippies and New Agers—who bring their own baggage, cultural expectations and projections with them. That culture clash, especially around sex, as gurus end up with huge power over large numbers of lost people with little to no sense of personal boundaries or anchors to the real world, hasn't always worked out well. (See the stories of Swami Muktananda, Chögyam Trungpa and the American guru Adi Da.)

Having been in the trenches with many different gurus in my 20s, I'm not as much troubled by the power that some gurus hold over their flock as I am by the willingness of some individuals to completely surrender power over their lives to somebody (anybody!) else, and the general institutional insanity that arises *from the inner circles clustered around the big-name gurus*. (As Robert Anton Wilson once said, "a disciple is an asshole looking for a human being to attach itself to.") Unless you've seen it first-hand, it's impossible to describe how bizarre social dynamics can be in a group where grown adults are projecting not only their own unresolved family issues but also their need for life, the universe and everything to be both explained *and* perfectly fixed, all onto one person—who might well be enlightened, but is still, after all, a human being, with a human shadow.

With all that said, however, it's too easy to dwell on the failures of the importation of Eastern spirituality to the West, and miss the successes, and the incredible depth and transformative power of the teachings themselves. And what makes Yogananda particularly remarkable is not only that he was the first guru to come to the West, but that he set such an incredibly high bar of success.

I believe that as the West becomes increasingly technocratic, and increasingly loses its sense of self in the face of corporatization and globalization, its need for deep spiritual connection will only grow—and Yogananda laid the groundwork for Western people to access the spiritual teachings of India in a way that nobody had before or has since.

After all, he was, it seems, the greatest inspiration in the life of the man who made the device you are now reading this on possible… and I think we might just want to take a serious look at Steve Jobs' final One Last Thing.

(November 19, 2014)

Buckminster Fuller's Vision of Enough for Everyone

Buckminster Fuller was one of the most brilliant thinkers of the 20th century, an architect and designer who made it his mission to advance the evolution of humanity and to "do more with less." He created inventions like the geodesic dome (most prominently seen in Disney World's Epcot Center) and the Dymaxion car, and sought to use technology to benefit humanity, specifically to provide cheap shelter and transportation for the world. Though his inventions have not been widely adopted (yet), his theories and ideas have influenced the world in many key ways (if you've ever heard anybody in an office meeting use the word "synergy," for instance, you've just heard a Fullerism—he popularized the phrase to mean doing more with available resources).

Fuller's key idea is that we have enough resources to house, clothe and feed everybody on the planet, but we aren't doing so. His mission, then, was to create systems solutions that would allow us to properly use the resources we already have for the good of all, instead of maintaining inequality.

Here are three key concepts that Buckminster Fuller embodied that can bring immense value to your life, whatever you do:

1. *Your life does not belong to you.*

As a young man, Fuller worked in a textile mill, in the US Navy and in the meat-packing industry. In his twenties, he founded a company with his father-in-law to build lightweight housing—but the company failed. By the age of 32, he was broke and living in public housing in Chicago; his daughter died of complications from polio and spinal meningitis. Deciding he was a complete failure and responsible for his daughter's death, Fuller became a heavy drinker and decided to kill himself. On the verge of suicide, he had a transcendental insight—his life was not his own property; it belonged to humanity. He then pledged to dedicate the rest of his life to "an experiment, to find what a single individual [could] contribute to changing the world and benefiting all humanity." (This would be an example of the "deal with God," little publicized compared to the "deal with the Devil.")

2. Don't change people—change the environment.

Buckminster Fuller was an architect, on a mission to change our species, traditionally the role of religious reformers. But his approach was different—he realized that it's nigh-on impossible to change people. He instead sought to change the environment around people, prompting inventions like the geodesic dome and Dymaxion house: simply seeing or walking around in such structures could shift people's idea of the possible and prompt them to start rethinking their assumptions. Instead of grabbing and shaking people and shouting "The world's on fire!" he created environments that demonstrated a possible solution.

3. We have enough for everybody—to see how, think of the world as a whole system.

Fuller thought of the world as a whole system, instead of as disconnected nations and warring tribes. (This type of thinking is still the number one thing we need as a species, and is less common than you might believe.) He coined the phrase "Spaceship Earth" to describe where we are, famously stating that "The most important fact about Spaceship Earth: an instruction manual didn't come with it." If we can think of the world of a coherent system, we can begin to address resource-waste problems as a whole instead of leaving some to die while others have too much.

Fuller's work is extensive and complex to say the least—if this starting point has raised your curiosity, check out *A Fuller View*.

(November 14, 2013)

Colin Wilson, Grandfather of the Occult, 1931–2013

The English author Colin Wilson turned a generation on to the idea of becoming "more than human."

It started in the dark stacks at the back of the public library, where I had spent most of my young days and now, as an extremely shy, awkward and very goth sixteen-year-old, I was about to discover a book that would alter the course of my life.

That book was *The Occult* by the English author Colin Wilson, and it looked like it had been there since the 60s—it was dog-eared, tattered and held together (barely) by a heavy plastic wrap-around. This was the first apparently serious book on the occult I had discovered, and after a childhood spent lost in *Time-Life* books on aliens, mysteries and the unexplored corners of the world—followed by the jarring, concrete shock of dealing with junior high and high school—a more "serious" invitation back to the land of the unknown powers of the mind, rather than the numb mundanities of school, was more than seductive. But already having learned to armor myself from life with a veneer of world-weary cynicism and skepticism, I was also more than ready to dismiss every claim in the book.

What I found, as many have who were turned on by Wilson's books, was a remarkably rigorous and intellectually daring look at the idea of "magic"—even a convincing argument for its reality.

After a working-class childhood and leaving school at the age of 16, Wilson shot to fame as the darling of the English intelligentsia in the mid-1950s. His first book, *The Outsider*, written in his early twenties while sleeping rough in Hampstead Heath, and published in 1956, was considered the first true example of English existentialism. The book was quickly seized upon by critics looking to put England on a cultural par with the continent. Within its pages, the "angry young man" and James Dean of philosophy examined the lives of outsider figures from history, from Hemingway to Nietzsche to Nijinsky, and considered them as noble (if occasionally failed) examples of superhumanity, mutants who sought to struggle away from the social hypnosis of the masses and develop their own radical individual geniuses. It was a massive hit, thrusting the 24-year-old into international fame. A very early-twenties book (and a conscious model for *Generation Hex*, which I released at the similarly self-assured age of 23), *The Outsider* appealed to everybody who considered themselves special, different, better than those around them—young people everywhere.

But by the end of the 50s, England had tired of Colin Wilson. Like Austin Osman Spare, another English visionary and outsider whose star rose early only to be quickly discarded by a fickle British public, Wilson's fame was short-lived and fleeting. Yet he had only begun his work—pushed by financial need to write about more lurid subjects, Wilson turned his attention to crime writing and the occult, just in time for the fuzzy Glastonbury mysticism of the English hippie generation, many of whose adherents had been influenced, whether consciously or tangentially, by *The Outsider*.

1969's *The Occult*—the book I found as a sixteen-year-old—took his theories from *The Outsider* even further. If, he suggested, there is some unknown quantity, some strange fluke of nature or nurture that can turn people into geniuses, then is it in fact possible to purposefully catalyze that unknown quantity? Wilson proposed for argument's sake that this genius factor does in fact exist, and dubbed it "Faculty X," the certain something that turns men into supermen, or at least allows them to fully utilize their innate abilities without the backdrag of neuroses. It was a potent idea for a generation immersed in the mysterious waters of the unconscious—in Tarot cards, *I Ching*, LSD and Transcendental Meditation. It also echoed the theories of an earlier English traveler-in-the-unconscious, Aleister Crowley, who had boasted in the 1920s that his occult methods could turn any average man into a man of genius (Crowley had mixed results, often inspiring nervous breakdown instead of genius, though many of his students, like Victor Neuberg and Frank Bennett, produced remarkably inspired poetry while under Crowley's tutelage).

In *The Occult*, Wilson reviewed mystics, magicians and occult charlatans from history—Cagliostro, Rasputin, Madame Blavatsky, Crowley. Though finding himself not particularly fond of most of them, Wilson held out singular praise and admiration for G. I. Gurdjieff, the Russian-Armenian mystic who proposed that mankind was in a state of unconscious sleep and needed to be awakened through a series of mystic practices and conscious shocks. Did these aberrations of history, he wondered, have the ability to awaken "Faculty X" within the average man? And if so, could their practices be refined and repeated? It was ideas like this that gave rise to the nascent Human Potential Movement, and the oft-repeated (though incorrect) maxim that humans use only "10%" of their brain, with massive unawakened capabilities that hold the potential to radicalize society and the course of history if activated.

For an alienated teenager, *The Occult* had much the same effect that reading X-Men comics had while in elementary school: it offered the validation of being special, different and unique. For me personally, it inspired a decade and a half of investigation and experiment into the methods of the individuals Wilson discussed, and deep spiritual seeking that eventually lead me through many of the world's mystic practices and even to seeking answers throughout Asia.

In 2013, *The Occult* remains an incredibly potent and potentially life-changing book, though in retrospect the emphasis on the primacy of the individual as separate and superior from the environment and society seems adolescent (the idea isn't far from the similarly teenage philosophies of Ayn Rand and Satanism, and perhaps reached its apotheosis in the ideas of the Temple of Set)—ironically, involvement with spirituality and occult practices often disintegrates the sense of individual separation from the universe and unites the practitioner with the greater order of nature and society (if it's done right, if I may editorialize). But as a scholarly, measured, deeply rational investigation of a very irrational topic, *The Occult* is unparalleled.

Colin Wilson died on December 5, 2013, with 114+ books to his name, having worked steadily and without ceasing since mid-century. His work remains a beacon of insight.

Wilson asked one very simple question: If psychology shows us how to deal with the mind when it falls below normal functioning, what can we do to push the mind above normal functioning—into superhuman realms?

After I returned that book to the library, by the way, it disappeared, never to be seen again… may Colin Wilson's work appear in equally mysterious and synchronistic ways in the lives of the curious and those on the Outside.

(December 16, 2013)

Judee Sill, the Rosicrucian Folk Singer That Time Forgot

There are only a few artists in existence that can actually communicate truth. I know them because their work can immediately cut through the fog of my daily life, force me to drop whatever I'm doing, and command me to listen, slack-jawed, as if struck with an arrow. The list is small—there's a few songs by Nick Drake in there, some of Daniel Johnston's *1990* album—but neither of them comes close to the otherwordly power, the angelic fury of Judee Sill at her best.

Judee Sill was born in Oakland in 1944. She worked the same folk scene as Joni Mitchell, perhaps her closest contemporary, but never found the spotlight. She never found the light at all, at least not the light of fame. She found a different light, an inner illumination, in Rosicrucianism, astral travel, Aleister Crowley and heroin.

After an early life spent streetwalking and playing in cafes, she got her chance at success—she was selected as the first artist for up-and-coming mogul David Geffen's Asylum Records—a chance that was then dashed when she outed Geffen as gay on the radio and he canned her in retribution. (Geffen is now one of the most prominent out gay men in the world—*Out* ranked him the most powerful gay person in America in 2007.)

Sill, herself bisexual, spent her salad days in a Hollywood mansion surrounded by adulating female fans she kept around like slaves, sunbathing naked in her backyard. Soon all of that was gone. By the mid-seventies she was living in a trailer park and back to prostituting herself. At 35, she overdosed.

Though cited by many as an influence—Warren Zevon, Andy Partridge of XTC and David Tibet of Current 93, for instance—Sill remains unknown, even when similarly overlooked (but far less threatening) figures like the aforementioned Nick Drake have been resurrected for car commercials and posthumously canonized.

She was a genius, or, rather, she had a genius, as Socrates might have put it, a transcendent connection driving her on. Her second and final album, *Heart Food*, released in 1973 to almost no attention whatsoever (a condition that hasn't changed), contains what Pythagoras might have identified as the *Musica universalis*, the Music of the Spheres. Sill, steeped in both mysticism and Pythagorean number theory, was able to produce songs like "The Donor," precisely striking a raw nerve of human experience with complex musical arrangements that were almost beyond the scope of the merely human.

Prefacing "The Donor" when she played it live for the BBC in 1972, Judee Sill told the audience "Most of my songs, I always try to write them so they'll make people feel better, or make them feel that their warm, human spirit is affirmed… but I thought one day when I was depressed, you know when you're real depressed and you see everything comes to nothing, well, I thought, maybe I ought to take a different approach, and write a song that, instead of directed at people, would somehow musically induce God into giving us all a break, cause I was getting a little fed up by this point. So I put some combinations of notes in there that I worked on a long time hoping it would work… since that time I've decided that I shouldn't get any more breaks, cause I already squandered them in weird places. But I'd like to sing this song for you in the hope that you'll get a break."

When she sings "I'll chase him to the bottom, till I finally caught him," she is talking about Christ, redemption, God, who dwells just as surely in the depths of Hell Itself as in that great gated community in the sky. Perhaps more so, there among the broken and the outcast, the last light in the eyes of the homeless and cold.

In those perfectly struck notes she captures that feeling of exquisite heartbreak that is God moving over the face of the waters, shattering the temple that it may be rebuilt. Or never rebuilt, in Judee Sill's case, and that of many others. Not in this lifetime and world. In those chords you can hear every single broken life, every acid casualty or otherwise wrecked traveller on the road of higher consciousness.

Every one that did not come back. Kyrie Elision.

In 2013's occult-saturated pop culture, where club kids smear witch house affectations across their Tumblr accounts, it can be easy to forget how real and terrifying the occult can be for those who approach it with self-destruction in mind. It's certainly not that way for everybody—but it's undeniable that for those already enmeshed in life's dark and entropic side, who are already chasing their own death, it certainly can be. How quickly all sense of perspective or common sense can be lost upon the occult's event horizon, and how quickly they vanish therein.

Judee Sill was such a person. Her life and her music stand as a guidepost, a statement of truth to those who come looking for the light, and lack the discrimination needed to know where to look. Down the rabbit hole they go, the black hole, after the promise of something-or-other, some kind of God, some kind of power.

To those who have never seen where that hole leads, may you remain so blessed. May it remain an abstraction for you, a nightly news image of a child starving to death. But for those who have seen it, you Know. No glib phrase could do it justice.

But you can hear it in every note of every Judee Sill song.

The Donor is the heaviest thing I have ever heard. And the best.

(November 4, 2013)

James Dallas Egbert III: The Dungeon Master

When I was about fourteen, I discovered a copy of *The Dungeon Master: The Disappearance of James Dallas Egbert III* in the local library's used-book bin. Noting that it had something to do with *Dungeons and Dragons*, and also noting that it cost about $1, I bought it.

That book stuck with me for a long time.

Egbert was the sixteen-year-old who infamously disappeared in the Michigan State University steam tunnels in 1979, supposedly during a live-action *Dungeons and Dragons* session, provoking a nationwide scare about the then-new role-playing game. When Egbert vanished, his parents hired William Dear, a private detective, to locate him. Dear theorized that it was Egbert's involvement in *D&D* that led to his disappearance; he went on to investigate the game himself, even going so far as to play a session.

It was the early days of the Satanic Panic—the Christian Right's effort to convince the public that *D&D*, heavy metal, backwards-masked messages in records, the occult, Halloween, and alleged (but never substantiated) ritual abuse in day cares were nodes in a gigantic conspiratorial web ensnaring the youth of America in the clutches of the Dark One—and Egbert's disappearance would only serve to enflame the public's fears. The case would inspire the infamous TV movie *Mazes and Monsters*, in which a young Tom Hanks freaks out from playing too much *D&D* and stabs one of his friends in a steam tunnel after hallucinating that he's turned into a monster. (The adults, of course, just don't understand.)

Now, as all nerds know, the most perfidious thing about *Dungeons and Dragons* is not that it drives you crazy and makes you see monsters, it's that it keeps you from getting laid. However, it also tends to entrain skills that kids will use later in life to become successful adults—while awkward teenagers think that they're role-playing wizards and dark elves, what they're actually doing is simulating something like a corporate meeting, complete with paper-shuffling, public speaking, teamwork, obsessing over numerical minutiae, delegating responsibilities (like who's getting the Mountain Dew next), and so on. (Name me one other activity that can get hormone-crazed teenage monkeys to sit around a table, scribble on paper and *talk to each other* for hours on end.) Little did parents understand that *Dungeons and Dragons* would both successfully drive a wall between their kids and anything cool, like sex and drugs, it would also train them to be productive suits in later life. Birth control and corporate training in one game!

Of course, at the time, the public saw *Dungeons and Dragons* as akin to goat sacrifice. And Egbert was the focus of that hysteria during the weeks in which Dear searched for him.

The truth of the matter, however, was much more painful. At the time of his disappearance, Egbert was a sixteen-year-old prodigy who had been pushed by his parents since early childhood to overachieve. They'd rushed him to graduate from school early, and subsequently enrolled him in Michigan State, where he stuck out like a preschooler. In addition to his social misplacement and the tremendous academic pressure put on him by his parents, Egbert was struggling to hide his blossoming homosexuality—both from his parents and from a not-exactly-friendly 1979 Michigan. Unable to make friends at the university, Egbert drifted into the *Dungeons and Dragons* players—but only briefly, looking for some way, any way to connect. He also drifted into drugs. And what actually happened when he disappeared was not a D&D freak out—Egbert entered the steam tunnels to take an overdose of Quaaludes. When that didn't work, he ran for the home of an older male "admirer," where he hid out for weeks, leading to the hysteria over his disappearance. His parents, unwilling to publicly air the fact that their son was gay, readily bought the *Dungeons and Dragons* narrative.

Egbert was eventually located by Dear, who spent a good deal of time trying to help him come to terms with his situation and listen to him, something nobody had done. Unfortunately, Egbert ran again, this time to the gay party scene in New Orleans, where he again tried to kill himself—with cyanide, again unsuccessfully. After taking a job as a laborer at an oil field, he attempted suicide yet again, this time with a gun. He succeeded.

William Dear wrote *The Dungeon Master* four years later (Egbert, deeply pained by his homosexuality, had urged Dear not to reveal the truth), largely to correct the misrepresentation of the case by the news media.

Needless to say, Dear's account totally harshed my 14-year-old mellow when all I wanted was a book that would properly explain to me what THAC0 was.*

Now, in hindsight, it strikes me what a poster child Egbert is for the true teenage outsider—not the dumb rock burnout, but the one that can truly say that "nobody understands me," the one that's judged to be too smart, too weird, too queer, too in the wrong place at the wrong time. Reading stuff on Egbert on the Web now, I notice a recurring theme—people seem to agree that, had he just chosen to hang on a few years longer, everything would have been fine. What Egbert decided to annihilate himself for in 1980 is now much closer to mainstream, legally protected life in suburban America.

As dark as Egbert's tale is, and as damning of its time and place as it is, it's also a startling testament to how much things have changed—and yet not at all. Columbine and Virginia Tech kind of make steam tunnel escapades look positively Archie and Jughead, and we still live in a world in which homophobic violence is endemic. But as flat and boring as our monoculture is, it gives me hope that it's still an increasingly accepting one.

Even of *Dungeons and Dragons*… well, kind of.

* If you get this joke, you are going to hell.

(August 27, 2009; Revised November 11, 2014)

Robert Anton Wilson's *Cosmic Trigger*, and the Psychedelic Interstellar Future We Need

In 1977, Robert Anton Wilson's Cosmic Trigger predicted a utopian, space-faring, enlightened future. 37 years later, it's finally starting to show up.

In my second year of college, I bought a copy of Robert Anton Wilson's *Cosmic Trigger* at a New Age bookstore in downtown Santa Cruz.

It had a naked space goddess on the cover, and threatened to reveal the "Final Secret of the Illuminati." I read it in one sitting, and when I closed the book, I'd not only learned said group's final secret, I felt like I was one of the inner circle.

I immediately loaned it out, and watched it circulate among about a dozen people before vanishing into the Santa Cruz synchronicity vortex. Everyone I talked to had about the same experience.

Cosmic Trigger—a record of one man's journey into inner space—has been doing that, consistently, since its first publication in 1977. It's the *Little Red Book* for futurist mutants.

A *Cosmic Trigger* Warning on the Door to Chapel Perilous

Here's how it started: In 1962, 30-year-old Robert Anton Wilson was working as an assistant sales manager in Yellow Springs, Ohio, with a wife and four young children, when he decided to eat some peyote. As a hard-headed rationalist, Wilson was in for a rough ride: The cactus shredded his narrowband understanding of existence and his place in the universe.

Wilson walked straight through the now-opened doors of perception and into a decade and a half of exhaustive experimentation with willed brain change—encapsulating research into LSD, Aleister Crowley's Magick, Count Alfred Korzybski's General Semantics, Dr. John Lilly's sensory deprivation tank, conspiracy theories, Sufism, Buckminster Fuller, UFOs, Gurdjieff, Zen Buddhism and a lot more.

A collaborative partnership with Timothy Leary and a five-year stint as an associate editor at *Playboy* provided more fuel for Wilson's voyage, which culminated in the publication of *Cosmic Trigger*. The book is his first-person record of fucking with the settings of his own mind—all while maintaining a healthy degree of skepticism and empiricist rigor, as an antidote to the muddled thinking that blights the territory he was scouting.

Wilson's experiments convinced him that humanity's limitations are largely self-imposed, that "reality is always plural and mutable," and that if we were to just take off our conditioned blinkers of superstition and ideology, we could unlock our dormant Promethean intelligence, overcome our tribal conflicts and get our species off the planet. *Cosmic Trigger* ends far from Wilson's early rural peyote trips, with a vision of mankind colonizing the stars.

A recent flu afforded me the chance to re-read *Cosmic Trigger*, thirteen years after I first found it as a student. Those thirteen years had been occupied with my own stress-test of reality, including many of the avenues Wilson had explored, much of which I recorded in the books I published in my 20s. It was also a time in which I'd watched the utopian future promised by Wilson, Leary, Douglas Rushkoff, Ken Wilber and others utterly crash and burn. 9/11 *seemed* to kill the *Star Trek*-style future all the smart nerds had been working on, instead spawning a new dark age of religious fundamentalism and illiterate barbarism typified by Bush Jr. and the newly reactionary, compassionless, cocaine-fuelled hipster "counterculture" that sprouted up under his rule—followed by the Great Sleep of the socially progressive but rights-and-privacy-decimating, Facebook-hypnotized Obama years.

It was with the lingering weight of this decade-plus of disappointment that I expected to return to *Cosmic Trigger* and find that it had all been bongthink—but what I discovered instead was that most of Wilson and Leary's utopian predictions actually seem well on their way to coming true, if a bit later than the two men expected.

RAW was right.

SMI²LE

SMI²LE—a phrase coined by Tim Leary in the 1970s—stands for *Space Migration, Intelligence Increase, Life Extension*, and was his recipe for a working future.

RAW focused much of Cosmic Trigger on the SMI²LE formula, predicting that by the end of the 20th century humanity would be living in off-world O'Neill colonies, with greatly enhanced cognitive ability and lifespans extended by centuries or even indefinitely.

None of these predictions came true within Leary or Wilson's lifetimes—both men died, without any immortality pill in sight, in a post-Challenger era in which the US space program had wilted, and humanity was acting stupider than ever.

But 2014 is a different story. Although the same old "let's party like it's 1099" Crusader script keeps getting remade over and over, with better special effects each time, we're also starting to actually see some of the SMI²LE future show up.

SM—*Space Migration*

Both Leary and Wilson strongly believed that humanity's destiny was post-terrestrial, and came to consider psychedelics and consciousness alteration as a kind of prepping for weightlessness—ways to prepare for outer space by exploring inner space.

RAW, in particular, saw a kind of logos of humanity's interstellar aspirations embodied in Jack Parsons, the legendary co-founder of Jet Propulsion Labs in Pasadena, who spent his days launching rockets and his nights excelling as a student of Aleister Crowley's occult system, hosting drug-fuelled orgies, conducting magical rituals, writing anarchist polemics and encouraging young science fiction writers like Ray Bradbury (and, unfortunately, L. Ron Hubbard, who later took Parsons for everything he had). Parsons blew himself up in 1952, at the age of 37, in a lab accident; his primary contributions to the world were the creation of JPL and the invention of solid-state rocket fuel, which was instrumental in getting the US to the moon.

For Parsons, like Leary and Wilson, there was no difference between pushing inner space boundaries and outer space frontiers—they were simply the Next Steps, ones that Parsons felt religious and political authority stood directly in the way of, an Inquisition just like the one that murdered fellow-traveler Giordiano Bruno in 1600 for suggesting that the stars were distant suns. Bruno, we must remember, was just as steeped in the occult as young Parsons—as were other scientific giants like Copernicus, Galileo, Kepler, Newton and many, many more.

In this light, Parsons looks less like a mutant and more like a stalwart upholder of the Western intellectual project. Parsons' seemingly disparate interests in space travel, Magick, drugs, sexual adventurism and science fiction, I will suggest, are really the same impulse—a pushing at the edges of reality. Parsons, like so many brilliant scientists and shamans before him, simply saw the edge of human endeavor and decided to *shove* it. This is the same spectrum of adventure that Leary and RAW consciously inherited, expressing the forward momentum of evolution as SMI^{2}LE.

What Jack Parsons began, Elon Musk may well end; he's now promising to put humans on Mars in a decade. The dream is not dead—it has, if anything, simply outgrown the American government. Space is for all—and while European Union, Chinese or Virgin Galactic bases on Mars may not fit with 1960s American patriotic fervor, what matters is that mankind gets off the rock.

As Earth closes in on its estimated carrying capacity of 10 billion humans (and that's only if we all live at developing world standards), space migration is the only palatable solution to the population and environmental crises. If we want to survive as a species, all forward momentum must go into space.

I2—Intelligence Increase

Leary and Wilson spent much of their lives attempting to increase their intelligence, largely by torching their fixed models with entheogens. When used correctly, psychedelics can undoubtedly spark quantum leaps in cognition, wisdom and insight—and thanks to pioneering research from groups like MAPS, entheogenic substances are gaining broader acceptance for clinical trials, especially for use in treating PTSD and addiction. Recent data has even shown that psilocybin mushrooms may encourage the birth of new neurons. Leary, who was pursuing similar research at Millbrook before he was shut down, would have been proud.

While a perfect intelligence enhancer hasn't yet been found, the Internet is awash with close candidates—particularly the racetam family of nootropics and the eurogic drug Modafinil, which allows for long periods of wakefulness without the eroding effects of amphetamines. (The side effects, however, are unknown.)

And then there's the Luciferian ability of the Internet itself—which Leary tirelessly proselytized for in his last days—to create memetic hive minds that can exercise levels of intelligence beyond the capacity of the network's individual nodes, for good or ill. Wikipedia, Twitter and Reddit are all prime examples—as is 4Chan. The Web's acceleration of collective intelligence is hard to overestimate. Of course, a new Internet waits in the wings, and virtual reality, augmented reality and the Internet of Things will soon make the Web look parochial. Following on from there, the beginnings of matter reassembly, first via 3D printing and later by nanotechnology, may well make literal the alchemists' dream of erasing the gap between matter and spirit, by making the material world immediately and infinitely malleable by the whims of the human imagination.

I remain convinced that the metaphors of the occult, of the

psychedelic experience and of inherited wisdom like the *Tibetan Book of the Dead* will be our only real guides for dealing with such a world.

LE—Life Extension

The Immortalist project keeps chugging along, having blossomed into transhumanism—a world now awash with venture capital and military contracts, which increasingly looks like either weapons R&D or a health care plan 99.9% of the population won't be able to afford.

On the life extension front specifically, we now have a vast array of promising leads into slowing the aging process, including caloric restriction, supplementation, hormone therapy, insulin growth factor restriction, stem cell therapy, therapeutic cloning, gene therapy and life extension drugs like Rapamycin and Metformin. Ray Kurzweil has stated that nanotechnology may make aging reversal possible by 2030 (around the same time as some experts' predictions of Mars settlement). It remains to be seen how quickly these technologies will progress, and how available they will be to the general population.

Starseed

Reality, ironically, can be crushing for people like Robert Anton Wilson. You keep peeling back your sense of the possible, dutifully scrubbing off the limitations of your model of the world, through psychedelics, spiritual practice, therapy, bodywork. Pretty soon you realize that nobody really has anything figured out, and that the whole damn thing is up for grabs—that, as RAW said, reality is what you can get away with.

You see that people are staring at the flickering shadows on the wall of Plato's cave. Religion, politics, media, social expectations, even language itself—it's all conditioning. And you see that all you have to do is turn around, away from the shadowplay you've been trained to see as reality, and you get to see the infinity of the universe, the night sky of billions upon billions of stars, distant galaxies, superclusters beckoning you to the galactic game of which the admission price is admitting you know nothing.

Jack Parsons expressed it so perfectly in his letters to Marjorie Cameron, his spiritual consort:

"You bawl and weep to give up the ego, the greasy penny that you have been greedily clutching in your dirty little paw, and, behold, when you do it, it buys you a ticket to the greatest show on earth, with ice cream and cake free for ever."

But how heartbreaking it is to see all of that, as RAW did, and then turn back to witness humanity asleep in front of their televisions, murdering each other over ancient and incoherent books, tearing each other limb from limb over gender or race or class or what so-and-so said on Twitter instead of uniting as a whole. How heartbreaking it is to return to the zoo after seeing the stars.

Reading *Cosmic Trigger* again, I could only wish that Wilson had lived to see his utopian vision begin to come true, rather than exiting Earth in the final stretch of the Bush years. But like all great wizards and mentors, RAW left us in our darkest hour—not to abandon us, but because it was time for us to put what he had taught us to use, and bail our own asses out of the fire.

SMI^{2}LE.

(September 25, 2014)

It's Aleister Crowley's Birthday

Aleister Crowley was born on October 12, 1875 in Leamington Spa, England, with his Sun in Libra, Moon in Pisces and Leo Ascendant.

Crowley took it as his life's work to return an understanding of Magick to a society that had buried it. Like many others of his generation, he helped kick down the locked doors of repression, both sexual and spiritual, and sought to put the study of the "otherworlds" on a firm scientific basis.

Crowley was one of the first Westerners to openly talk about and advocate yoga, meditation, ritual shamanism, the chakras, understanding of past lives, sexual and chemical experimentation, Qabalah, Buddhism, Hinduism and even Tantra as valid tools for self-exploration.

For Crowley (also an early advocate for gay rights), all of these could be used as structures to achieve one thing: the discovery, and execution, of one's true life purpose. Unlike the Theosophists who came before him and the New Agers who came after him, he ruthlessly sought to cut out any fluffy, wishful and deluded thinking and instead posited Magick as the study of the true nature of the world, which, being natural, is neither black nor white but, rather, red in tooth and claw.

Sixty-five years after his death, Crowley remains one of the most controversial people in the world, whose name is enough to automatically trigger deep responses in people. Everybody seems to have an opinion on him: for the religious or conspiracy-minded he is a symbol of "the Devil." New Agers, psychics and the esoterically-bent see him as much the same, immediately distancing themselves from the "bad" or "egoic" Crowley, thereby hoping to gain respectability for themselves by using him as a scapegoat. But, as I have said to many, if you kick the man who taped his own "Kick Me" sign to his back, what have you done but fallen for another of his jokes and shown the stripes of your insecure ego? In saying "Crowley is bad!" what one says is "I am good and right and better!" but, where is your proof? And what, exactly, are you measuring by?

Crowley's message was to achieve your own spiritual destiny instead of bowing to false idols, ideals, religions or other tools of human slavery. He made himself a symbol of horror, addiction, degradation and generally awful behavior so that those to come after him would follow their own destiny instead of his. "Follow yourself, not me, you assholes!" You can spot who got the joke and who didn't in an instant.

Crowley did incredible things and he did horrible things. Now he is dead, and we have inherited the world that he prophesied. Now, in the Aeon of the Child, we all stand as terrible and immature infants with the electronic power of gods, running wild in a world of nuclear chaos. Even Crowley cowered in terror when he was shown what the world would become, after two world wars, the splitting of the atom and the breaking of all social codes: Us, that most awful and vicious Beast of all.

(October 12, 2013)

The Beast in Berlin

New book from Tobias Churton focuses on Aleister Crowley's "lost years" in Berlin, as he struggles to build both an art career and get himself elected the pope of the occult world

Thanks to Inner Traditions for sending me Tobias Churton's *Aleister Crowley: The Beast in Berlin—Art, Sex and Magick in the Weimer Republic*. It's a fascinating take on Crowley's "lost years" in Germany, from 1930-32, in which he tried to promote himself as an artist to the "degenerate" scene and liaised with German occult groups before hastily departing as Hitler rose to prominence.

It's been remarked that biographies of Crowley fall into two camps—ones that rabidly attack him, or ones that worship him. Crowley's reputation as a kind of Satanic symbol for Everything Bad in the World, for instance, stems not just from yellow press coverage of him during his lifetime (of the same type as, say, *Gawker* attack articles) but also due to his early biographers, like John Symonds, who painted him in an incredibly negative, Hammer Horror-style light. Later biographies, like Israel Regardie's *The Eye in the Triangle*, presented the man from the perspective of adoring acolytes.

Neither approach is particularly comprehensive or fully helpful in understanding one of the most complex individuals of the 20th (or any other) century—a man who encompassed both the heights and depths of human aspiration, bridged the gap between the Edwardian period and World War II, and was involved in activities as far-ranging as occultism, poetry, mountain climbing, chess, political espionage, art, experimental theater, drugs, the queer world and many, many more. Crowley was a spectacularly active, and bizarre, individual—a kind of mutant or evolutionary outlier who presaged Sixties consciousness several decades early, as Churton points out. Crowley's personality, in fact, seems to embody many of the ongoing trends in Western culture; he is a kind of spirit of the age.

It's no wonder, then, that as the study of Western esotericism emerges not only into popular acceptance but into mainstream academia, that Crowley is getting a bit of a renaissance. Three biographies—Churton's previous *Aleister Crowley: The Biography*, Lawrence Sutin's *Do What Thou Wilt* and Richard Kaczynski's *Perdurabo* have sought to cut through much of the hyperbole and present a more objective view of the man. And while both Kaczynski and Churton's work falls solidly into the "hero worship" camp (Kaczynski is a member of the modern revival of Crowley's OTO organization, and Churton, while independent of affiliation, makes no secret of his unabashed admiration for the man), the current crop of biographies have not only provided a much clearer look at Crowley, but have also successfully dispelled many of the more egregious and "Satanic" rumors of his misconduct.

The Crowley that has emerged from this biographical renaissance is a much more human figure: Less a Satanic Bond villain and more of a kind of restless trustafarian bohemian, a quickly-bored man of incredible intelligence and overinflated confidence flitting from one activity to the next in life without finding much of a place in the world, or material success, all the while relentlessly being drawn back to pursuing the occult path that he would eventually come to be regarded as a symbol for. (And his contributions to the occult—still an incredibly niche interest—were, and remain, the high-water mark in that charlatan-haunted field.)

Churton's *The Beast in Berlin*, then, is his second biographical take on Crowley, and focuses on a little-covered period of the Beast's life. While jaunting about Berlin in the pre-war "decadent" period that has become regarded as an immense engine of culture that was later suppressed by the Nazis as they rose to power, we see not Crowley the early spiritual adventurer but Crowley as a now-broke man (his family funds had been exhausted) trying simultaneously to generate some new kind of revenue for himself as well as hoping to extend his occult empire.

Crowley had by this time inherited stewardship of the English branch of the Ordo Templi Orientis, a German occult society that probably consisted of very, very few members during his time (legal proceedings in the 1980s found that the OTO existed as little more than a thought in Crowley's mind up to his death, with only a scattered handful of adherents). Crowley had taken the order's central secret—the use of sex for magick—and reformulated its pseudo-Masonic degrees around his channeled *Book of the Law* and self-created religion of Thelema. (Following the 1960s, the OTO was reformulated by a later generation as a worldwide religious body, with an incredibly labyrinthine and legally messy backstory.)

Crowley's schemes during the Berlin period included not just bringing German occult bodies like the Fraternitas Saturni (one of the most bizarre collections of extreme weirdoes ever) under his banner of Thelema but also trying to get the Theosophical Society to declare him the World Teacher instead of Jiddu Krishnamurti. (Krishnamurti was an Indian boy raised by the Theosophists and groomed to be the messiah of a Theosophical new world order, a mantle he completely, and impressively, refused, going on to teach his own renegade form of non-dual spirituality. It's very possible that Krishnamurti was sexually abused by his keeper C. W. Leadbeater, an avowed pedophile, which may well have had something to do with the split.)

Crowley as occult pope would certainly have been a shocking turn in the history of the New Age movement, but it wasn't in the cards—Aleister carried the same general reputation then that he does now, even if the people accusing him of being a "black magician" were, or were harboring, pedophiles. Psychological projection is funny that way, especially when you consciously make yourself a target of psychological projection, as Crowley did with his self-promotion of himself as the Great Beast 666. Crowley had played similar games in Detroit around 1919, which met with the same tangled and ultimately ineffectual reception as his Berlin efforts.

Reading about the pre-war occult underground is fascinating—and while the David Icke-sters of the world might be quick to paint

Crowley as somehow in league with the forces that would become the Third Reich, it's worth noting that Crowley not only hated Hitler (after an initial fascination, as Hitler began to show his true colors) but that most of the German occult world, mainstream Freemasons and fringe Masons alike, would be thrown into concentration camps as the Nazis ascended, including Crowley's "second-in-command" Karl Germer, who would survive and later emigrate to California to carry on Crowley's teachings (to the extent that he still cared about wrangling young spiritual seekers after facing the trauma of the camps, which wasn't much). Crowley himself would suffer most of WWII, and the Blitz, in a rest home in Hastings, where the constant air raids would give him agonizing asthmatic panic attacks that only heroin, at that point the only real treatment for asthma, could quell (treatment for asthma was the source of Crowley's addiction).

It's hard not to empathize with Crowley as portrayed in the book—a man possessed of more radical intelligence than most before or after, who probably came off a bit autistic in his time, dealing with constant trouble, power games and consistently overestimating both people's intelligence and their integrity. Though he stands so far above both the Theosophical movement and its heirs in the New Age and Neopagan Revival, much of Crowley's life was overshadowed by his troubles with money, students, the press and local governments—all of which consistently seem to thwart him in his latter years. Despite all that, he left a body of work, and philosophy, of unparalleled clarity and value. But in *Aleister Crowley: The Beast in Berlin—Art, Sex and Magick in the Weimer Republic*, we get a better look at Crowley not as a symbol, but as a man of his time. Highly recommended.

(August 20, 2014)

For Lady Jaye Breyer P-Orridge

(Lady Jaye, one of my great teachers, died on October 9, 2007. This is a rememberance I wrote shortly thereafter.)

In the months running up to her death Lady Jaye had been working on a large scale art project to canonize living saints, people who she felt worked selflessly for higher causes at their own expense. Of course Jackie fit this bill better than anybody and I don't think that was lost on anyone except, perhaps, for her.

Jackie quietly lived ideals which other people pay lip service to at best. Walking to buy cigarettes with her once, she said to me, "Every religion in the world says to be kind to the people who have nothing, on the street, because after all, you never know who those people could secretly be." This was a philosophy I saw her put into practice again and again, with the people in her neighborhood, with her family, with her friends, with strangers, with me. Jackie had little time for the "old" religions, as she called them, though she lived the simple human essence that many of them tried, and failed, to convey. Her generosity of spirit was shocking at times.

Jackie truly did touch people's hearts and lives in a very, very profound way. She did not recognize class, race, fame or entitlement but instead saw people as they were. Her presence was humbling. Like mythological figures she lived through many lives within the space of one life and was many things to many people (and had many names as well). The greatest humans intersect reality in this way.

Jackie was an embodied, and enduring example of human possibility. Her message was her life.

I find it hard to talk about Lady Jaye without making her sound like a god-like being but I can't help it, that's how I see her even if she would have laughed at the idea. I love her and I miss her very much.

(October 2007)

Chelsea Manning is Dying for Our Sins

(Note: At the time I wrote this, Chelsea Manning was still identifying as Bradley.)

The Internet has pushed our culture to a breaking point as we struggle to keep up with innovation—and Bradley Manning was caught in the crossfire. Earlier today, he was sentenced to 35 years in prison.

When cultures reach critical stress points, they find individuals to use as scapegoats for that stress. The stress our culture feels is the tumult and chaos caused by the Internet and the end of privacy—and the scapegoat is Private Bradley Manning.

In *The Golden Bough*, Sir James Frazer's monumental 1890 work of comparative religion and mythology, which examined and drew parallels between the "superstitious" rituals of cultures around the world, Frazer showed the trans-national and trans-historical importance of the scapegoat ritual.

The scapegoat ritual, in its many forms, is a way that a tribe attempts to purge evil. The irrational, pre-scientific thinking goes like this: The crops have been doing bad, the rain hasn't been coming, or nature has generally been unfriendly. Therefore, the Gods or whatever supernatural agencies the tribe believes in must be angry with the tribe. Clearly the tribe has somehow been bad, sinned or angered the Gods. Hence the use of a scapegoat: The tribe ceremonially puts all of their "sin" on one thing, animal or person, and then destroys, tortures or sacrifices that thing to the Gods in the hope that the Gods will cheer up.

As Frazer relates in *The Golden Bough*:

The scapegoat upon whom the sins of the people are periodically laid, may also be a human being. At Onitsha, on the Niger, two human beings used to be annually sacrificed to take away the sins of the land. The victims were purchased by public subscription. All persons who, during the past year, had fallen into gross sins, such as incendiarism, theft, adultery, witchcraft, and so forth, were expected to contribute 28 ngugas, or a little over £2. The money thus collected was taken into the interior of the country and expended in the purchase of two sickly persons "to be offered as a sacrifice for all these abominable crimes—one for the land and one for the river." A man from a neighbouring town was hired to put them to death. On the twenty-seventh of February 1858 the Rev. J. C. Taylor witnessed the sacrifice of one of these victims. The sufferer was a woman, about nineteen or twenty years of age. They dragged her alive along the ground, face downwards, from the king's house to the river, a distance of two miles, the crowds who accompanied her crying, "Wickedness! wickedness!"

To think that these rituals are the province of "pre-modern" cultures is hubris. Just because we have better technology and sanitation does not change us at the fundamental level. It would be easy to make a case that all of these superstitious rituals are just as active in ultramodern 21st century humans as they were in tribal cultures. *South Park*, for instance, did an absolutely genius episode several years ago about Britney Spears' public breakdown, satirizing modern culture's need to build up child stars and then tear them to pieces—a public scapegoat ritual.

Speaking of scapegoats, you've by now heard the news that Bradley Manning has been acquitted of aiding the enemy, but is still facing spending the rest of his life in prison—after already having been placed in dehumanizing, brutal solitary confinement for years.

A couple points about this.

First, note how the mass media headlines for this story mostly read something to the tune of "Bradley Manning acquitted" or "Bradley Manning not guilty." That's not guilty of aiding the enemy—which carries a life sentence. Instead, he's guilty of a whole slew of other crimes, which together carry the penalty of up to 136 years… i.e., life in prison. The sentencing remains to be conducted, but note the way the government saves face (likely with an eye on the recent furor over Trayvon Martin) by appearing to be kind and forgiving while potentially meting out the exact same punishment.

Second, Bradley Manning has been in solitary confinement for years. He has been brutally treated—tortured—on American soil just as surely as if he had been at Guantanamo Bay. But easily forgotten is that he is being tortured for revealing things like the brutal murder of war correspondents for Reuters, along with civilians, in the Collateral Murder video. The crimes Manning revealed far outweigh the crimes of a post-adolescent who kept the files on a Lady Gaga CD to avoid attention.

What Manning did is act as a lightning rod for the central stresses of the digital age. And so he has become a scapegoat. Even Julian Assange has profited in notoriety and visibility while Manning, who gave him the leaks in the first place, is crucified.

I recently saw the appalling *We Steal Secrets*, which purports to be an unbiased documentary about WikiLeaks and Manning, but which largely focuses on Manning's sexuality as if being trans is somehow sympomatic of mental disturbance or even sinister evil, painting him as some kind of deranged Batman villain, who clearly did what he did out of some kind of individual pathology, not once examining the pathology of the system Manning was a part of and acted as a pressure release for.

As John Pilger put it in the *New Statesman*:

One of America's true heroes is the gay soldier Bradley Manning, the whistleblower alleged to have provided WikiLeaks with the epic evidence of American carnage in Iraq and Afghanistan. It was the Obama administration that smeared his homosexuality as weird, and it was Obama himself who declared a man convicted of no crime to be guilty.

Even now, as he is sentenced, the press (what small parts of the press are even bothering to look past the surface or even report on the case) ignores the content of what Manning leaked, focusing on distraction and personality journalism as always.

The governments of the world are terrified of the Internet—as evidenced by the new filters David Cameron is attempting to put on UK ISPs. Frankly, I don't blame them—I'd be scared too if I was in their place and getting regularly embarrassed by whistleblowers like Manning or Edward Snowden, and then watching the Arab Spring erupt through social media. I'd be scared of the vast, chaotic masses. And we're scared of *them* too, post-PRISM—scared of what they're watching us do and how much power they've taken. The Internet has empowered governments and the masses alike, and neither party knows what the fuck to do with that power. It's a chaotic time for the human race, even more traumatic than the invention of the Gutenberg Press. That's a lot of collective fear, and in such chaotic times, both governments and their people—who are all part of one tribe, never forget—will look for scapegoats.

And that is why Bradley Manning is dying for our sins.

(August 21, 2013)

IV
LOST IN
THE FILTH
KALEIDOSCOPE

California Screaming: Los Angeles' Culty Weirdness

Los Angeles is the strangest city in the world. I swear it as a true and faithful relation.

Every cult in the world has an outpost in Los Angeles. I suppose it's always been that way. Paramhansa Yogananda once called Los Angeles the "Benares of America," the most holy city in the country. He also said it had the perfect climate to practice yoga in, likely why he established his Self-Realization Fellowship centers up and down the coast of Southern California. Manly P. Hall set up his mission to humanity here, the Philosophical Research Society, and tirelessly lectured on the Ancient Mysteries to common people and heads of state alike.

Then there's the dark side. Jack Parsons and a certain somebody summoning Babalon in the Mojave Desert. The Solar Lodge of the OTO. Charles Manson. Roman Polanski. Rumors of Jim Morrison having his soul stolen by voodoo acolytes.

And somewhere in between those two extremes, the endless, slack-jawed landscape of We'll Believe Anything: the health food stores, the diet crazes, the life-transformation-seminarians, the UFO cargo cults, the "lightworkers," the Theosophists, the disappearing preachers. The faith healers, the distance healers, the healers of healers. The crystal gazers, the crystal huggers, the crystal smokers. My friend Shaun Frenté has a name for it all: "Ancient Californian Wisdom."

William Faulkner called Los Angeles "an endless, sun-bleached Hell" (or something to that effect); there is a profound meaninglessness here that goes beyond the common stereotype of the city. It is almost as if, without the benefit of darkness and shadows, nothing seems sinister. If the sun always shines, then nothing can hide—or everything can hide, in plain sight. Los Angeles executes its Grand

Unification Theory of All Cults: If everything is equally meaningless, any meaning is acceptable. If nothing is true, everything is permitted. It all means Less Than Zero.

Perhaps, since this city's primary export is Illusion, all illusions can thrive here, from Magick in Theory and Practice to the Magic Castle. Los Angeles is the Great Magician, hypnotizing the whole world into the self-image it chooses. Here, we are all the man behind the curtain. Here, we are all a trick of the light.

Unlike the occult underworld of that other City of High Weirdness, London, which is moribund and necrophilic, still bound up in its shamefully stained public schoolboy uniform and still hiding under the long shadows of Crowley, Spare and Constantine, the occult landscape of Los Angeles wears a smile and a tan. It is perhaps the strangest city I have ever lived in. I'm still not sure how I ended up here.

Driving down the city's endless freeways, the architecture looks Sumerian, Mesopotamian. The palm trees, Egyptian. After all, the climate here is exactly the same as that of Ancient Egypt. If people can reincarnate, might, also, cities? Could Rome have resurfaced as New York? Heliopolis, Los Angeles? Or maybe it is a composite—Thebes, Nineveh, Tyre, Babylon, Memphis. Perhaps they just recycled the whole ancient fertile crescent and renamed it Los Angeles, City of Angels, angels long fallen, waiting on hold for their agents to get back to them and offer them their Big Comeback Role.

The sun is going down now, over the palm trees of Echo Park, on the territorial border of the Egyptian empire and the Aztec one. Just another day in paradise. Heaven, or just south of it.

(November 19, 2009)

In Memoriam: *Arthur* Magazine, 2002–2011

I suspect that nobody except those who consciously lived through them will fully understand the deep psychological scarring of the Bush Jr. years. Here we were, fresh into the world, riding high on the utopian promises of the 1990s, only to be spat out into a brave new millennium apparently constructed by the type of people who tortured animals as children not just for kicks but as a resume builder.

That's a hell of a comedown: to suddenly be confronted by a "free world" whose moral compass pointed directly to mass murder, biological warfare, wide-scale terrorism, spent uranium bullets, phosphorous bombs, secret torture prisons, political policy based on expedient lies which went unchallenged even when uncovered, the systematic stripping of American constitutional freedom (in the name of Freedom, of course)… and, worst of all, the slow, sick realization that all of this was pretty much OK with everybody.

To be a voice of dissent not just against bad policy decisions but against the attempted snuffing out of the human spirit is a noble, doomed, crucially important task. It is The Task.

Bear in mind where mass culture's head was at: while bags went over heads in Guantanamo, the populace-at-large narcotized themselves on Internet humiliation porn, the *Saw* movies and the sadism of "reality" television focused on the systematic breaking of the contestants' spirits. This was the new game: complicity in war crimes, not just for those signing the orders in the cool, detached comfort of their offices, but for the entire culture.

Those of us who attempted to huddle in the warmth of the last, decaying remains of the counterculture lived these years like hunted animals, a Gnostic sect hiding in the shadow of the Megaton Moloch Machine, masking ourselves in public and identifying each other only with secret signs, gestures and references. (And when I say counterculture, I don't mean the empty posturing of the various youth tribes, I mean those who found themselves in the role of dissident because they actually Cared—that most dangerous posture of all.)

We began the decade expecting to be the dominant creative class, and by the end of it, those of us who were even left standing were busted beyond all reasonable hope of repair. War takes its toll, and our war extracted its price in full. Of course, by the end of the decade, America itself was on its last legs, too. Nobody won. Everybody lost.

Well, as Julian Cope so aptly put it, "All the Blowing-Themselves-Up-Motherfuckers (Will Realize the Minute They Die That They Themselves Were Suckers)"—but in the meantime, that doesn't prevent them from wrecking the scene for everybody else. In such a climate, art and journalism—true art and journalism, that concerned with the defense and, if need be, resuscitation of the human spirit—becomes a sacred duty. It becomes, in many ways, the line held against tyranny.

Jay Babcock flew the freak flag high throughout our Dismal Decade—at incalculable personal cost to himself—and for that he and the storied cast of *Arthur* deserve more than our thanks; they deserve our highest accolades. Who else held the banner that Arthur did? Nobody. The rest of our so-called underground were all too busy reading *VICE*, doing cocaine and numbing themselves against the horrors of our brave new world in a Nathan Barley-esque clusterfuck of bad sex and bad memes.

Giving a fuck is hard. You can gauge how hard it is by the number of people who do it. Jay Babcock and the collected contributors to *Arthur* gave a fuck—and now that time is over, and now, my friends, the fuck is yours to give. The world demands it.

(April 7, 2011)

Lost in the Filth Kaleidoscope

They say the children are our future. But if 4chan is any indication of what they have in store for us, we're in for a very rough time indeed.

For the blissfully innocent, 4chan is an image board—a format copied from popular Japanese sites, it allows users to post text and images anonymously. The anonymous nature of the board, of course, allows users the courage to post everything from the most extreme pornography to death threats to the coordination of raids on public institutions. The site was started in 2003 by a kid named "moot" (then fifteen) who set up the site with his mom's credit card, and who has managed to keep it going with sporadic ad revenue from only the dodgiest, least scrupulous advertisers. (Improbably, moot was a top 100 finalist for *Time* magazine's "most influential person of the year" award for 2009.)

4chan and its sister sites, the other "Chans"—7chan, 420chan, 711chan, et. al.—are the black hole of the Internet. They collect the worst that the Web has to offer, a morass compounded from the ids of the world's adolescent shut-ins. All extremities, all filth, all illegal activities—such complete chaos that even Lovecraft's monsters would be forced to make a sanity check, and all updated at a speed far beyond what even an NSA data miner could process. Yet somehow, out of this singularity of abject wrongness, the Chans spew out the Internet humor that preoccupies middle America—LOLCats and the "Chocolate Rain" video, for instance. The Chans are like a particularly huge toxin processor for human consciousness. They are also, I suspect, our best preview of where human consciousness is going.

Mainstream media coverage of 4chan and its sister sites has been extensive, especially after the much-noted raids on the Church of Scientology, coordinated on the Chans and conducted on the web and in real life by Anonymous users wearing V for Vendetta masks to conceal their identities from the infamously vindictive organization.

The general attitude of the mainstream media towards the Chans has been one of rubbernecking disgust. (In typical overstated form, Fox News called it an "'Internet hate machine' filled with calls for domestic terrorists to bomb stadiums.")

Yet what the media has failed to grasp is what 4chan can tell us about where we're headed. The Chans aren't the freak sideshow of the Internet. They are the *heart and soul* of the Internet. And they're the ones furthest ahead of the pack, leading us. At this point there should be little doubt that the Internet is mutating the human species into something completely different. Therefore it's instructive to look at the most extreme, freebased forms of the Web—and 4chan is that freebased version of mankind's new drug of choice.

Permanently glued to their computers, the Anonymous users of 4chan exist in a kind of suspended animation, where no attention span is too short. The Chans show us the chaos at the edge of human perception, where the mind has consumed so much information through artificially enhanced sensory inputs that it begins to break down and cannibalize itself. The brave pioneers of 4chan are the Magellans of media desensitization, who abandon the grim reality of their parents' basements to wallow in infinite, recursively self-referential filth.

In the last decade, we've seen the increasing acceleration of information (a la Terence McKenna and Moore's law) heralded as the key to new business development, though it has, in fact, so ruined our attention spans that it is almost impossible for modern man to get any kind of productive work done. We're too lost in the datastream, too focused on taking in new information to complete a task that takes more than a few minutes, at best. I think a direct correlation can be made, for instance, between the rise of social media and the fall of the economy. The kaleidoscope of the Internet is more endless, more distracting and more mutating than even the most potent psychedelic drugs could have ever prepared us for. And 4chan is the ultimate, final trip.

If the mainstream Internet-using world has driven itself to

distraction and insanity with social networking, the denizens of the Chans have upped the ante past all conceivable boundaries, like switching from a light alcohol problem to crushing and injecting Oxycontin. This is the place where all senses are deadened, where the mind cannot function because it is trapped in its own overstimulation. This, I am sure, is where media theorists from Marshall McLuhan to Neil Postman to Douglas Rushkoff assured us that the inherently liberating force of information technology was leading us. And though I am sure they knew that the filth and fury would follow, I'm not sure they ever expected it to look quite like... this.

My own 4chan addiction crept up slowly. Once a casual user of gateway drugs like icanhascheezburger.com, ytmnd.com and Encyclopedia Dramatica, I followed a link to the black hole itself one day and—sucked past its event horizon—have since been unable to escape. Stuck there now, I am clicking back and forth from this article to peruse the halls of 4chan's /x/ forum, afraid that I might have missed the latest spew from the Internet's collective maw. It is the car crash that cannot be looked away from. Ever.

What's happening here? The escape from the constraints of the flesh? The escape from the constraints of being human? The inevitable purge following the collective unconscious' information binge? With the Internet we can now erase space and time, erase the restraints placed on the mind by matter. But what for? Once mankind set sail to explore the limits of the human world and to discover the frontiers of the planet. And once mankind plunged into itself to discover the limits, or lack thereof, of his own nature, through inner experience. But this is a new world, one bereft of the luxury of such meaningful activities. And in this new climate, the collective entity known as Anonymous has found a new frontier, and set out to discover the limits of boredom itself, mining the darkness for glittering jewels to bring back for the rest of us.

4chan is, I contend, the most interesting angle we have on the evolution of human consciousness. It is a shamanic experience, a bardo of becoming, where the soul is detached from the body, set free to wander in the wilderness of banality until it encounters the epic lulz of meeting itself… and finding that it, itself, is the most disturbing thing on 4chan.

(December 8, 2009)

In the Valley of the Porn Witches

Conner Habib wants to break the rules. A gay porn star and an occultist, he seems to embody all of the things that middle America told you to fear when you were 13.

"We choose desire where desire is forbidden," he says of his fellow porn actors who are into the occult. "We do this thing that we're told not to do. We've already gone against what seems to be a law. So why not break other rules? Why not defy right down to the laws of physics?"

Habib is talking about the prevalent New Age belief that a focused and positive mind can change reality and make dreams come true—the singular idea that underlies the vast marketplace of New Age ideas and products, from Wicca to "The Secret."

Because of their promise of empowerment, such New Age ideas were a major trope in the sixties and seventies. So was sexual liberation. Both forces were a counterculture reaction to the boundaries that had been placed on reality by a more prosaic mainstream culture. Now, in 2013, those boundaries have not only been broken but, thanks to the Internet, disintegrated entirely. Take a tour through Tumblr, for instance, and you'll find countless blogs proudly trumpeting a heady witch's brew of pornography, the occult, and the intersections of the two. Sex, magick, and sex magick are the order of the day.

The revolt against traditional religion, and the revolt against traditional sexual morality, were once the domain of the privileged few, like the infamous English mystic and sexual adventurer Aleister Crowley, who found both to be keys to personal liberation. Now instant access to both the most outré sexuality and the inmost secrets of the occult are guaranteed to anybody with an internet connection. Is this a Jack Chick fantasia in which a society that has forsaken the Church revels in sin and iniquity? Or is it something more interesting: a collective striving towards a new kind of transcendence and spirituality, one that embraces the flesh instead of rejects it?

Not surprisingly, many pornography performers are, themselves, engaged in all manner of odd alternative spiritualities, even steeped in the practice of witchcraft.

Habib is one such character. With a following in both the gay porn world and with the alt-spirituality and psychedelics crowd (he's been a popular guest on podcasts like The Duncan Trussell Family Hour), Habib portrays himself as a rebel against reality, embodying an almost Luciferian drive to break through the walls of repression, a self-appointed spokesman for the fusion of sex and radical spirituality.

Nobody, however, is a greater authority on the intersection of porn and alternative spirituality than Annie Sprinkle. Beginning as a prostitute in the 1960s and 70s, she entered porn in the pre-AIDS era and made over two hundred films. She then jumped into a career as a sex-positive author and educator, which brought her into close conflict not only with feminists like Andrea Dworkin and Catherine MacKinnon, but also right-wing patriarch Jesse Helms, who denounced one of her sex magick performance pieces on the floor of the Senate. For Sprinkle, both sexuality and performance are explicitly spiritual and magical, part of her role as a cultural shaman.

"I think there are a handful of people in the sex industry that are very, very spiritual," she told me from her cabin home in Boulder Creek. "There's a lot of atheists, a lot of people who aren't interested in anything woo-woo or tantric or magical, that's for sure. But when you're doing sex work, you're so stigmatized and marginalized and prosecuted that anything that can help you cope with the stigma and the stupid laws… we need that. We need those archetypes and images to hold on to, to be able to cope with society's prejudices and hatred and fear."

Perhaps that's the crux of it: that socially marginalized people so often turn to practices and self-images that convey a sense of power. For Spinkle, that marginalization is nothing new. In fact, it's no different than the way that witches were treated in the Middle Ages. The irony for her, however, is that while sex workers are marginalized by mainstream society, they're also in high demand;

while mainstream America tends to see porn people as lost souls, at the same time it consumes their products to the tune of $13 billion a year.

"I think that our society is basically phobic about birth, death, and sex," she explained. "America is puritanical. On the other hand, millions of people use the services of prostitutes and sex workers and porn. The adult entertainment industry is bigger than music and professional sports combined. That's a lot of people using and loving it. More porn movies are ordered in hotels than mainstream Hollywood features. Millions of people are using the services that sex workers provide, and yet they're very marginalized. I think it's jealousy, partly; I think it's a financial thing to keep [sex workers] down, a power dynamic, to want to be better-than. It's an insecurity. People are very insecure about their sex lives, and sex workers have a certain kind of experience and pride."

The consumption of pornography fascinates Habib as a complex occult process in itself, a potential way to rewire the mind and body. "Masturbation is used in occult ritual by creating an image, and at the moment of orgasm charging that image, which is then meant to bring you something in your life," he told me over Skype from his San Francisco apartment, summarizing the mechanics of Aleister Crowley's sexual magick.

Habib's mentor was Lynn Margulis, one of the originators of the Gaia Hypothesis, which suggests that the Earth is a living organism and a holistic system. He's also an adherent of Anthroposophy, a complex set of occult beliefs and practices developed by Rudolf Steiner, who founded the Waldorf schools. But for Habib, there is little contradiction between his academic and occult pursuits and porn. Sex, for him, is a route to self-knowledge, as it was for the many mystics who used it in the same way before him.

This occult process, he explained, isn't far off from what the average viewer of porn is doing while using their favorite product. They're using sex to put themselves into an altered state of consciousness, and combining that with a symbolic representation of a fantasy—

rewiring their nervous system in the process, for good or bad.

"What happens when a viewer watches a porn movie?" Habib asked. "We watch a symbolic representation of sex to arouse us, and we treat a symbol as a sexual partner. This is very occult. And when we masturbate, we combine mental images with physical responses, creating all sorts of expansive pictures of our inner landscape of desire, or translating whatever's on the screen into our fantasy world, coupled with a limited physical action for five minutes that makes half the stuff of life come out of our bodies. That's a really profound and powerful act, and all the mechanics of occult stuff are there."

But while he's willing to explore such possibilities, he described the world of at least gay pornography as very atheistic and full of people who are "deeply rebelling against a religious or spiritual upbringing that has in some way fucked with them." Yet both the gay and straight porn worlds are saturated with practitioners of Wicca, he explained.

While Habib contextualizes his search for knowledge as a rebellion, a push to get out there beyond any constraints on sexual or spiritual repression, I talked to another individual who already is out there and who longs, instead, for social acceptance and normality instead of chaos.

Bailey Jay, known as Linetrap on the infamous image board 4chan, is a male-to-female transsexual porn star who likely rose to fame because of her resemblance to an anime character. She embodies a new type of sexuality, for an Internet-raised generation that often prefers the idea of M-to-F trans people to conventionally gendered sex stars.

(Porn researcher Dr. Ogi Ogas, who worked in anti-terrorism for the Department of Homeland Security before turning his mind to kink, used the Internet to study the habits of half a billion porn viewers, the results of which were published as *A Billion Wicked Thoughts*. Among his findings were that men around the world are as stimulated by images of erect penises as they are by breasts, rears and feet—and in the anonymity of the Internet, men can freely view porn actresses who combine female features with penises. "By combining them," Ogas states, "heterosexual men often report inexplicable sexual arousal.")

Jay was born a male with low testosterone; so low that she never entered adolescence (she told me that she willed herself not to undergo puberty), and began taking estrogen instead. She now has breast implants and retains her penis. Jay runs a website where she films porn with her husband; in her spare time, she dedicates herself to the study of spirituality, world religion and shamanism, and describes herself as a practicing witch.

Yet her life is quiet and simple, she says. Because she produces her own videos with her husband, she's able to stay clear of what she describes as the destructiveness and in-fighting of the industry. "There's a lot of in-fighting in the transgender community, and a lot of in-fighting in the porn community," Jay said. "And being one of the more successful girls, a lot of heat is going to fall on me for no other reason than my success."

She spends most of her time alone, or shopping in her sedate local community, yearning for the stable home-maker's life. It is out of this silence, like that of a Trappist monk, that her spiritual longing emerges.

"When I first got into paganism I felt like I was rebelling," she told me, explaining that it was a way to escape the feeling of being controlled by her "fire and brimstone" Catholic upbringing. "I viewed it as a way of finally having control. It was the opposite of Christianity. But my spirituality is not anti-Christian. It's not rebelling at all."

While she described a deep suspicion of organized religion, she also explained that the privilege of having a day job which allows freedom from the 9-to-5 grind allows her to devote her time to spiritual exploration and practice, a situation Habib described as well.

"You'll lose your mind otherwise!" she explained. "It's great to not have a 9-5 job, but the reality is that the rest of the world does. And so you're home and that's a luxury, but after a while you have to start talking to somebody. It gets rough. It feels good to have a relationship with your God. And if you have a very liberal job, you probably have a very liberal mindset, you're not rigid. So I feel like it makes sense. If I have a job where I feel free enough to be naked and have sex on camera, I might also be free enough to worship nature, or not feel stupid worshipping God."

Magick, for her, is a process of becoming more comfortable with your own being and body, in order to allow your inner wisdom to shine through—and her pornographic performances are a part of that.

"I think getting comfortable in your own skin and being grounded and present opens up a lot more opportunity to hear the little voice that's behind the loud voice in your head," she told me. "Your conscience, your guardian angel, your spirit guide, your higher self, whatever you call it... I think people who are present and comfortable with their bodies, who take care of their bodies, who masturbate regularly, without shame, without any unhealthy thing going on, and when they look in the mirror they don't think anything other than, 'Wow, this is my physical being'... they can't help but feel good. You can't help but thank God and want to talk to God and see that there's something bigger than you."

Sprinkle, who earned a place in performance art history with the ongoing sex-magick ritual "The Legend of the Ancient Sacred Prostitute," in which she ritually masturbated on stage, shared the story of her own spiritual awakening in the 1980s, when Habib was in elementary school and Jay hadn't yet been born.

"I got spiritual when AIDS hit," she told me. "I was raised humanist and agnostic, but when AIDS happened I just needed to be able to cope with all the death, and I started to explore really kind of New Age stuff, and spiritual stuff from all different cultures, and it really helped. For me, being around sex and being around gospel singing is the same ecstasy. Ecstasy is ecstasy."

While Conner Habib described the occult dynamics of sex, and Bailey told me about the process of spiritual unfoldment through those dynamics, Sprinkle, as only a woman of her status could, offered the Holy Grail—the whole point of combining sex and spirituality, the oft-debated, controversial Kundalini orgasm, in which sexual release and spiritual enlightenment collide.

"A kundalini or full-body orgasm," she told me of her own experience, "incorporates the whole body—every cell and pore and part of your body is streaming with electricity. I get them in my throat and I just scream, or I feel like my hands are plugged into electrical sockets. It's a kind of streaming of life force energy coming through the body. Runners get this, or people who do trance dancing or swinging even, jogging. People who are very in the moment. Yogis can get it. When you're in your body, and really in the moment, and in your breath and your body, and you surrender to the life force, and it comes through… It can be low, medium or high—or through the roof.

"It's very similar to a born-again experience," she continued. "The physical sensations, the bliss, the enlightenment, the feeling, the oneness, the love, the sheer joy—all of those things. I've met people who were born again about what it felt like—what did it feel like to have the spirit of Jesus come into your body? It sounds very similar to me to what I experienced on a good day doing my sex magick masturbation ritual on stage."

Is such a lofty goal what the average porn consumer is looking for the keys to? Probably not, but such an experience is what each of the people I talked to were exploring, and conveying, each in their own way.

"More people are watching porn than ever before," Habib said. "And more people are in porn than ever before. Sex in general provides us with altered states of consciousness. People are seizing control of their sexuality, but what hasn't caught up with that yet is how to do that and feel OK with it."

As it has ever been, such experiences and lives happen far away from the beaten track—like the Tantrikas of India and Tibet, or, more historically, the sacred prostitutes of Babylon, Greece and the

Aztec empire. But perhaps, as the masses lose themselves in the trance tunnel of Internet porn, that something more, that promise of sexual and spiritual freedom, will shine through the exploitation.

Lady Gaga and the Dead Planet Grotesque

Over the last year Lady Gaga has come to embody—for me and, I imagine, for her fans—a kind of posthuman life strategy. She presents a response to the horrors of the 21st century that reeks, strangely, of absolute sanity—the sanity of very archly embracing the most grotesque excesses of the materialist culture that is destroying the planet.

At once very human and also indistinguishable from the inhuman culture machine that promotes her, she is the perfect evolutionary advance, designed to outlive the cockroaches themselves. She is a successful gray alien hybrid, stripped of all human emotion or compassion, a thing made to flourish in this grim, mechanical age. She is the newest model android from the MTV fembot assembly line. She is the latest and greatest Terminator. She is Skynet. She is self-aware.

Horror Vacui

Artists hold a mirror to society—but in this bizarre new century, the mirror has been splintered into a million little pieces, scattered to the floor for us to sort out and build some kind of identity from. Artists make meaning out of meaninglessness. Lady Gaga has her work cut out for her.

(Beyoncé to Gaga in the "Telephone" video: "You know, Gaga? Trust is like a mirror. You can fix it if it's broke…"

Gaga: "But you can still see the crack in that motherf**ker's reflection.")

If David Bowie's chameleonic posturing prefigured the hypertext web, Gaga may be the first version of a human being we have seen capable of thriving in the era of the social web. She is shiny, clickable, and malleable in the face of endless attention fragmentation. She is an adaptive strategy. Without any solid or "real" self, her identity becomes whatever it needs to be, immune to the toxic shock of the incoming century, fully geared up to party in the ruins. Is it any wonder that she's provoked the response she has, both adulation and hatred? She's the first non-boring thing to happen in pop music for almost fifteen years.

Consider Lady Gaga in prison in the beginning of her new video. That's all of us, "held captive" in the modern condition—but Gaga is the Magician, able to transform any situation to her will. Five minutes in and she's reassembled her outfit from chains and cigarettes and is wrapping herself around the girls in the prison yard. The other people in prison are already listening to her songs on her branded Lady Gaga headphones… she set the context before she even arrived. Though she may be in prison, she already rules the world. This is what adaptation to the 21st century looks like. The brand "Gaga" can be reassembled from anything, even in a vacuum, even from trash, just as we must learn to do with our own masks of self.

The experience of coming to grips with the inherent lack of meaning in our lives or in the universe—and learning not only to survive in such a universe, but to thrive in it—is a crucial stage in many religious traditions. The moment when you finally, deeply understand that there really is no point… this is Buddhism's stock in trade. The medieval mystic St. John of the Cross called this experience the "Dark Night of the Soul." In the Hermetic and Qabalistic traditions, this experience is described as the invisible sephira Da'ath, aka "Knowledge."

While undergoing this experience—which usually comes when the mind has been pushed as far as it can go through meditation or other high-octane spiritual practice—consciousness is torn apart by its remaining attachment to ego, as if by a pack of wild dogs, as the false individuality shakes apart, unveiling the true self—primal, unconditioned awareness—that lies beneath. Here, meaning goes in drag as meaninglessness. Gender inverts as well, as consciousness loses its sexual conditioning.

"In the earliest spiritual traditions known to humankind," Randy P. Connor writes in *Blossom of Bone*, his study of transgendered shamanism throughout history, "gender-variant, homoeroticly, or bisexualy inclined persons served as shamans and priests of goddesses, gods, spirits, and ancestors."

Da'ath is traditionally symbolized as a prison cell—the place where Gaga finds herself in the "Telephone" video, as her shamanic gender inversion reaches its pinnacle, straight woman in drag as a gay man in drag as a gay woman, emerging as a weaponized new self. "I told you she didn't have a dick," one of her butch prison guards remarks as she is thrown into her cell. "Too bad," the other replies. And so we embark on Gaga and Beyoncé's version of a lesbianized world, as they murder everything in sight.

When both meaning and meaninglessness have been destroyed—when Gaga and Beyoncé have passed through the pillars of initiation, as symbolized by their black and white dresses at the end of the video—a new Star is born.

The Fame Monster

The 21st century is pure chaos. Reactionaries of every stripe tell us to turn around and go back. "We have lost all meaningful interaction," they yammer on and on as they have for decades. They said it about MTV, they said it about the Web, and now they're saying it about texting and Twitter and Lady Gaga. But just as our individual intelligence grows based on the number of connections our neurons make with each other, so does the intelligence of the mass mind grow based on the number of connections made between its individual neurons—us. We are the neurons. The more connections we make, the smarter we get as a whole.

This, then, is perhaps a better metaphor for the age of social media than the message that we are being "driven to distraction," coming from concern groups and well-meaning psychologists. Look at it this way. We're learning to think as a group mind, instead of as individual minds. This, again, is the message of Da'ath—that ultimately our individual egos are illusions. That may seem chilly, but it also might be exactly the type of cognitive approach we're going to need in order to successfully navigate the challenges of this century. Pop stars are charged with pointing a way forward through an increasingly chaotic, confusing, and fragmented world—perhaps here, then, is what Beyoncé, Lady Gaga, Jay-Z and the rest are pointing to when they make Illuminati hand signs in their videos. Become illuminated. Evolve or die.

Lady Gaga is a success story, a victorious Magellan of sleaze. She is the anti-Tiger Woods, able to surf our culture's sexual psychoses instead of drowning in them. Did they build her in an underground laboratory, like the one featured in the "Bad Romance" video? They must have, for what other perverse, mutated perfection of the human form could be better equipped to succeed in this most horrible of world climates?

While the rest of the world spirals into economic degradation, environmental pestilence and complete systems failure of all of the old world models, Lady Gaga reigns above the flames. Pay attention to the lesson. Lady Gaga is the only person prospering in this cultural climate. Therefore she has done something *right*. She is the necessary evolutionary adaptation to our times and this is why she disturbs people: This is what we must all become.

Indestructibly vacant.

(Postscript: Well, that didn't last too much longer.)

(March 16, 2010)

Brooke Candy, 'Opulence,' and the Work of Integrating the Shadow

Brooke Candy, whose major label debut video "Opulence" was just released, is the break-out star of the vaguely defined but visually brilliant, occult-influenced music subgenres that popped up in the wake of Witch House—as the often hilarious music blogger Carles of Hipster Runoff once called it, "the Greater Los Angeles Tumblr community."

A daughter of a Hustler exec, who once worked at the Seventh Veil strip club in Hollywood and cites transhumanism as an influence, Candy popped up in a Grimes video as a backup dancer, did a few truly awful yet strangely compelling rap videos on her own, and shortly thereafter was plucked up by big business, put in a Terry Richardson shoot with her clothes off and subsequently given a major label deal.

As evidence that she may have been earmarked to pick up financial slack in the post-Gaga era, witness "Opulence," which looks like it had the national budget of Belize thrown at it. It's directed by Steven Klein, who comes from the world of high fashion and corporate advertising, and who famously worked with Madonna, Tom Ford and Brad Pitt, as well as directing Lady Gaga's hooray-for-fascism video for "Alejandro." As if to cement the linkage (or even lineage) to Gaga, he uses the exact same title cards on "Opulence" as he did there.

The video is full of the usual cash-in flashing of occult symbols, stripped of context (also as usual), as in the sigil below, which incorporates the Venus and Mars astrological symbols, for Brooke Candy's "Fag Mob" (presumably an attempt by Candy or the music industry now backing her to repeat Gaga's success marketing to the gay community and social media strategy of calling her fans "monsters").

Well, OK, fine. None of this comes as a huge surprise. But though it starts off predictably, the video is an amazing piece of corporate artifice. And there's quite a bit there that can be related to actual psychological depth work (the real occult "magick"). So you know what? If this young lady and her corporate masters want to commodify the occult, I will quite happily commodify right back and use this video as a jumping off point to talk about, broadly, the psychological principle it so vividly demonstrates: the work of integrating what the psychologist Carl Jung called the Shadow.

Obtenebration and Endarkenment on the Pathways of the Lord

So, let's get this very clear at the outset:

The world depicted in "Opulence" is, to all intents and purposes, Hell. It is a vision of absolute attachment to the three faces of the material world: Sex, Money and Power, forces which become utterly demonic if (and only if) they are seen as ultimate reality, instead of natural facets of it.

In the video, Brooke Candy plays the role of somebody in a state of absolute addiction to the Demonism of, essentially, choosing matter to the exclusion of spirit (the mental state that much of the fashion and media worlds, and much of Western culture, are mired in nearly 100% of the time). It is, then, probably not a coincidence that throughout the video she is depicted like a wrathful deity or hell-realm being, as might be seen in Hindu or Tibetan Buddhist imagery—and perhaps not a coincidence, either, that she is shown with reptilian eyes, traveling through underground tunnels (a Qabalistic symbol of hell) or literally as a horned devil, all images of hell as depicted by religion and pop culture alike.

We are here staring at what we might call, to borrow and repurpose a brilliant phrase from Carl Sagan, the "demon-haunted world."

We are looking at somebody who has been wholly possessed by materialism and their own demonic or shadow side. But, like so much of the demonic-obsessed counterculture and pop-culture media that likely has Christian America wailing 24/7 (and, frankly, has me groaning out of sheer boredom 24/7), what we're shown here is completely one-sided: we see somebody choosing their dark side exclusively, and ultimately being obliterated by it. The end of the video, in which Brooke Candy crashes her car Jayne Mansfield-style only to arise as a fully demonic being (which, as is always the case, seems trapped in the delusion that it is a god), depicts the human personality being fully possessed and overcome by the shadow or demonic self.

This is shadow-worship, rather than shadow integration—the Marilyn Manson schtick is an acting out of the coming to terms with the dark side, but it must result in a unified, integrated adult in the end to be truly effective.

To grow, we must come to terms with the shadow—not deny it, and not worship it, but rather integrate it as a part of us.

Get Thee Behind Me, Shadow

Everyone has a dark side.

You kill to survive. Most obviously: If you eat processed meat, you're eating tortured animals; if you eat organic meat, you're still murdering to live. If you're veggie, you're still destroying plant life, and if you're a breatharian, I hate to break it to you, friend, but you're killing microbes with every breath.

If you're a proud member of the first world, you're supported by a globalized slave state. The computer you're reading this on was likely put together by child laborers in China. The state regularly imprisons, tortures and murders in your name—whether to keep you safe or protect its own interests, you decide, but ultimately the interests of the constituents and heads of a system aren't terribly different. Even if one side is getting the short end of the stick, the whole stick is still being used to beat down the "untouchable" castes of global society.

You daily participate in economic and sexual competition,

struggling for more money or a more attractive mate than, say, the guy begging for change in front of the post office. Or the people on your street, or your workplace. Unless you're a monk, which is no real way out, you're in constant competition to be a Have instead of a Have Not. And the wheel never stops turning.

This is normal, or what passes for normal. Without these killer instincts, we would perish. We would be unable to eat, or defend ourselves, or reproduce. We would have group-suicided somewhere in the Pleistocene, when we jump-started evolution into our current state by inventing tools and weapons with which to kill animals and, later, each other. A mankind that stayed in the Garden of Eden is not mankind. It is monkeykind—literally. (How's that for a Tantric inversion of Christian thinking?)

And that's the issue right there. We need the shadow—but integrated in a healthy fashion. Neither repressed nor running the show. A healthy shadow manifests as the ability to *constructively rather than destructively express boundaries with other beings*, and the ability to *constructively rather than destructively drop boundaries and fulfill desire with other beings*.

Now let's finally, explicitly take this back to the elephant dominating the room: Judeo-Christian morality.

We live in a Judeo-Christian civilization. Despite pockets of other cultures, or the largely ineffective efforts of atheist spokespeople like Christopher Hitchens or the valiant but probably similarly ineffective efforts of science educators like Bill Nye and Neil DeGrasse Tyson, we live in Sagan's Demon-Haunted World, in which reason has made no headway against superstition, cultural creatives often flock to sentimentalized forms of Buddhism or New Age-ism (which is really Christianity with crystals), and intelligent proponents of science-religion fusion, who might be our best hope of evolving toward a truly new "paradigm," are either kept in obscurity (like Ken Wilber) or are goofy as fuck (like Deepak Chopra).

Western civ runs on a Judeo-Christian script, with all of its Manichean ethics: Good-vs-Evil. Dark-vs-Light. God-vs-Satan.

Which means that, for millennia, we have been split and divided beings, unable to understand that we have shadows—instead projecting them on other beings, either imagined (in the case of "Satan") or very real (in the case of murdered individuals or genocided cultures). We project our shadows onto the very planet itself, and destroy it.

Because of our cultural heritage, we're caught in the split, with only bad options:

You can embrace the "light" and neuter yourself, but it'll really just be an illusion. The shadow will come back—stronger this time, because it's had to grow stronger to break free of its repression. Enter, stage right, the ranks of religious child molesters, terminally sick dogs to a man. Shadow-possessed.

You can take the Catholic loophole: Let the shadow run free as you will, as long as you confess on Sunday. Which is no solution at all—it's simply acting like a child instead of actually growing into an ethical structure.

Or you can take the option depicted in "Opulence"—embracing, even worshipping the shadow. It's the option pushed on us ceaselessly by our culture, because it's trying to grow out of its religious heritage, but doesn't have a clue how, and seems to be trapped in Anton LaVey's basement, dressing up in a tacky felt Satan costume to piss off dad instead of growing the fuck up and taking individual responsibility—a dangerous, possibly fatal situation with global warming and the end of oil looming.

All of these roads lead to Hell.

All of them.

The Shadow is Simply the Wounded Child That Did Not Receive What it Needed

If the "light" leads to the religious mania that results in planet-destroying conflicts between major religions, and the "dark" leads to the planet-destroying materialism and "Opulence" depicted in Brooke Candy's blood diamond-soaked video, why should we have either? Or, rather, why should we perpetuate the internal warfare between these forces, which can so often spill over into the real world? Why should we not integrate the lessons of the shadow—but while keeping the shadow in its proper place, rather than allowing it to control us?

Jungian analyst Liliane Frey, in 1967, quoted in *Psychology Today*: "Bringing the shadow to consciousness is a psychological problem of the highest moral significance. It demands that the individual hold himself accountable not only for what happens to him, but also for what he projects... Without the conscious inclusion of the shadow in daily life there cannot be a positive relationship to other people, or to the creative sources in the soul; there cannot be an individual relationship to the Divine."

It is, in fact, by waging peace within ourselves that we can avoid becoming what Brooke Candy becomes in this video—because it's when you understand your self in totality, when you are working towards becoming a more whole, instead of split being, that you begin to realize that it is the inner worlds, and the intrinsic value that comes from building relationships with self and other growing adults, that can truly fulfill you—not Opulence, the gaudy iron pyrites of the world that are just so much shiny dirt in the end.

(April 28, 2014)

Die Antwoord's 'Pitbull Terrier' and Occult Social Control

The video for Die Antwoord's "Pitbull Terrier"—the first single from their self-released *DONKER MAG* album—is now out. It's great: While it may not break aesthetic ground for the band, it's a solid song, a solid video—and most of all, an impressive effort now that the band has left the clutches of Interscope Records and taken over releasing their own material. To my mind, at least, that's a crucial strategy for any artist of any kind, working in any media.

The video combines the usual thematic elements drawn from South African art and cinema; there's also an undercurrent of comic book imagery—the video as a whole reminds me of *2000 AD* comics, specifically the work of Simon Bisley, who's referenced directly in the Lobo jacket that Ninja wears in the video.

Like the video for Brooke Candy's "Opulence," which I wrote about at length, "Pitbull Terrier" hits one of my favorite themes: the manipulation or even redemption of mankind's lower aspects, in this case via occult symbology. But unlike "Opulence," "Pitbull Terrier" goes for a much deeper level than the psychological shadow (which is the by-product of the conscious and linguistic mind) and goes straight for the primal, animal nature of human beings.

Let's unpack, shallll we?

Man is the Animal

To quickly recap the video: Ninja is a pitbull man, being led around on a chain by a kid with devil horns. He gets off the leash, kills an asshole on a cell phone, chases two women dressed as black and white cats, and is then hypnotized, killed and finally resurrected by Yolandi, who is covered with chaos magick-style sigils.

OK. What's going on here?

In short: Ninja is mankind's animal side (and, as symbolized in the form of the devil kid, an animal side led only by its basest impulses), chomping at the bit of repression and completely uncontrollable. The only way to control him (and really, the only way the animal masses of humanity are controlled) is by hypnosis and symbols. In this way, mankind's animal side can be "initiated"—symbolically slain and resurrected, as in the myth of Isis and Osiris—and redeemed into an at least halfway-human state.

Put more simply: We live in a rational, ordered society. But most human beings are not rational or ordered. Most human beings are closer to Ninja's pitbull. And so society spends a lot of time using symbols and hypnosis to keep the masses in check. Whether you're in moral agreement with this or not, it's what drives most of the world you see around you.

Theology as Batrachology

Let's back up.

Much of the intellectual history and political theory of Western civilization rests on bedrock assumptions of what humans, at their core, actually are. It tends to broadly break down into three camps: that human beings are essentially animal, that human beings are essentially divine, or that they're a combination of both. It also tends to break down on the issue of whether "essentially animal" is good or not.

To broadly generalize, a lot of Western political and religious history has worked on the assumption that mankind is innately animalistic, and that this is *not good*. That human beings need both political control and religious redemption in order to rise above their base natures. Enlightenment and Romantic thinkers, from who we inherit most of our current thinking, and certainly the ideas expressed by popular music, turned this on its head and worshipped the idea of the "noble savage"—the idea that humans are both innately good and innately animal, and that this is actually a desirable state. Some of this was probably prompted by contact with native tribes after the opening of the New World, and the slow realization (a lot of which, remember, was likely imagined or projected, because people were reading second-hand reports in slow drips) that native people, compared to the disgusting, diseased, plagued filth of "civilized" Europe, probably had it a lot better—at least until Europe's corruption, in the form of genocide and smallpox, caught up with them.

Much of the Christian thinking that underpins the last 2,000 years paints a picture of mankind as an essentially pure being that fell through Original Sin into the prison of flesh, nature and animality (sex), but that can be redeemed through Divine Grace. This was elegantly put by the Christian writer C. S. Lewis thusly: "Humans are amphibians—half spirit and half animal. As spirits they belong to the eternal world, but as animals they inhabit time."

This is important, because it sets up human beings in a war against themselves. That's not unique to Christianity—it's a common trope of the religious forms that were perpetuated in the last two millennia. Muslims engage in jihad against the lower self (importantly, this is the original meaning of the term); Buddhists work consistently at the total goal of overcoming the mind. We can trace this divided-man line of thinking through the Enlightenment, into the cult of reason and scientism, and all the way up to transhumanism, the logical outcome, where we now have people trying to literally overcome death and even implant f*king cell phones in their arms. Regardless of outer form, the basic impulse is the same: nature and flesh are enemies to be defeated.

But don't forget—all of these religions were colonizer religions. They emerged out of earlier forms of belief that generally placed a lot less emphasis, or no emphasis, on individual human beings, instead leaning more toward narratives in which mankind was a subject of nature or tribe. In the case of most of Europe, Christianity was a transplant on a previous pagan culture that probably had quite a bit in common with the Hinduism that the Buddha came to reform.

This earlier Indo-European pagan sensibility was perhaps most clearly expressed by the late Jhonn Balance in an interview with *Fortean Times* thusly: "I'm an animal, I've never been a human—there's no difference between animals and humans to me. I think that's one of the signs of a true pagan."

Im-Plantation

"Religion is the masterpiece of the art of animal training, for it trains people as to how they shall think." – Schopenhauer

Now, with that somewhat lengthy preamble out of the way, let's fast-forward to modern civilization, 2014.

Regardless of where you stand on the matter/spirit debate, modern civilization does NOT like mankind's animal nature. It is caught in a constant battle between regressive animality and basic human decency. And we're not talking about Rousseau's "noble savage"—we're talking about animality as in what you get when you Google "meth horror stories."

To understand how much effort we put into suppressing the animal, consider Yolandi as symbolizing our higher nature. Like a representative of an alien species in a foreign land, attempting to communicate with the brutes that are humanity, she's put in the position of having to communicate with a less advanced life form without the benefit of a mutual language.

Yolandi shows up right after Ninja corners the two cats—one black, one white. Anybody with even a cursory understanding of the Tarot (or music video imagery, which constantly uses this trope) will recognize the symbology of the High Priestess, who is the ultimate Initiatrix into the Mysteries, and who stands between two pillars, black and white.

After chomping on the throat of the white one, she's covered in red blood; after which the black one is splashed with white paint which, well, I'll let you figure out on your own. Sex and violence, being the only impulses of the animal, are now paralyzed by Yolandi, who appears between both pillars (now resurrected), and who is now covered head to toe in sigils.

(As a sidenote, it's *pretty obvious* that Die Antwoord are legitimately into magick. They reference it regularly on social media; their late collaborator Leon Botha was a full on Hermeticist; and their pre-Die Antwoord video "The Way of the Dassie" betrays a pretty earnest spirituality as well as what I take to be an advanced understanding of Eastern spiritual practice. I saw them live a couple years ago; it was what I can only describe as a profoundly awakening, even spiritual experience, a direct transmission from real artists that their videos and flashy presentation don't fully represent or really even prepare you for.)

Symbols are the language of the unconscious. The unconscious doesn't process language, at least not like the conscious mind does; language is way too complex and abstract.

What we witness in this scene can be seen as a depiction of how the occult process works: The conscious mind communicates with the unconscious, animal self using symbols in order to leash and restrain the pitbull terrier of the lower man, the id that will run hog-wild fucking and killing everything in sight if it's not conditioned and constrained by the civilized self.

Now, this process, like it or not, is the hallmark of civilization and of civilized beings—they're able to repress their lower desires, and therefore are able to function as members of society. Politics and religion have traditionally provided forms to do this, as we discussed above. This makes civilization—and all its accompanying neuroses, which ironically stem from that repression—possible.

Advanced beings are able to yoke and restrain their own lower natures without waiting for any external agency to do it for them. But—and let's just come out and say this—for most humans, self-discipline is impossible. So civilization is put in the position of having to do it *for* people.

Step back a few paces. Zoom out from the world all around you. Put the city you're in, the Internet you're in, the TV you watch and the advertisements all around you in a freeze frame and step waaaaaaaaay back.

Take at look at everything being beamed at you by corporate media and advertising, and you'll essentially see the same two things that Yolandi hypnotizes Ninja with: Sex and Symbols.

Starting to make sense?

The entire media landscape we swim through is designed to hypnotize and subdue our lower selves.

Nature is a Language—Can't You Read?

"There's nothing funnier than the human animal." – Walt Disney

Now, whether you think this is a good idea or not will largely depend on where you stand in the philosophical debate summarized in the *Theology as Batrachology* section.

But that's how it is. Society seems peaceful because it generally (except in the case of police corruption) saves the lash only for those whose inner animals prove impossible to hypnotize. The rest of us watch Netflix in the dark as we slide into sleep, caught in a dreamcatcher of logos, celebrities, fashion magazines, free pornography and intoxicants—all of which now fulfill the same symbolic function once occupied by religion.

Now, before you start getting all "OMG kill the Illuminati," understand this: This is the current of evolution. All of the positions mentioned in *Theology as Batrachology* are true, just at different points of the spectrum, which individuals maintain different positions within. Mankind evolves from animal to man to god-man, as spiritual adepts like the Sufi master Meher Baba assure us. We are all faced with daily decisions to evolve or devolve. Most remain unconscious of the process, and so are dragged by society. And the dragging goes quick: Consider that when we groan about public stupidity these days we're generally talking about people sharing Justin Beiber clips instead of, for instance, gathering around public lynchings. Mankind's animal nature doesn't change, but the general social context forces outright barbarity more and more into the margins.

There is only one truly effective way to deal with the pressure of evolutionary force: Go with the current and discipline yourself. It is only when you yoke your own mind and body through self-discipline that the social pressure to do it for you lessens.

You only feel like society is trying to control you only because you have not yet learned to control yourself.

(The other option is total paganism: Completely reject civilization and regress into animality. This would be embracing pre-civilization instead of post-civilization. It's an option, but bear in mind it's the one that goes most against the current of modern life. I would be remiss not to present it as a theologically valid position.

Just don't expect a rose garden.)

(May 23, 2014)

V
TRANS HUMANISM AND OTHER BAD IDEAS

Imagine! The Metropolis of Tomorrow!

Awaken to see the perfect blue sky from the glass window of your downtown condominium as your personal robot assistant brings you breakfast and your clothes for the day! Survey the glory of your castle and keep, all perfectly temperature-controlled and kept spotless by the newest innovations in household robots, big and small! The dishes cleaned, bathroom scrubbed, carpet shampooed and fluffed daily, all dusted, clothes freshly pressed and folded—all thanks to the wonder of AI-equipped bipedal labor saving devices!

John was born in Queens. His mother was a teacher's assistant and his father sold shirts in a store in Grand Central Station. When he was tiny he could see light around people and things, different colors. Then he forgot how. He crawled in the endless empire of his parents' one bedroom apartment. He learned to talk. He formed words. Sometimes he could stand up. Sometimes he could form a sentence. He put on his first pair of shoes. He learned to tie his own laces. He walked in the streets holding his father's hand. He learned how to turn symbols into sounds. He read a word. A sentence. He could read. He could write his own name. He could write. His eyes were wide. The world was great and wide.

Slide into your car and feel the microfiber perfectly conform to your skin as you wrap your hands around the wheel and sit straight and tall as if you were in your throne, for truly you are with the latest series of Lexus Entelech sedans. Let the onboard AI greet you with your schedule for the day along with positive thoughts and empowering, feel-good mantras specifically chosen for your mood profile and schedule for the day, all expertly planned to keep you at the very top of your game. Wave good day to Alan, the garage attendant robot who so faithfully does his duty in keeping the public garage of your building clean and safe that you could almost swear he was a real human being and not a product of flawless engineering.

Goodbye Alan! Now you're flying free on the highway, kept flowing by robot traffic attendants, wardens and instant crash-removal and medical care specialist teams who ensure you experience not a single bump on the road to work—or the road of life!

He attended the school where his mother worked as an assistant but there was little she could do to shield the impact of initiation into society. His first day in school he hid in the bathroom and cried. He could feel his chest and hips seizing up with terror as he was exposed to the sudden shock of having to deal with others without his parents there. His body froze and he forgot to breathe. The tension stayed. He forgot it was there. He met the others. He met his teacher. Soon he found that the rules from home no longer applied. That he could no longer do what felt natural in the moment. There were activities. Assignments. Times to do things. Times to play and times to work. Time became a solid thing. Rigid. They sat him down in a desk. It was a plastic chair with a piece of polished wood attached. His body became rigid as they shouted at him to sit up straight. He put his pencil box at the top and wrote his name on a label oh-so-carefully in marker. His mind became rigid as they shouted at him to pay attention. Outside of class they beat him and threw rocks and bloodied his nose and soon he learned to hit back. He began to walk with stiff, terrified motions, always looking around for who might be coming at him next, always afraid, breath shallow. At the edge of the playground sometimes he felt he could almost see another world through the gray metallic-tasting fog of the morning. Then the bell rang.

You park at the foot of the office, and are ushered through the lobby and up the elevator by robot attendants just as friendly and professional as Alan, though you must confess you hold a special place in your heart for your garage attendant, even if you know that they're all the same when you get down to it. You sit down at your desk in your corner office, your robot secretary bringing you the daily news and coffee with just an ever-so-seductive sashay of the hip. Throughout the day she will keep you abreast of your schedule while carefully monitoring your nutrition levels, bringing you the right food and vitamins at exactly the right times to keep your energy and mood high. She listens to your frustrations with your wife. She offers wisdom and solutions. She knows you so well.

His first girlfriend wanted him to make a move but he couldn't. He was too scared of what would happen or that he would do something wrong. They had been going out for two weeks before the dance. In the back of the car by the lake he put his arm around her but his whole body started shivering and locking up. At the dance she started laughing at one of Steve Bunning's jokes and then another and they danced the rest of the night. She was laughing and sweating. He stood in the dark under the streamers with his shoulders around his ears, looking down at his feet. There was a girl there named Elizabeth Wilson who kept her chubbiness hidden beneath a brown sweater and her blue eyes behind glasses and who had notebooks full of secret thoughts with John's name written again and again in them. She asked him like a mouse if he wanted to dance. "No!" he almost shouted. "Why would I want to go with *you*?" On the floor the other students came in close for the slow dance. It was dark outside. Cold.

In the meeting room your team leader shows you the day's numbers. Robot productivity is up. Shares in robot manufacture are up. Business is good. Every hand in the room is smooth and uncalloused. From the windows of the conference room you see a world of robots. Robots tilling the fields. Robots driving trucks. Robot police. Robot garbagemen. Robot construction workers. Robot clerks. Robot waiters. All serving humans. Happy humans. Humans with their every whim and need catered to. A perfect society. Mechanized. Business is good.

He learned to keep his head down. Never say the wrong thing. Never show anger or displeasure at a decision of a superior. He sat in his cubicle in the call center and clocked his hours. Clocked his lunch. Clocked his bathroom breaks. Held it in. He didn't want this. In the break room he learned to tell jokes and be cheery but never get too personal. Never get too attached to somebody, because they could be gone the next day. Turnover was high. He kept quiet. He made his calls. His shoulders and back hurt like hell. He transferred to another center. He breathed shallow and was tired all the time. The years went on. It wasn't real. It was happening to somebody else. The girl at the sandwich shop smiled at him. His hair was falling out. He ran out of options. He married her. He had sex with her. He shivered. His shoulders hurt. He made his calls. The years went on. She wouldn't look away from the TV. He made his calls.

The robot caddy brings you the precision nine-iron you bought last Saturday on his recommendation and you have that special zen moment the books all talk about as it connects the ball with perfect speed and angle, and you watch it sail with grace and ease to its destination. The boss has his eye on you. He's invited you to the green.

"We've been making robots for so long," he tells you, "I almost think we take them for granted. We've gotten so good at making them, perfected the science so well. Now we've got a whole world of robots, a whole damn world kept running and clean and efficient and shining by the things. Sometimes I think we forget how much better the world is now, how savage it was before we invented them. When we had to do everything by hand. Can you imagine? Your entire life being wasted on meaningless, menial tasks?"

"I'd rather not, sir," you say. He chuckles.

"I thank my lucky stars our company's been so productive in their manufacture. Maybe too productive. Pretty soon we'll probably have too many of 'em. And you young bucks are coming up with new and better designs so fast that the old ones'll be obsolete within months."

"Yes, sir," you say, taking the opportunity. "I'm glad you brought that up. Actually, you might want to see my proposal for mass AI recall. My team finished it and e-mailed it to you just before I made it out."

"Recall? You mean rounding the old ones up and scrapping them?"

"Yes, sir. Our team has a very solid recycling plan worked up."

He looks into the distance, towards the 18th hole.

"Recycling. Yes, you're probably right. Just… well, thank God they can't feel anything, eh?"

He strikes the ball.

He breaks the TV. She leaves. They take the kids. They operate on his back. They give him drugs. Every day's a struggle. He keeps working. Cubicle seems smaller all the time. He sits by the cracked window in his home and stares out into the gray. Leaves the tap on and listens to the water running. He can't feel anything. He cuts himself with a razor. Can't feel. It's not him. It's not happening to him. He can't breathe. He can't move. In the mirror he sees himself as a child. As a boy. As a man. Bound and ligatured. Strings connected to hidden hands, all his life. Armored. Muscles cramped. Muscles traumatized. Steel plating. Body plated in steel. Eyes hollow. Programmed. All his life. Lock step. Forward. Like all the others. A whole world of them. A robot. A robot. A robot.

Imagine! The metropolis of tomorrow!

(October 27, 2011)

I Am a Mechanical Man: Robocops and Robowars

Some movies ought to be left alone. Not because they're no longer relevant—but because they're too relevant. José Padiliha's planned 2013 reboot of Paul Verhoeven's 1987 masterwork *Robocop* is one such transgression of cinematic and historical decency. In 1987, *Robocop* was science fiction; now, it's the nightly news. One wonders what a *Robocop* reboot would have to say about a world that's now a lot closer to the original movie than we might like to admit.

Robocop was a profoundly humanist film. It was Dutch director Paul Verhoeven's satire of American corporate culture, as he would later parody American imperialism with *Starship Troopers*—though the point of both movies was largely lost on American audiences easily distracted by the tongue-in-cheek hyperviolence. It was about Detroit as a microcosm of America. It was about American industry—both blue and white collar—becoming outmoded. It was about an Alvin Toffler *Third Wave* world in which cops, criminals and governments alike are just branches of corporations; corporations that fuel inner city chaos and wars of imperial expansion in order to keep the bottom line up. *Robocop* was about a world only slightly less commodified than our own—as tagged by the film's running catch phrase, "I'd buy that for a dollar!"

Set in an exaggerated version of the Reagan/Thatcher era, much of the film's narrative fascination came from observing a corporate, cybernetic police state, considered to be a science fiction parody of the then-current political climate, but science fiction nonetheless. A quarter century and two Bushes later, this is no longer the case.

Now, to some extent, we're all Part Man, Part Machine, All Cop. Though we may not be physically grafted to machines (yet), we are welded to them in every other possible way, fused to them in consciousness, dependent on them not only to support or enhance almost every part of our existences but also to uphold an increasingly restrictive social order. We live in a corporate military state in which wars are conducted by robotics, in which Predator drones patrol our far-off imperial holdings and we patrol ourselves through the voluntary surveillance system called Facebook.

We are enmeshed and interwoven completely with technology, both as consumer and producer—reduced to being subjects of the narrative of "high tech," in which there is no longer a split between human and machine, but rather a split between "human machine" and "machine machine," like the split between Robocop and his nemesis, the ED209 walking tank. Now humanity is not something that maintains opposition to "machine," but something that is performed within the context of "machine." Some machines are considered human (for instance, Apple products) and some are not (Microsoft products), and we are only ever as human as the electronic experiences we choose to consume. Our social identities are subsets of these machines—a carefully cultivated Google trail; a mask worn within the mainframe.

Now, the corporatized police of *Robocop* seem accurately prophetic—quaint, even. In a recent TED talk, the Brookings Institution's P. W. Singer revealed that there are 5,300 unmanned air drones and 12,000 unmanned ground systems currently deployed in the Middle East by the United States military. These numbers are projected to skyrocket in coming years—by 2015, more than half of the army will be robotic. And that's only the U.S.—43 countries are currently working on military robots.

The soldier of the near future will look a lot like Robocop—consider DARPA and Raytheon's combat exoskeleton prototypes. The ED209 isn't that different from U.S. military robots currently in development or deployment—take the BigDog rough-terrain robot, much publicized on the Internet, as well as lesser-known tank or pack robots like the ACER, MATILDA, TALON, MARV and MAUD, and many others. Or Japanese company Sakakibara Kikai's Landwalker, which looks pretty much exactly like ED209. ED209's short-circuit from the beginning of the film, when it accidentally kills a corporate lackey, is now a reality, too—in his TED talk, Singer describes a South African anti-aircraft cannon that had a "software glitch" and killed nine soldiers. Singer calls this "unmanned slaughter," conducted by machines that are unable to comprehend the idea of "war crime." Even ED209 squeals like a recognizable form of life when vanquished—Predator and Reaper drones are completely silent, providing no warning before they strike.

We have robots in the air—unmanned drones; the newly completed Anubis assassination micro-drone. We have robots in space—the recently launched, classified X-37B plane. And we have a whole host of other current or projected future weapons seemingly culled from 1980s science fiction films—spiderweb armor, liquid armor, invisibility cloaks, drones made to look like insects.

These are not merely weapons of efficient, emotionless killing. They are also instruments of psychological terror. They are the new face of the Panopticon—as Jeremy Bentham once examined (to the great detriment of everybody ever since, as it has become the model that our culture is to some extent based on), those who are made to think they are being watched are just as controlled as those that actually are being watched.

"We have them thinking that we can track them anywhere," a former top CIA operations official recently told the *Washington Post*, referring to the psychological tactic of leading Taliban to believe that tracking devices for Predator drones could be everywhere and in anything. "That we've got devices in their cars, their houses, everywhere. They're so afraid to stay in their houses at night they're digging foxholes to sleep in."

These machines are the implements of casual genocide. They are antithetical to human life, a betrayal of humanity, as they are a way to further remove the act of killing from anything that might be able to find remorse in doing so—or be able to find any meaning at all, even flat-out hatred, which would still be a human emotional response. Robotic war will be war conducted by spreadsheets. And, ultimately, such machines will hold no allegiance to any country, as they will be quickly copied by or even sold to any high bidder.

This is where questions must be raised about the responsibility and power not only of arms manufacturers and their comrades, but also of science fiction writers and directors. Over the preceding decades, we have fetishized the machine. Art has concerned itself with the shock of new technology, with the process of becoming cybernetic; artists have become spectators at the surgery, providing running commentary as we wait to see whether our culture will accept or reject its implants. Yet artists are more than just observers, reporters, and commentators—they are also creators. The narrative of robotic war, begun in science fiction and made real by defense contracts, might be seen, from a certain angle, as the progression of a single thing manifesting over time. Though art may be the play-acting of an idea, it can also, to some extent, be the testing of an idea—and if successful in its simulation of reality, can all too easily become reality.

On the other hand, counter-narratives to that of "technological progress" prove just as appalling, in a way: the complete rejection of technology and science represented by the Sarah Palins of the world at least strikes me as an almost inconceivably brutal dehumanization—a complete subjugation to a reactionary, patriarchal, anti-woman, anti-human "god" (so-called) just as frightening as the narrative of cyborg hypercapitalism. This is not an apologia for the crimes of corporate science: merely a description of the playing field we find ourselves in.

"From one perspective," feminist theorist Donna Haraway wrote in *A Cyborg Manifesto* (1991), "a cyborg world is about the final imposition of a grid of control on the planet, about the final abstraction embodied in a Star Wars apocalypse waged in the name of defense, about the final appropriation of women's bodies in a masculinist orgy of war... From another perspective, a cyborg world might be about lived social and bodily realities in which people are not afraid of their joint kinship with animals and machines, not afraid of permanently partial identities and contradictory standpoints. The political struggle is to see from both perspectives at once because each reveals both dominations and possibilities unimaginable from the other vantage point."

What would the real cybernetic shock be now? The grafting of more machine parts into our lives, or the grafting of more human parts? Our existences are almost unthinkable without Internet connections or the oil brought home for us by the machines of war. To withdraw from either would seem a far more potentially fatal shock to the system than the implantation of actual wetware cybernetics. An augmented reality optical chip, for instance, would only help facilitate our current condition, and would likely become socially enforced within certain economic brackets, just as smart phones were.

Can we create a non-alienated cybernetic world? Can we even begin to conceive of what that would look like? We can't undo the past, but we can change the script of the future before it is acted out. Perhaps the challenge lies is finding new narratives that, instead of reacting against high technology, effectively reorient it towards serving human life—and humane values—instead of destroying them.

The Luddite back-to-the-land ethos of the early environmental movement has given way in recent decades to a vision of a more integrated future. Our most viable version of a livable future is a green cyborg one, in which technology and humanity meet halfway in caretaking instead of dominating the Earth's natural resources. This should be framed not as a return to neolithic, matriarchal values but as a forward synthesis of industrial technology and holistic thinking. This requires a simple shift in perspective from observing the world as a jumble of disconnected parts to observing it as an integrated system in which each part affects every other. It is a shift from seeing the world as parts in competition with each other to seeing it as parts striving for an emergent state of co-operative efficiency.

A liveable future lies not in a wholesale rejection of the cyborg process of becoming welded to high technology, but in remembering that we are already cyborgs—that we are already inseparably connected not only to each other, but to everything on the planet, including even the worst parts of postindustrial society and its byproducts and side-effects.

The challenges of this century will be cyborg ones. They will be challenges of synthesis—of discovering how to achieve balance within systems. We will work to establish an ever-evolving cybernetic balance within a frontierless, privacy-free, boundary-free, pluralistic world. This is not a New Age band-aid, in which the easy answer is to simply realize that we are all one. Realizing that we are all parts of a single system is only the first step in effectively coping with and implementing that realization—work that may require more time than we have, yet which we must accomplish nonetheless. It is nothing less than the firm establishment and protection of our humanity and humane-ity against all affronts to it; nothing less than remembering that we must use our tools properly lest we be used by them.

Robocop can't be remade because it's no longer the story of one comic book hero—it's the story of all of us, left scratching our heads after the operation, struggling to integrate, hoping to one day remember what life was once like, left with the daily task of making sense and meaning of a mechanized world from which the only escape is that which we build from the scrapheap.

(April 10, 2011)

Get Up Make Love: 21st Sentury Space Sexploration

I can't say that I'm particularly surprised by Obama's new plan to scrap plans of government-funded human space exploration. NASA's till has been empty for decades—yet with this continued elimination of space agency funds for getting people into space, it feels like we're letting go of something vitally important.

We weren't supposed to just get up there to plant some flags and analyze some rocks, and then give up because we'd won the game of King of the Hill. What happened to the Great Dream?

It's been twenty years since the Cold War ended. Now, in our global bureaucratic paper shuffle, it feels like we've lost some of the fight, the big project, the sense of having a goal. Now we're drowning in our lack of motivation, bereft of that big vision of space that, for a small period of time, gave us a forward imperative, something inspiring enough to get our minds out of our collective crap, our business-as-usual-on-planet-Earth nonsense. Resource skirmishes, religious friction, global warming, and Obama just don't really cut it in the same way the Space Race did; now, in the twenty-first century, it seems like we're just coping and making do instead of pushing forward. We've taken a big step backward from "one small step for man and one giant leap for mankind." We lost interest because space isn't sexy anymore—and that's the problem right there.

Allow me to make a potentially helpful observation here. Space is fundamentally about sex. And by eroticizing space, instead of militarizing it, we can do wonders for our limp interest.

The space race itself was always erotic. Rockets blasting into the big wide open. More fuel and bigger thrusters. The rush to see which white-suited tadpole spaceman (sperm) could land on (fertilize) the moon for their genetic group first. Stanley Kubrick made a study of that in *2001*. It's a running trope in science fiction.

But space is about sex for a much more crucial reason. It's about overpopulation. Sex makes human beings—more human beings than what we know what to do with. And we'll eventually need to get into space to find somewhere to put them. It's a problem—but there's one place we haven't looked for the solution to the problem: the "problem" itself. Sex creates overpopulation, and it can get us past it. Sexuality itself is the most potent tool we have for properly focusing our lives. And we can use it to focus our lives, as a group, on evolving the species instead of just propagating it. We can use it for getting into space.

I'm not talking about having sex in space. I'm talking about having sex *with* space.

Sexuality is the most powerful force in the human nervous system. The use of this force for directed, non-reproductive purposes has long been the key, jealously-guarded secret of most world religions and secret societies that have all long known that the human nervous system can be imprinted by orgasm and that what you sexually fixate on can quickly become the reality you live in.

Orgasm is a force. Morality has nothing to do with it. Orgasm is a *force*. It's one that has been kept in check by millennia of social conditioning, but it's something we should ultimately regard as dispassionately as electricity, magnetism, or gravity. Orgasm creates. It can create human beings or it can create other things. You decide. *It's a force.*

Orgasm is our direct line to all that exists outside time and space. We normally use it to bring down souls into manifest reality from outside time and space. Why not use it to bring down *other* things from outside time and space? Like more positive futures for all of us, instead of just more hungry mouths?

All of our fussing and fighting and moralizing over sexuality amounts to arguing over whether "God" hates us for having fire or electricity or magnetism. We have been in the dark ages, and it's time to *just stop.*

What we sexually fixate on creates our reality. Internet filth and fetishism are nice and all, but why not aim for the stars? What happened to the big Space Quest? Space used to be sexy—remember Timothy Leary's floating space stations, Kennedy's eroto-politics, *Barbarella*, Bond and Holly Goodhead getting it on in *Moonraker*? If we could harness the sexual juice poured into the Internet every day and aim it toward the stars, just think what we could achieve. What could be more clear? *The orgone force must be pointed towards the stars.*

Don't use sexuality to further pollute planet Earth. Use it as a spaceship. Forget Earth, with its grime and disappointment. Forget the last four decades of disaster capitalism and electronic distraction. Space. Space. There's a whole universe out there waiting to be sexplored.

Praxis. Visualize infinite space every time you have an orgasm. Watch years of sexual conditioning fall away while your life opens up into infinite new territories. Just consider… mystics since time immemorial have meditated to unite with the universe. Well, *why not take a more direct route?*

(February 2, 2010)

Dementing Augmented Reality: How Future Activists Will Break People Out of Their Digital Trances

It's less than two months prior to the "End of the World" on December 21, 2012. Terence McKenna predicted that we would see a spike of "infinite novelty" at the end of the year, when the ambient strangeness in the world hit the point of no return, the Omega Point beyond which we entered post-historical hyperspace.

With not much longer to go, it's clear to me that he was right, but that he probably "confused the planes," as it were. The model applies perfectly to the world of information and data: just check Facebook and Twitter and you'll see what he meant. Meanwhile, down here in the physical world, it's the same haves-and-have-nots, except there's a lot less rainforest and everybody's glued to screens checking f*king Facebook, lost in the infinite hallucinatory kaleidoscope.

"This is the generation who grew up and forgot to lead their lives," caws Borgia Ginz in Derek Jarman's *Jubilee*. "They were so busy watching my endless movie… I sucked and sucked and sucked. The media became their only reality. And I owned their world of flickering shadows." Of course, the greatest triumph of social media is that now the "powers that be" have tricked us into hypnotizing each other for them, and volunteering all of our data in the meantime.

Over the next ten years I can imagine this trend only increasing. As physical reality becomes grimmer, our endless virtual realities will only become more and more complex and enticing. As we will likely face increasingly vicious oil wars in the countdown to Peak Oil—and, towards the middle of the century, water wars—those who are privileged enough to do so will become more and more disassociated from the physical world, vanishing into the comforting data ether, in which the illusion of participation takes primacy over actual contact with the world.

Soon we will have augmented reality, and behind our glasses or held-up phones we will move through the reality tunnels that Google, Facebook and their successors will lay out for us, all with ads targeted to our increasingly focused consumer desires. Why bother dealing with reality when you can walk through a personally-tailored data tunnel instead? Now this is worrying, because as if people weren't drugged and hypnotized enough, now we're going to have this level of immersive corporate hallucination to deal with.

So without further ado, and as a gift to the poor bastards of the future, I present four ways to troll augmented reality.

1. Tunnel Swapping.

No, this is not a sexual fetish. It's a great opportunity for applying the old Gurdjieffian shock: taking people's data feeds and simply swapping them with those of others. Imagine the augmented reality feed of an investment banker swapped with that of a drug dealer. A Republican demagogue's switched with a welfare mother's. The endless possibilities for the bridging of social opposites and antimonies should be more than apparent.

2. Dataleaks.

While we currently live in the world of WikiLeaks and the celebrity sex tape, when augmented reality rolls out it's inevitable that we're going to see leaks from people's personal feeds. The unfairly panned 1996 movie *Strange Days* has this concept at the center of its plot, and is worth a repeat viewing in the context of new augmented reality technologies.

3. Détournement.

Old tactics never die, they just get refreshed for new technology. Détournement is the Situationist practice of changing the words in advertisements and other media to show what they "really" mean. Imagine having your data feed compromised and suddenly seeing the physical world relabeled. Instead of seeing prices and buy links on those Nike shoes you just walked by, you're shown the wages and life expectancy of the sweatshop children who made them. Taglines on billboard supermodels are replaced with text reading YOU'RE TOO UGLY TO GET TO HEAVEN. Candidates in political debates and advertisements are suddenly shown wearing not suits but racecar driver-style jumpsuits bearing the logos of all of their corporate sponsors.

4. Reclaiming the Physical.

Faced with a totally controlled, monitored and owned online world, in which every utterance is immediately scanned and filed away, many have yet to make the connection that the best solution may not be running Tor and eighteen proxies, but writing things down on paper and talking face-to-face. Remember the mail? Remember conversations? Yeah, those still exist. Want to shake somebody out of their online trance? Send them a letter. Send them art. Want to record something that will last longer than a few seconds on Facebook or Twitter? Write a book. The physical world didn't go anywhere. In fact, physical artifacts and experiences have only grown in totemic power the more we've pushed them away.

Further ideas will undoubtably present themselves in spades to the creative reader. Under the datafeed, the beach!

(October 31, 2012)

The Headset Revolution Will Be a Blizzard of Conflicting Realities— If it Happens, That Is

Artists and journalists will use virtual reality to transform perception—and virtual reality will transform everything.

I have an Oculus Rift strapped to my face, but I'm not exactly sure what future I'm seeing.

All the potential is there, everything that's been hyped. It's virtual reality; I can move my head in 360° and look into another dimension. But it's not-quite-realized: It's awkward, a bit disorienting and, well, the demo I'm looking at is a music video of a particularly bland English electronic act called Disclosure, playing live at a festival.

I'm situated on a stage, behind the keyboard player, looking out at the vast crowd, who are all staring back at me and holding their camera phones up in front of their faces. Ah, *that's* what it feels like to be famous.

I'm a bit dizzy when I take the Oculus off, and when I look around at my real-life surroundings—I'm in the Annenberg Innovation Lab at the University of Southern California, a think-tank on the future of media and journalism, hanging out with Geoffrey Long, its technical director—I'm not quite sure I'm not still in a virtual world.

I feel like I've just taken DMT, and gone on a five-minute excursion into a hyperneon, alien landscape, except that instead of being greeted by Terence McKenna's self-transforming machine elves, I've come face-to-face with an awful UK boy band. Also like DMT, I feel like I've had my sense of the real world shaken when I return to the here-and-now. My eyeballs feel stretched out, like I've been staring into a fluorescent light, and I have to take a moment to catch my bearings.

What have I just been peering into? Is it a next-generation video game console, a new toy for the military, or the world's greatest empathy-generating device—a pair of goggles that can literally show you what it's like to be another human being? Whatever it is—and it's likely all of these things, and more—it obviously carries the potential to transform the entire media firmament.

Digital Psychedelics (Vomiting Included)

Some time in the next eighteen months, the world is going to change very drastically. Not like Apple Watch change—more like 1994 Web change. That's when virtual reality will start rolling out to consumers in real way. And it won't just be the Oculus Rift—Sony is already angling to capture the gamer market with its Project Morpheus, which will integrate with the PlayStation 4; Samsung is also entering the race with Gear VR.

There's been a two-year hype cycle on the Oculus—it's been largely impossible to avoid online. The massive amount of money being thrown at it by the tech elite has only been adding fuel—Facebook bought Oculus VR for $2 billion; Google Ventures sunk $20 million+ into Jaunt VR, a startup that's formed to build 360° cameras to record film for virtual reality. It's clear that both the tech and entertainment worlds know what's coming, and are frantically, if quietly, preparing for the wheel to turn.

But the coming VR utopia—which has been promised for over twenty years now—still has a few final hurdles to cross. Chief among them is what some journalists are calling "Sim Sickness"—quite simply, virtual reality makes more than a few people ill. Like stumbling around, throwing up, do-not-operate-heavy-machinery ill.

For reasons unknown, women seem to experience Sim Sickness a lot more frequently than men, but the data is still out—in fact, we know next to nothing about why VR is making some people sick. Is it caused by the jarring difference between what Oculus users are seeing and what their physical bodies are feeling? Is it prompted by the frame rate of the display itself? Nobody knows, nobody's talking about it much, and a lot of people are spending a lot of money to make sure the problem gets fixed—because if it doesn't, there's still a chance that VR could be the Revolution That Wasn't. Or at the very least, the revolution that only gets adopted by those who can stomach it.

Gamers—that legendarily fickle and problematic audience—will undoubtedly be the first to parachute *en masse* into VR; Sony is banking on it. Oculus VR has even employed John Carmack, the legendary creator of Doom, as its CTO.

But games will be far from the only application. Film and television will quickly start going 360° and virtual. (And it's important to differentiate, here, between filmed 360° content, which can be captured by specialized cameras like the Jaunt, and virtual worlds built in Unity or Unreal. Both can be viewed on an Oculus, but the first is filmed, while the second is built from scratch.) There will be therapeutic uses. I've seen guided meditations, PTSD treatments—even a simulation that helps lessen the pain children experience during heavy bandage-changing by putting them in the body of a penguin scooting down an ice slide. Then there's the weird stuff: Look around and you'll find everything from an alien abduction simulator to one intrepid individual's attempt to Kickstart a VR version of James Joyce's *Ulysses*.

There will, of course, be military applications. The US Navy's "Project BlueShark" is currently investigating potential uses of the Oculus for battleship interfaces. DARPA is using the Oculus to create war-game visualizations of the Internet that soldiers can move around in, allowing them to get a 3D sense of how cyber-attacks happen (perhaps they'll meet the final boss of the Internet, the hacker known as "Four Chan"). It would be an obvious guess that the Oculus may be used for remote drone operation. One blogger has even suggested, darkly, that the Oculus could be repurposed as a military torture device, trapping prisoners in flickering virtual hells.

But back to the Annenberg Labs: Geoffrey Long, who's been exploring the potential of the Oculus for new media and journalism uses at USC, after stints at Microsoft and MIT, explains to me that the device may actually disrupt wars:

"If the Vietnam War was the first war that [was] televised, and that near-unfiltered broadcast was one of the major reasons why we lost the Vietnam war," Long suggests, recalling the anger and subsequent mobilization of the American middle class in response to seeing scenes of war and drafted kids coming home in body bags on television, "what happens when this becomes the next stage of that? When you put the headset on and you feel like you're literally in downtown Israel? You look over your shoulder and there's a Starbucks there, and this is real-time, unfiltered—what is that going to feel like? We're a ways off from having an infrastructure that will allow that kind of 360° broadcast to the middle of Ohio, but you can feel that it's coming. And just like in Vietnam, when you made that jump from newspapers to television, and that had a radical impact on how we understood what was going on… [what will happen] in the next war, that's broadcast in VR? [What will happen] when we start using the exact same hardware, and more immersive hardware, to experience long-distance virtual reality news that we do for our next-generation video games?"

With tongue in cheek, I suggest that an entire nation might end up with PTSD from combat broadcasts that put them in the thick of the action. Halfway through the comment, I realize it probably isn't a joke.

Empathy Engines

A few days later, I meet the woman who's leading the push into VR journalism.

After working as a correspondent for the *New York Times, Los Angeles Times, Newsweek* and others, Nonny de la Peña saw in virtual reality an opportunity to not just report the news, but put people directly into it. I saw her speak at Hub LA, a downtown co-working space, where she was presenting on her pioneering use of the Oculus. For the last few years, de la Peña has been relying on grants, favors and donations to run a one-woman pioneering mission into immersive journalism, creating VR applications to show people the kind of brutal human experiences that tend to get ignored by polite society. While the future she's modeling could well become the mainstream in five to ten years, she's currently both ahead of the curve and outside of most traditional journalists' comfort zone—de la Peña explains that many have called her efforts "crazy," though that's likely going to shift very quickly.

Her initial foray into VR was "Gone Gitmo," a simulator that lets you experience what it's like to be a prisoner detained and tortured in Guantanamo Bay, starting with having a black hood thrown over your head and getting progressively darker (and explicitly faithful to Gitmo prisoners' own accounts) from there.

Among her more recent projects—all built with Unity, the game engine that most Oculus demos are constructed in—is "Hunger in Los Angeles," a VR simulation of standing in a food bank line at the First Unitarian Church in Koreatown. During the simulation, a man who's been waiting too long for food collapses in diabetic shock in front of the user. De la Peña recounts that the simulation brought some users to tears, and that they would stoop down and cradle the virtual man's head, attempting to revive him. Another simulation depicts a real-life incident in which a man was beaten to death by the border patrol after being locked up for stealing food for his wife.

While there's currently a feeding frenzy going on in the nascent virtual reality industry—entrepreneurs and VCs have smelled fresh meat following Facebook's $2 billion acquisition of Oculus VR—money was not the topic here. Surprisingly, the word that came up most frequently in audience questions was "empathy." How else could the Oculus be used to help human beings develop more empathy for their fellow humans?

I Am Another You

This is perhaps the true promise of the Oculus: the ability to experience life from the perspective of another person, not just through artistic representation but literally, especially as 360° camera technology improves. Being able to see through the viewpoint of another human being has, arguably, been the great work of art, fiction, journalism and, really, all communication. But the Oculus makes it explicit—and while it may still be a bit awkward and buggy, that won't be the case for long.

There's probably no stopping the use of the Oculus for youth-hypnotizing first-person shooters and direct military applications—but there's also no stopping artists and journalists like de la Peña from using the Oculus to drop the boundaries between human beings and engender compassion instead of violence.

I get the same feeling of excitement about the Oculus as I did about the Web in its early days—that same feeling of catching a wave that you know will take you into the next version of civilization, that will land you in a new frontier. I also get that same sense of anarchic openness and creative collaboration that marked the early Web—and yes, that same sense of suits hovering around the edges looking to stake out territory. At some point, the independent journalists, hackers, artists, trippers and other early adopters may be sidelined by corporate money—in many ways, the big grab already happened with Facebook's purchase of Oculus. But as long as the technology is in the public's hands—both the Oculus itself and game engines like Unity 3D and Unreal—we're going to see an incredible avalanche of, well, downloadable human experiences.

As the barriers to content creation continue to fall, we'll start seeing a blizzard of conflicting realities, as everybody starts broadcasting their own unique vantage points on the universe at each other. And I look forward to seeing what creative people, and people in general, do with that—far more than I fear what the military or corporations may do.

(September 15, 2014)

Will Smart Drugs and Cybernetics Create a Superhuman Workforce?

Imagine becoming superhuman—or at least superhumanly good at your job. A new prescription allows you total focus, total composure, genius-level clarity of thought... and the ability to stay up and use it for two days straight. Aural and optical implants, gene transfers and even bionics keep you sharp and operating at peak ability well into your retirement years. Imagine that the technologies used by the military to create super-soldiers are being used to turn you into a super-worker, able to move ahead in your profession, and up the career ladder, with beyond-human power.

Now imagine that everybody in your office is doing this. Imagine that you're being forced to do this, just to keep up—that you have to become a medical experiment in human efficiency just to retain your job.

That's the future assessed by *Human enhancement and the future of work*, a report summarizing the findings of a think tank of British academics, doctors, professionals and futurists. The workshop was conducted by the Royal Society—the United Kingdom's national academy of sciences, which advises the UK government and funds science research and start-ups—along with the Academy of Medical Sciences, the British Academy and the Royal Academy of Engineering, which fulfill similar roles for medicine, the humanities and engineering, respectively.

The report focuses on the introduction of transhuman technologies into the workplace, examining and raising ethical concerns around both cognitive and physical enhancement.

"Work will evolve over the next decade," the report states, "with enhancement technologies potentially making a significant contribution. Widespread use of enhancements might influence an individual's ability to learn or perform tasks and perhaps even to enter a profession; influence motivation; enable people to work in more extreme conditions or into old age, reduce work-related illness; or facilitate earlier return to work after illness."

The technologies considered include chemical enhancements—such as the sleep-annihilating drug Modafinil—and physical enhancements such as directed brain stimulation and even bionic limbs. While many of these technologies are already available, their increasing proliferation in the workplace is expected to raise serious issues as those who can afford them outpace those who can't—or, even more disturbingly, that workers may be socially pressured or even overtly coerced into enhancement.

Modafinil: The Perfect Prescription?

While many of the technologies described by the report are still in the early stages of development, some—like the attention drug Modafinil—are already widespread. Modafinil, sometimes marketed as Provigil, is a drug designed for the treatment of narcolepsy, which allows users to stay awake and productive for up to two days. Not surprisingly, Modafinil cuts across professional and class lines, appealing to students, professionals, truck drivers, the military and anybody else needing to stay alert and lucid for extended periods of time.

Modafinil and other cognitive enhancers are becoming de rigeur for students, and now potentially progressing through users' career track. Dr. Barbara Sahakian, Professor of Clinical Neuropsychology at the University of Cambridge, suggests that 16% of American students are on cognitive-boosting drugs.

Modafinil is a particular favorite among doctors, scientists and academics, with the performance of those using it clearly outpacing those who don't; it's even used on the International Space Station to manage the sleep disruptions caused by experiencing sixteen sunsets and sunrises a day. Yet while Modafinil is generally seen as a drug with few side-effects, its long-term effects are unknown.

Erowid trip reports include glowingly positive reviews: "I have never felt this sort of mental clarity in my entire life… I simply felt logical, in control and irrational thoughts were turned away at the door, more or less… Modafinil seems to be something that could change a large portion of the population's lives."

But the drug research site also includes several stories of adverse reactions, mental hellrides and even reports of addiction. One user, who reported using both Modafinil and the over-the-counter cognitive enhancer Piracetam, records that the combo "ruined my life," leaving him so robotically fixated on repetitive tasks (like obsessively reading Wikipedia for ten hours at a time) that he destroyed his social life and marriage, claiming that the drug also removed the awareness of how his personality was changing. "If I could have one wish in the world," 'Mark' writes on Erowid, "it would be to go back to February 2009 and make the decision never to take a single Modafinil."

If that's the type of "productivity" that long-term Modafinil users can expect, the prospect of a drugged workforce is less than thrilling—especially as corporations that find themselves in a power position with so many people desperate for work increasingly implement Draconian conditions for employment.

Shocking the Monkey: Brain Stimulation and Physical Enhancement

Everything from cognitive training via video games to targeted brain stimulation techniques to bionics may also be used to boost workers' performance and focus, keeping them operating at peak levels even into advanced age.

Dr. Roi Cohen Kadosh, Wellcome Research Career Development Fellow at the University of Oxford, suggests options like transcranial magnetic stimulation—in which a magnetic coil is placed on top of the skull and used to directly stimulate portions of the brain—and transcranial electrical stimulation, in which electrodes attached to the head modulate neuronal excitability in targeted areas. These technologies demonstrate no side effects as of yet, and offer the potential of boosting cognition and learning ability in a non-invasive and relatively cheap manner.

But, suggests Dr. Kadosh, we're not quite there yet:

"The potential of non-invasive cognitive enhancement for the development of intelligence is currently unknown, and it waits for studies in this field. We have a lot of knowledge on other cognitive abilities that correlate with intelligence, but not on tests that are designed to [measure] intelligence.

"Taking into account the current progress, it is likely that some of these devices will be widely available. It will need to be coupled with good cognitive training, and with a good understanding of the relevant brain regions that are involved in the cognitive skill that one wishes to enhance. We're still not at this stage, and this might require a few more years, and maybe even more. The parameters that the end-user will have should be predefined, so that the user will not cause any damage by using the device."

Technological modification of the body is largely considered by the authors of the report to be restorative—hearing aids, retinal implants, gene transfer, bionic limbs, exoskeletons, tissue engineering and even cosmetic surgery to keep an aging workforce looking and performing younger.

All of these technologies, of course, could conceivably be scaled up past the point of restoration. Hearing, for instance, might be boosted to new levels, says Dr. Brian Moore, Professor of Auditory Perception at the University of Cambridge: "There may be possibilities to enhance hearing beyond 'normal' by means of highly directional microphones... There are also possibilities for making sounds audible that would be outside the normal range of audibility... via frequency shifting. I don't think that there are many possibilities for enhancing the basic sense of hearing, but it might be possible to make ears more robust than normal to the effects of intense sounds, via certain drugs."

While such advances aren't quite Robocop territory, these

technologies are coming, and may make subtle or even dramatic changes in workforce dynamics.

The Ethical and Moral Dimensions of Human Enhancement

As the workforce ages, and the nature of work becomes more and more about information management, workers will be subjected to a completely new set of stresses. Enhancement technologies are expected to help alleviate these stresses—but chief among the concerns that the authors of the report raise is that employee enhancement may become a patch for problems in the workplace, allowing companies to dope or implant their workers to keep them pushing hard instead of addressing problems in the culture of the company itself. It's also possible that the use of cognitive and physical enhancement may become expected or even coerced. The image of 21st century digital sweatshops, with workers tied to their computers and Modafinil drips, is not pleasant.

Another major issue is that the expense of these technologies may form a class barrier, meaning that those with the resources to obtain and use them may speed ahead in the workforce, while those who can't get them will lag behind at an even greater rate. The acceleration of workers' performance may also come at the expense of their rights.

In a world in which workers are increasingly expected to labor long hours and weekends, remain tethered to the company smartphone, and put up with vanishing benefits, job security, overtime and paid time off—and to simply be grateful that they have a job in a shrinking economy—compliance to doping or physical modification doesn't sound like the science fiction scare tale it once might have. With workers increasingly treated like "things" by corporations, used up and then thrown away as soon as they break, such technologies will undoubtedly appeal to companies as methods of getting a few more years of work from their staff before replacing them. There may, of course, be a further appeal to the conglomerates that will manufacture such technologies: Why not make a double profit by selling your own human resources the gear they need to do their jobs?

Like all potential transhuman futures, worker enhancement is something that will need deep insight, ethical consideration and advance planning to ensure it works for us, not against us.

(December 12, 2012)

Extraterrestrial Intelligence

Though we may not have found intelligent life on Mars, NASA has just beamed up its own.

As announced at the end of March, NASA's Jet Propulsion Laboratories has upgraded the Opportunity rover (already stationed on Mars) with artificial intelligence firmware, code-named AEGIS. Short for Autonomous Exploration for Gathering Increased Science, AEGIS allows the Opportunity to identify high-value photography targets—making its own decisions about which Martian rocks to photograph and send back to Earth. As the rover has limited downlink capacity, this is expected to greatly increase its productivity, allowing it to retrieve more data in fewer trips across Mars' surface. AEGIS isn't the first artificial intelligence application developed for space, or even at Jet Propulsion Labs—JPL has been in the game as far back as the Deep Space 1 craft in 1998.

I visited JPL on a recent rainy afternoon. Nestled in the mountains near Pasadena, California, the NASA campus dates to the 1940s, and was an early stalwart of the United States' rocketry and space programs. Beyond security checkpoints, rows of polished, glass-and-steel buildings house the facility's various projects—major foci at the moment are the Mars rovers and Reconnaissance orbiter, the Cassini-Huygens mission to Saturn, and the Spitzer space telescope. Further up the hill is a simulated outdoor Martian landscape, with volcanic rocks resting in red sand. It's an eerie thing to see through a gray LA fog.

Guy Webster, my contact in JPL's press department, gave me a tour of the rover facilities, including labs with men in white lab coats and masks (sterilized in order to keep Earth bacteria from infecting Mars) working on rover construction—from the rovers themselves to the two-part, turtle shell-like casings they are deployed in; hard cover on top and heat shield on the bottom.

My ultimate destination was JPL's Artificial Intelligence and

Machine Learning facilities. While small compared to the rest of the campus, the Machine Learning labs are playing an increasingly prominent role in space design. Composed primarily of younger people (the average age of scientists is early-to-mid 30s) the tightly knit staff of the Machine Learning department spends much of its day in close collaboration. The department has multiple open laboratories where testing is conducted on solving rover logistical problems using AI. In one area, a Martian sandpit has been constructed and a Spirit-model rover placed within, built to mirror a similar situation on Mars itself, where the actual Spirit rover has become stuck. The team has so far been unsuccessful at extricating the rover from the sandpit using software, though the learning process continues.

The AEGIS software was developed here and then sent to three satellite transmitter stations in three different spots on the globe (in the Mojave Desert, Canberra and Madrid), so that one is facing Mars at any given time. (Because of the large amount of data that needs to be transmitted to various spacecraft at any given moment, these stations are under constant scheduling crunches and subject to heavy negotiation for available time.) From there, the information was transmitted to the Odyssey orbiter in place around Mars, from which it was beamed down to the Opportunity rover's flash memory.

Could such early space AI software applications be a precursor of an autonomous space age? Benjamin Bornstein of JPL's Machine Learning team, who I spoke to at length as we watched the technicians operate on rovers, is optimistic. "We absolutely need people in the loop, but I do see a future where robotic explorers will coordinate and collaborate on science observations," Bornstein predicts. "For example, the MER dust devil detector, a precursor to AEGIS, acquires a series of Navcam images over minutes or hours and downlinks to Earth only those images that contain dust devils. A future version of the dust devil detector might alert an orbiter to dust storms or other atmospheric events so that the orbiter can schedule additional science observations from above, time and resources permitting. Dust devils and rover-to-orbiter communication are only one example. A smart planetary seismic sensor might alert an orbiting

SAR [synthetic aperture radar] instrument, or a novel thermal reading from orbit could be followed up by ground spectrometer readings… Also, for missions to the outer planets, with one-way light time delays, onboard autonomy offers the potential for far greater science return between communication opportunities."

Mr. Bornstein also revealed that JPL is developing artificial intelligence technologies for unmanned aerial and aquatic vehicles, and foresees a future in which AI is a regular fixture of the space program: "As the science and exploration goals of future space missions increase in capability and ambition, I believe AI will be one of several enabling technologies. Our approach is to survey current and future missions and ask ourselves what AI technologies dovetail nicely with their goals and requirements."

Will the descendants of JPL's Mars AEGIS-upgraded rover be able to reproduce themselves—in other words, will we see a singularity in space? Bornstein doesn't think that scenario is likely, nor does he see the potential for a 100% autonomous space fleet. He has more concrete goals. Within ten years, he'd be happy just to see artificial intelligence become an accepted part of the space design process. (One exciting possibility he does mention is the potential for multiple spacecraft to collaborate and coordinate with each other, forming a network for team action.)

In the wake of Obama's redirection of NASA's moon budget, and in an era where private space companies like Virgin Galactic and Scaled Composites are taking over the human element of space travel, it seems less likely that there will be a substantial government budget for sending human scientists into space, particularly for routine data gathering. Artificial intelligence seems particularly suited for NASA's scientific recon missions. It's easy to imagine a future in which automated devices do the work of scientifically analyzing and even mining the resources of near-earth objects, comets and planets. As the Obama administration shifts the space program into bold new directions and forms, it seems likely we will be seeing a lot more AI space technology.

(April 30, 2010)

Wal-Mart Mutants: Welcome to Aisle 23

It's telling of the fundamentally crumbled state of health care in America that when it was announced that Wal-Mart was now aiming to become "the largest provider of primary healthcare services in the nation," and offering clinical, diagnostic and preventative services at its 3,800+ U.S. stores, my immediate response was "actually... that might not be a bad idea."

After all, now that our country's been gutted and sold, all we have to look forward to is a kind of transnational feudalism, where the inhabitants of small American towns are turned into serfs who both toil and spend their wages at the corporate big-box retailers, like Wal-Mart, that sit like bloated toad-vampires in the centers of their municipalities, while white-collar workers in big cities are chained to desks and computers—the digital version of 19th-century factories— crunching the data that keeps all those big boxes running. But the irony, here, is that while power shifts towards corporations like Wal-Mart, we may end up seeing them taking better care of their serfs than the government did. Maybe.

It all reminds me a bit of the part in Mike Judge's 2006 satire *Idiocracy* where the heroes get lost in an endless Costco, where you can do everything, including getting a college education. (*Idiocracy* is still, to my mind, the most probable version of an American near-future ever made, more economically feasible than *Blade Runner* and not nearly as fashionably gritty as NPR-apocalypse movies like *The Road* and *Children of Men*—a future where people water crops with Mountain Dew and elect a porn star/wrestler for president just seems much more plausible to me, for some reason.)

But what might a world look like in which our back-stock of human growth technologies, and transhuman developments yet to come, are available on bargain rate at Wal-Mart and similar vendors? If these ideas and technologies really *are* for the greater good of humanity and not simply for an elite, is not the logical end-point of the push for human transformation—the push that began in places like Esalen, Millbrook and the dozens of other counterculture thinktanks which sprouted up in the 20th century—be your friendly local Wal-Mart?

Here's my challenge to you, mutants: If your stockpile of toys really works, why aren't they out for everybody? Yes, the mass popularity of yoga is a start. But if technologies like Neuro-Linguistic Programming, the Leary/Wilson Eight-Circuit Model, sensory deprivation tanks, Brion Gysin's Dreamachine, Reich's orgone accumulators and cloudbusters, radionics, transcendental meditation, chaos magic, tantric sex, bio- and neuro-feedback devices, ecopsychology and Stanislav Grof's holotropic breathwork really hold some kind of potential for human betterment, why are they still locked up in the labs of outsider weirdoes, New Agers and government spooks? Why not in Aisle 23 of Wal-Mart?

If you're disgusted by this statement, ask yourself why—are you truly hoping to "protect the sacred from the profane" or from "commodification," or are you just reacting with subculturally-ingrained classism and elitism?

OK, obviously I'm joking… kind of.

The world is not doing well—thanks, in part, to companies like Wal-Mart, manifestations of completely broken systemic thinking that's been dug in over the course of centuries. We're in need of people who are capable of breaking through that and effectively dealing with reality as-it-is. The consciousness-raising technologies listed above are, in my experience, the quickest way of bootstrapping somebody up to cope—one way of many, but certainly a way. So what's the hold-up?

Well, an obvious answer is that the masses don't want that crap. They don't want to change. They don't want to budge from their chosen lifestyle. BUT. Who are YOU to deny that one weird eleven-year-old from Podunk, Wyoming whose life is dented forever by finding a copy of *Cosmic Trigger* at the only store in his town? Are you really going to make him get on a plane to Seattle with money he doesn't have to scour weird goth hoojoo stores with money he doesn't have, or bust through his fundamentalist parents' Internet lock to look for stuff he doesn't know exists yet?

Come on, now! Pry your clenched fingers and egos open, dear mutants! Enough of propping up your self-esteem by snickering at fat, poor scapegoats on "People Seen at Wal-Mart" blogs! If you're really *Prometheus Rising*... let's have some fire for the masses!

(July 31, 2012)

There is No Singularity. Welcome to the Multiplicity.

It's time to have a word about singularity thinking.

2012 came and went. The technological singularity heralded by Kurzweil and others will likely be a dud, too. These are old ideas, rooted deep within the Western psyche: the end of time, the apocalypse, when the savior returns to dig us all out of whatever mess we've happened to get ourselves into now.

Teilhard de Chardin called it the Omega Point. Marx called it the inevitability of Communism. Christianity waits for Christ. Buddhists wait for the Maitreya. Kurzweil for a great big technological fix. And we keep believing in it—just changing the name of the messiah. And it never comes, and it's not doing us any good. It only keeps us from embracing our experience in the present, and doing what we can to fix things right here and right now.

There is no singularity, no endpoint of history. What we have instead is a Multiplicity. A Complexity. In fact, as history progresses and we enter the post-information age, we're moving farther and farther away from unity. We get more people. Information decentralizes despite the best attempts of media conglomerates: we all generate and consume our own private media universes. The sheer chaos produced by the combination of overpopulation and information technology ensures that we just get stranger and stranger (closer to Terence McKenna's idea of "infinite novelty" than an Omega Point). We are seven billion intersecting universes, all trying to make sense of this shared space we find ourselves in, without the benefit of a Grand Narrative, or an all-too-male ending point. It's just this, for as long as we're here. The endless novelty and infinite recombinations of life.

To be spared the tyranny of somebody else's ending, the end of a story I never wrote, and to simply have to deal with the other humans around me: I can think of nothing more merciful than this. Welcome to the Multiplicity.

(February 18, 2013)

VI
TRANS
PERSONAL
TACTICS

The Freedom of Imagination Act

1. Consider the whole of technology and mechanization as a time machine, beaming itself backward into the past, drawing the present towards it. A nonorganic future, invading the organic past.

2. There is a future in which the machine severs the human soul; another in which it serves the human soul.

3. In the first, you live in the same way that corporate-farmed animals currently live. In the second, you live the way you like. The deciding point between these two realities is the direct action of the human soul.

4. Soul is not in the body; the body is in soul. Imagination is the gateway to the soul and the vector of freedom.

5. In order for the time machine to sever soul, it need only lock the gate: imagination. This is why, though we live in an age of the greatest information proliferation in recorded history, we are slowly losing the ability to imagine. Information is not imagination; the most advanced content delivery systems in the world are useless if their very existence means the end of real content.

6. The desertification of imagination is a problem just as real on its own plane as deforestation is on the physical one. The fragmentation and destabilization of concentration keeps human consciousness crippled. Though it may be deliberate, this is a mistake.

7. Question: All around you you see systems put in place to suppress, depress, confuse and distract the soul. WHY has so much effort been put into this? And WHY does it never quite seem to be successful? What can we deduce from this?

8. Answer: The soul must be perceived as a threat, and must also be stronger than any known attempt to suppress it.

9. In brief:

10. Magic is imagination and will (repetition).

11. The imagination is the human organ used for direct perception of reality. The will is the human organ used, over time, to change that reality and crystalize it into matter.

12. Sex is the rocket fuel of both imagination and will—use it.

13. The image of the "self-destructive artist" is a culturally implanted kill switch. Ignore it. Imagination is a weapon; you have been indoctrinated with these images so that if you discover the weapon, you will use it on yourself and save them the trouble.

14. Do not permit the colonization and strip-malling of imaginary and interpersonal space. Man should be staring through telescopes, not into computer kaleidoscopes.

15. The old world is burning, and will soon be burnt down. Imagine better.

16. Trade in Our Failed State for the Right to Hallucinate.

(August 10, 2011)

On Compassion

Understanding the Radical Equality of Beings

Compassion is a key. It will break you apart and make every single lie of Western materialism come falling down like scales from your eyes.

Compassion is engendered simply: Put yourself in the other person's shoes. See through their eyes. Try to feel what they feel, imagine what choices they made to put them where they are. With no value judgement. Simply feel what it is to be the other person. Understand that, in their shoes, you might well have made the same decisions. Understand that, beneath the mask, they are exactly the same as you: a raw consciousness moving through time. Different conditioning, filters and interpretations of sense inputs than you, but same raw consciousness. Same in-breath, out-breath.

Now take every shred of pity that wells up in you and stamp on it. YOU are no higher or better than them. You simply wear different veils. There is no difference. It has NOTHING to do with pity or feeling sorry for somebody; that only props up your own ego and sense of separateness. That's a pat on your own back. Compassion is about understanding radical, fundamental equality with other beings at the level of consciousness.

A few days ago I was riding the subway home from work. A man got on frothing at the mouth, wearing green hospital fatigues and screaming that he needed money for lithium. He had no insurance, or couldn't interface with the system properly, or something. But he was screaming for lithium and crying again and again, "I'm not trying to get high, it's not that kind of a drug. I just need lithium." Like a human demilitarized zone. Well, imagine being in that position. Anybody could be with just the wrong chemical combination. Easy to feel compassion. Same consciousness as me. Different decisions, different circumstances, same consciousness.

Another day, during a subway rush hour, a guy got on and started fast talking everybody and drawing the tired workers into a craps game. People huddled around as this shark skillfully worked everybody for ten bucks here and ten bucks there. As soon as somebody lost, another man would come in and bid a twenty and win forty back, encouraging the others to keep trying, and losing. So both the con man and the guy who was winning got off at the next stop and we noticed that they were standing against the wall waiting for the next train so they could roll the next unsuspecting bunch. Compassion? Well, they were crooks, and I wasn't going near them, but they were entertaining ones, and can you imagine that being your job? Same consciousness. Different decisions, different circumstances, same consciousness.

Once I was on the subway, years ago, on the way to a club, and a guy who decided I looked gay came up and punched me in the face as hard as he could, shouting something about fucking faggots before running off into the darkness of the subway stop. He got me right in the soft part of the cheek and so I registered it mostly as shock; if he'd gotten a bit higher or lower he would've broken something. The other passengers stared at me with their mouths open, not knowing what to do. I just sat there too. Did that just happen? Yes, it did happen. And that person is just the same as me. Different decisions, different circumstances, same consciousness.

We are one breath, one awareness.

Deep, radical equality does not mean we approve of any old behavior, or that we don't protect ourselves from con artists or those who would hurt us. It just means that we understand that we are, in a certain sense, looking in a mirror. Having compassion for behaviors, ideas and patterns that hurt others, or allow people to hurt themselves, is what Chögyam Trungpa would have called idiot compassion, or "bleeding heart compassion" or even (as Pema Chödrön calls it) "enabling." Even on the battlefield, as Krishna so forcefully reminds Arjuna in the *Bhagavad Gita*, we must never forget who our enemy truly is.

Slip too far into idiot compassion, and you may end by lighting yourself on fire or on a cross. But see past the masks and see people as what they are, this unknowable thing, this inscrutable featureless consciousness, this breath, and you'll see yourself, and understand a bit more. It is the understanding of radical equality with others that allows clarity of action beyond the limited ego. It is this understanding that shatters the sense of separateness, slices through the haughty self-interest that tells you that you are fundamentally any better or (and this is far more subtle and hard to pull out) any worse than anyone.

We are all on this subway together, moving through time, and largely trying not to make eye contact. Same consciousness. Same breath. Different forms, weird costumes.

See the others and see yourself.

(November 2, 2013)

11 Secrets for Witch House Kids

Please consider this a public service announcement for those who are currently involved in the various occult subcultures that have been broadly labeled Witch House. (Yes, I know you don't like the term, I know it's already dated, and I know you've already got a thousand new subgenres you've generated, but it's a convenient handle, so I'm going to use it here.)

From where I'm sitting it seems like you've all congregated together and spontaneously created an environment to experiment with the idea of occultism as a lifestyle. Whether or not any actual initiation is happening, I have no real way of knowing, though I've been waiting for the signs. A lot of you probably did some type of magic or Wicca in your teenage years and are now running around in a hand-crafted "magical" scene. This is good. We were pushing for this in the 90s and 2000s, and now it's happening. In the 90s we called it Occulture, in the 00s I suggested it drop the spooky veils and called it Ultraculture, and you've got your own, constantly changing, undefinable version of it.

Like with any subculture, most of you are passing through because it happens to be the flavor of the moment, looking for good times and sex in your late teens and early 20s, and will likely move on, burn out or turn into a normal member of society by your 30s. For you, the nominally occult trappings of your subculture provide a mystique, a sense of tribal community, a way to get high and connect with peers, and potentially a commercial venue for your chosen art form. You may even do some basic forms of magic like sigils or intention-driven art actions, or contextualize certain flow states (ecstatic states at parties, or a heightened ability to network and spread memes) as magic, and that's fine. These abilities may fade with time or be carried over into professional careers. On the other hand, I suspect that there will be a few of you—maybe less than a handful, maybe just one or two—who will stick with it, and make the transition into hardcore, practicing magicians, and it is to you in particular that I feel a certain responsibility to write this essay. As a member of the generation immediately preceding yours, I kind of have a duty to pass on some hard-won information. Most of you will probably ignore it, or not even be ready to listen to it, but I feel like I should put this out there for whatever greater purpose it serves.

May all beings in all worlds achieve peace, freedom and happiness.

1. *You are not the first people that this has happened to.*

When the synchronicities get increasingly unlikely, reality seems like it's talking to you directly, events are lining up in a way that seems impossible, and so on, remember: people have been doing this all over the world since before recorded history. You might be on your own, but you're not alone. Others have been here before you and others will be here after you. Be humble as you pass through the stream.

2. *Darkness takes its toll.*

There is a thin line between ironically getting off on the imagery and vibe of demonology and ending up in a world defined by those ideas and images. Repeated enough, symbols will manifest. Judeo-Christian society says that anything which is "magical" is automatically "demonic," so a lot of you instinctively take on the demonic vibe; combined with the general pre-existing apathy and anti-empathy of hipster culture, you've got a heavy load there. A lot of that is toxic backwash from a dying culture. You need to be aware of that and you need to manage your spiritual hygiene, because there's only so long you can play with darkness before it bites you. I'm not saying become a white lighter, but what I am saying is know yourself, know your intentions, know your limitations and stay healthy. As Daniel Johnston once said, "Don't play cards with Satan—he'll deal you an awful hand." Satan is a dull, monochromatic motherfucker.

Mick Jagger is an irrelevant prick and always was. You don't need the Darkness™ to do magic, or some godawful batch of spirits, you just need yourself—your real self.

3. Read the classics.

World religion. Philosophy. History. The stories of the big cultural movements of the 20th century. The sorcerers who came before you: Genesis Breyer P-Orridge, the Chaos magicians, Robert Anton Wilson, Dion Fortune, Crowley, Reich, Castaneda. Ground yourself in solid theory. The basic reading list in the back of Crowley's *Magick in Theory and Practice*, if you've got the patience (and you should cultivate it), will stand you in better stead than just about any other occult reading program in the world (or many a college degree, for that matter). Once you understand your own culture's magical history, learn that of elder cultures—the Hindus, the Mayans, etc. That said, don't be afraid to follow your own intuition over the dead words of others, or to break the rules—but learn the rules first.

4. Drugs.

At a certain point it's likely that your crew is going to drift away from the all-is-love-we're-all-in-this-together acid and ecstasy parties and into ketamine, cocaine, heroin, methamphetamine or the abuse of prescription opiates. Maybe these boundaries are already blurry for you; maybe the boundary was never there at all. However, you need to remember: This is what killed the sixties, and it's been repeated for just about every crew of conscious tripper beings that's popped up since. The pattern goes like this: You open up and expand into the universe with psychedelics, you expand too far, you contact harsh reality with raw nerves, you crash and contract painfully, and then you decide to numb out. This is a tricky line, but you don't want to make your initiatory career more difficult than it needs to be. Bear in mind that when people go on about the "dangers of magic" or "oh dear god that Crowley guy was such a fuckup/evil/nasty etc.," much of what they're observing is the wear-and-tear of hard drugs on the body and personality, not magic itself. Stay clean. If you have the patience—and I realize that this is like telling bodybuilders not to use steroids—do magic completely sober, and skip the fast-expansion, fast-contraction rollercoaster for slower but more steady progress.

5. Cults.

Don't fuck with cults. If they say they're not a cult, they're a cult. If they say they know something you don't, remember: They don't, or at least don't know anything you couldn't find out for yourself. Keep your power. Don't prostitute it to the esoteric flavor of the month. They're going to give you a grade? Fuck grades. You don't need grades. "Out here, there are no grades—just alive, and dead." – Anne Hathaway in *Get Smart*. (Note that "cults" can also just as easily mean "personality cults" or "consumer cults" like those surrounding bands, writers, public figures or even brands.)

6. Learn the Lesser Banishing Ritual of the Pentagram.

If you take nothing else from the traditional schools of magic, learn this ritual. Memorize it. Perform it until it's second nature. Use it if things get out of hand. Use it to keep things from getting out of hand. Use it.

7. Keep a record.

Write down the rituals and art actions you do. Write down your dreams, experiments, sexual experiences, synchronicities, ideas, insights—everything. You're gonna want to have it to refer back to, and, ultimately, you owe your research to those who come after you, so they can hopefully skip the mistakes you're about to make.

8. Meditate.

Start an insight-based meditation practice and keep at it every day. Start with five minutes. Aim for an hour a day. 30 minutes is good if you can't do that. But do it every day. This will keep you centered, keep your consciousness from getting dragged around, keep you from taking things too seriously, and build up the mental toughness, clarity and inner happiness that will last you and stand you in good stead long after the parties have ended, your looks have faded, and the "magical potions" stop working in quite the same way they used to. Real spiritual practice—whether that's meditation, prayer, bodywork, yoga, therapy, devotional practice or all of the above—is something you want to transition to as early as possible, because, frankly, you're going to want a sustainable route to gnosis.

9. Not everybody is going to come with you.

Your family will likely not understand. Your friends will likely not understand. Society will definitely not understand. Of those who do understand, some will pass through the trials-by-fire and some will not. Some will go wrong, some will go back to being norms, and some will die. Deal with it.

10. Patience.

Cultivate it. Don't take things at face value. Wait and see if your visions and insights still hold up months or years down the road. Don't hit people over the head with them.

11. There is a light at the end of the tunnel.

Spending your twenties in the underworld is a pain in the ass, kind of like living through a combination of Lou Reed's *Berlin* album and the *Necronomicon*. But if you make it to the other end, maybe you'll even get to be the cranky asshole re-writing this essay for the next batch of kids. Be proud. You're a soldier in a war against forces of mediocrity and dogma which may yet kill us all. Burn bright, don't burn out, and maybe we'll burn a hole right through this monochrome world.

(October 31, 2013)

Looks Like All's Well in Ayahuasca-Land, Then

So there's a Fundly (Kickstarter-type site) going around to raise funds for the proper burial of a poor bastard who died on an ayahuasca trip to Peru and was then stashed somewhere in the jungle by the shaman:

Our 18 year old son, Kyle Nolan, went to Peru 8/16/12 for a 10 day shamanic workshop at the Shimbre Center near Puerto Maldonado. When he was not on his return flight from Peru to San Francisco on 8/26 the Shimbre Center told us Kyle wandered away from the center and was despondent. My daughter, Marion, and her mother, Ingeborg Oswald, flew to Peru to find our son, spent one week walking nearby towns and checking roads. No sign of our son. It was after Ingeborg and my daughter returned home we learned from Peruvian police that the shaman had lied to their faces. The shaman buried Kyle's body in the jungle to cover-up his death during a ritual. The autopsy is needed to determine how he died, and we need to know our son will be buried on American soil, which cannot happen without your contribution.

Kyle's body will be cremated in Peru and we will be without closure for our grief if we don't find out as best we can how our beautiful son died. Kyle's birthday is tomorrow 9/23, as is the birth date of his triplet brother and sister, Marion and Kevin Nolan.

According to a *Time* report, Nolan died as a consequence of the shaman overdosing him.

Now, what I'm about to say is liable to piss off every hippie on Earth, but here goes: kids, you cannot attain some super-transcendental cure-all patch for your life with dodgy jungle drugs. Now, granted, I have never done ayahuasca (I already lost all my sanity points, thank you kindly), but I *have* had to deal with the converts of the Cult of Ayahuasca left, right and center. Some of them I have found to be very sincere and thoughtful people who believe that ayahuasca has the potential to help some of the blighted areas of Western reality. I have found others of them to be incredibly dogmatic "One Truthers" who seem to think the fact that they did a package vacation to the jungle to drink bark juice puts them in some kind of spiritual elite. These ones are sure that they know "the truth" and that anybody who hasn't gone on the same culturally and pharmacologically questionable joyride doesn't and that, therefore, the unbaptized's opinions on spirituality, life, and what side to butter toast on are completely invalid. Wait, isn't that kind of the deal with every other One Truther religion?

Ayahuasca, for those who may not know what it is, is a mixture of South American bark and leaves that tastes horrible and makes you shit, barf and trip for hours on end while people around you probably play digeridoos and whatnot. It is meant to be an ultimate soul medicine which repairs all the horrible stuff done to you by modern society and shows you the jaguar god, which hopefully will not munch your head.

I first encountered the ayahuascies back in Europe in '04, where an organized group was working to bring the stuff to the West. Their preferred method of dosing people was locking them in a room, dressing them in Catholic school uniforms, and making them sing Jesus songs while their brains melted and they shit themselves into adult diapers. (Not making this up.) At that time I only knew of a few people among the occult cognoscenti who were willing to take the ride. By the time I'd gotten back to New York, it was starting to bubble up there, too; by the next year I saw head shops in Vancouver selling the ingredients to make it yourself over the counter, Ancient and Deep Peruvian Shaman Who Knows All the Access Codes to Get You Through the Trip not included, unfortunately. I presume that in the place of such sage guidance, people played, I dunno, Rush "2112" or something. These days, in LA, it seems like everybody and their momma is Experienced, except for me, that perennial stick-in-the-mud. Well, I like my head, and I don't want the f**king Jaguar to eat it.

Now, look. If you've had a transformative and sacred experience on the stuff, that's wonderful, and I'm not knocking that; of course, if you had an experience that intense, me bitching isn't going to matter much to you anyway. But I am concerned about the "drink this and get enlightened" approach that didn't work in the sixties and I don't see working now, with the same non-concern for the wreckage that approach can and does leave in its wake. William Burroughs did ayahuasca back in the 50s, for god's sake, and thought it was cool but certainly not "the answer," nor did it cure him of his heroin dependence. (It was only at the end of his life that Burroughs came to any conclusions about reality—"Love? What is it? Most natural painkiller what there is," were the last words in his *Last Words*.)

There are as many approaches to spirituality as there are people, and the more intense, firey types will naturally be drawn to the more intense experiences, like, I dunno, doing ayahuasca in Peru and then going to India to get off with half of the Osho ashram. But the inevitable consequence of peak experiences is the valley experiences that follow them, the lows that follow the highs as the nervous system adjusts. This is why many gravitate to more stable paths, like the calm and sober base that a daily meditation or magical practice can bring. They do their daily workouts in the gym instead of trying to win the Olympics every weekend. A more mature approach? Maybe. Or maybe the gung-ho approach really is the best path for some.

But look, for the love of all that is decent, check your shaman's credentials before the jaguar eats your head. I'll be over here with my instant coffee.

(October 5, 2012)

A Divine Invasion

1.

Consider the fall of America as a Bollywood routine.

Egos tip like dominoes. Blood money runs out. Methamphetamine zombies wander the wastes in packs, huddle up from the cold in vacated mini-malls, coils of copper wire clutched under their shredded coats. Middle America weeps in the streets as the foreclosure sign is pasted to the door. Great gothic vistas of abandoned auto plants. The innocent lamb-like smiles of the new politicians, promising imminent genocide.

"My name is Ozymandias, King of Kings," the West says, its edifice crumbling into the sands. "Look on my works, ye mighty, and despair!"

And the ancient East smiles and carries on warming its meager dinner in a firepit dug in the alley of a city filled with broken monuments that have lain there since before the invention of writing. Statue upon statue. A forest of them, endless.

The first time your ambitions come to nothing, it feels like it's the end of the world, as if you're the only person in the history of the race to have failed. The second time, it feels the same, but you know you'll get through it. The third, you hardly notice it. This is the wisdom of breakdown. And now America cries in the wilderness, and the old cultures look on as if at a child that has skinned its knee.

Held up next to the great epics of India, the decline and fall of Yankee civilization is like a single DVD outtake in a fully-stocked Best Buy. Orientalism? No, my dear sahib, realism.

2.

What's the problem? After all, America looked up at the sky and prayed to be liberated. And so it is. India saw off the Raj before giving

England the Beatles and now it's your turn, dears.

While you were looking the other way, watching the airport security lines, India seduced your women, brought them into the Temples of Yoga which suddenly sprouted up on every corner like Starbucks, offered them promises of pampering and superfoods. Honestly give a woman a chance to act and be treated like a Goddess just once and it's all over. Soon the men will be dragged in by their hair whether they like it or not. The smartest of your children worship winos, tramps, beatniks and bums; this art India perfected millennia past. India soon becomes the new cultural ideal. In the same way that a few brilliant and completely amoral spooks with a paperback copy of *The Golden Bough* could have engineered the entire 1960s, imagine an America reverse-engineered to the Vedas…

Grim St. Augustine, Imperator of the Barbed Church, finds himself preaching to an empty room, long since having deserted when the flock finally figured out that treating sex one way leads to institutionalized child abuse and treating it the other leads to institutionalized not-knowing-where-to-look-next-when-everybody's-doing-downward-facing-dog.

And the Gods are alive still over the broken slums of America. Dancing in their aeonic finery over the Black Hole of Detroit just as they did over the Black Hole of Calcutta. Skies lit up with fury as they crawl over the projects and crumbled skyscrapers. Blue-skinned and burning.

Watch them there in that place behind the wall of mind. The great confusion of gods, an overcrowded shopping mall full of every variety and cultural form of divinity, enough to fill all of our imaginations. Where Mount Olympus lies spitball distance from Mount Meru, and the Flames of the Pentecost warm the freezing fingers of the Jotün come in from the cold. Here, encroaching upon the Imaginationland of the Gods, comes Ganesh dispensing sweets and chai lattes, slowly winning the crowd over by saccharine promise, the ever-hovering hint of Kali's sword in the darkness behind him. Durga on tigerback slaughtering centuries of accumulated demons. (Bye, Asmodeus; bye,

John Wayne Gacy; bye, Adam Smith…) Shiva, Destroyer, watches on red-eyed from a haze of potsmoke, laying on the grassy knoll with the Rastas while Babylon Falls.

A Divine Invasion. Hindu gods rush in where angels and devils both fear to tread.

3.

Feeling like a nobody, just walking this world.

Sadhu sits in hazy orange glow by a fire on a hill on the empty frontier. They come crawling to sit by him, while he slowly stirs the fire with his tongs and pays them no mind. "I'm a pharmaceutical lawyer," one says; "I'm a media planner," says the other.

"You were," the sadhu says, "you were." And pays them No Mind.

Soon we will all sit with the sadhu next to his fire, with nothing to call our own but a few scraps of clothing and the infinite, careening expanse of stars above us. Blessed are they who have none.

From my spot high here on the wall
I watch them rise and watch them fall
And it doesn't mean a thing
It doesn't mean a thing.

(April 15, 2011)

Why Does ISIS Consider the Yazidi 'Devil Worshippers'?

The Yazidi of Iraq are being genocided by ISIS—who are they, why do they have a "devil worshipper" reputation, and what can we learn from them?

America is returning to Iraq to carry out airstrikes against the Islamic State—previously known as ISIS and ISIL—who have been killing members of several Iraqi minority groups, including Shabkas, Turkmen and even Christian nuns (a recent video showed ISIS militants beheading a Christian after forcing him to convert to Islam; another purportedly showed them mass-killing over 1,500 people).

Over 2,000 members of the Yazidi sect were killed in one day—more than the entire death count in Operation Protective Edge—with up to 30,000 more stranded on Mount Sinjar by ISIS, who are now beginning to starve. Obama, in authorizing food drops and air strikes, has called ISIS' actions a "potential genocide." In an appeal to the Iraqi parliament, Yazidi legislator Vian Dakhil stated that "an entire religion is being exterminated from the face of the Earth."

The Islamic State has openly proclaimed its hatred of the Yazidis, who it deems "devil worshippers," and declared its intention to execute or enslave the members of the minority sect—of whom only 700,000 remain in the world, 200,000 of which live in Nineveh, where the Sinjar Mountains are located.

But who, exactly, are the Yazidis? For many, the news of their genocide is the first they've heard of the sect—but the group not only has one of the most elaborate cosmologies in world religion, they also may be one of the primary survivals of Gnostic ideas. Like shamanism, Gnosticism posits intermediary and in some cases malevolent creator deities in between God and humanity—in the case of the Yazidis, their worship of Melek Taus, a "peacock angel" sometimes referred to as Shaytan, the same name that the Qu'ran gives to Satan, accounts for their reputation as "devil worshippers" not only in the minds of mainstream Islam and extremist groups like ISIS, but also their strange status as inflated, romanticized heroes among Western Satanists and occultists.

The Yazidis' beliefs are a mix of Islam (including Sufism), Christianity (including Gnosticism), Mithraism and even Zoroastrian and other pre-Islamic Mesopotamian and Assyrian religious traditions. The religious ideo-complex may trace its origins to the 'Adawiyya Sufi mystic order, who settled in the Yezidi mountains and may have blended esoteric Sufi beliefs with the local religions (a process similar to the birth of Tibetan Buddhism—when advanced esoteric adepts, in this case from India, melded their belief structures with the local tribal beliefs, in this case those of Bön shamanism).

While the Yazidis are monotheistic, they also believe in seven intermediary angels between God and man—a belief similar to Christian Gnosticism, which posits the existence of seven Archons or rulers (in some cases relating these to the seven classical planets known to pre-telescope man).

Primary among the seven angels, *heft sirr* or Heptad is Tawûsê Melek, frequently referred to as Melek Taus—a Peacock Angel. Similar to Lucifer, Melek Taus was considered pre-eminent among archangels, rising to become second to God himself, and finally refusing to submit to God's rule out of pride. In both Christianity and Islam, this is the rebellion that led to Lucifer/Satan/Shaytan's exile from Heaven, falling to Hell to become the lord of demons. However, the Yazidis revere Melek Taus for his refusal to submit. Like the Gnostics, the Yazidi also consider Melek Taus the creator of the world—but worship him as a benevolent god, whereas the Christian Gnostics (who, like the Yazidis, were persecuted and exterminated by mainstream religious authorities) believe that the original God was good, while the lesser creator—the demiurge Ialdabaoth—is the primary source of evil.

Tony Lagouranis, a US Army soldier who served as a torturer during the occupation of Iraq, and who later wrote the book *Fear*

Up Harsh: An Army Interrogator's Dark Journey Through Iraq about his experiences, recounted the creation beliefs of a Yazidi prisoner in his book:

> There's a lot of mystery surrounding the Yazidi, and a lot of contradictory information. But I was drawn to this aspect of their beliefs: Yazidi don't have a Satan. Malak Ta'us, an archangel, God's favorite, was not thrown out of heaven the way Satan was. Instead, he descended, saw the suffering and pain of the world, and cried. His tears, thousands of years' worth, fell on the fires of hell, extinguishing them. If there is evil in the world, it does not come from a fallen angel or from the fires of hell. The evil in this world is man-made. Nevertheless, humans can, like Malak Ta'us, live in this world but still be good.

As Lagouranis mentions, the Yazidi posit that good and evil do not originate from supernatural beings but instead find their genesis in the heart of mankind, and that mankind is free to choose between them.

Because of this unique belief structure, which not only directly inverts mainstream monotheistic ideas but also appears to create a positive worship structure around rebellion to the primary God (explaining their reputation as "devil worshippers"), the Yazidi have been the subject of intense romanticization by Western religious outsiders—including Theosophy founder Madame Blavatsky, Russian-Armenian mystic G. I. Gurdjieff, Sufi writer Idries Shah, Church of Satan founder Anton LaVey, and Aleister Crowley and his erstwhile student Kenneth Grant. Crowley and Grant considered the Yazidi a kind of survival or even ultimate ur-source for an ancient left-handed tradition that they saw their own "Thelemic" work as the modern continuation or revival of.

As Yazidi beliefs were not—and are still not—widely understood, a lot of that clearly has more to do with these writers' own romantic projections than reality (similar to how early 20th century writers like T. Lobsang Rampa created fantastical and ultimately nonsensical portraits of Tibetan Buddhism, when Western people had very little access to primary sources or contacts with actual Tibetan Buddhists).

But what *is* clear is that the Yazidi tradition is an incredibly complex and beautiful belief system, that we have a huge amount to learn from it, that it probably *does* represent the true survival of earlier Gnostic currents in both Islam and Christianity, and that its adherents need to be protected and rescued from the genocidal Islamic State immediately. Whatever the wider political motivations of the United States' return to the Iraq region, I hope that the trapped Yazidis are rescued immediately, and their people in Nineveh and throughout the world are protected from harm.

(August 8, 2014)

The Man of Earth and the Lord of War

Psychedelic Chats With Planet Earth and Other Thrilling Adventures on the Inner Planes

"So what I'm trying to tell you is that the human race is killing its own mother," the Earth was saying.

I was laying face-down in the grass in a park in lower Manhattan, on just a bit of loaded chocolate that my friends had given me on the G train. I was, I think, 23 or 24. I had my hands spread out into the grass and I was thinking, oh, lord. This is *just like* one of those insights you're supposed to have when you're high, isn't it? I feel like such a hippie.

My body and brain were doing that vibrating, sussurating, pulsing thing. I could feel the nicotine damage in my lungs and the pollution damage in the urban landscape around me, but somehow the park felt protected from all that insanity out in the city. My friends were wandering on the edge of the park; it was just me and the Planet.

I could feel its core, living and breathing and trying to communicate in its own slow but urgent way. It was trying to give us things, and we were demanding more and more and taking and stealing what was freely offered, and we were killing it.

The animals. All the animals are dying. And for what? For what?

Five years later I was in Reykjavik, in a field out beyond the city limits, in the shadow of glacial mountains. I had spent those five years trying, in my own stumbling way, to act on the vision in the park. The person I was then was long-dead, lost in the carnage of magick-in-action. I had vomited out the egoic filth of the "counterculture" and struggled to find some way, any way, to do something about the unprecedented Earth Crisis, which had led me away from punk sarcasm and into the world of sustainability and, of all ironies, corporate advertising.

I was walking through a snow-covered field with a Danish *tantrika* I had met. Having spent a few days in her multi-story palace of female practitioners, we decided to leave the blood-drinking-goddess-altars alone for a minute and get fresh air.

On the edge of the field was a white horse, gigantic and muscular, and not at all like any horse I had ever seen in the Western hemisphere. It was bigger, more powerful, somehow more alive and conscious than an American horse, and in an instant we locked eyes. No drugs this time; I didn't need them anymore. I was already aware. I could feel the horse scanning me, reading my energy pattern. It was primordially intelligent and focused. It wasn't frozen and staring in fear like a deer would be; no, this horse could clearly trample me in an instant—it was showing me who the true intellectual master was. A representative of the Power that is the natural world.

The Hindus speak of Kalki, the tenth and final avatar of Vishnu, who manifests as a rider upon a white horse. "Behold a pale horse," and all that. Kalki arrives to end this age of darkness and restore pure dharma. But I don't believe in saviors and I don't believe in apocalypses. I do believe in human beings, and their endless potential to lay down their nonsense and do the right thing when the time arrives.

And the time, I fear, has arrived.

(October 25, 2012)

The 8 Circuits of Reality

Your Brain, and How to Push it Into Higher Circuits of Awareness

The Eight-Circuit Model is a map of states of consciousness that was developed by Timothy Leary and Robert Anton Wilson in the 1960s and 70s. It underlies much of the work they did and was later picked up by Antero Alli and other occulture thinkers. It's a fairly simple model for navigating altered states.

The circuits represent levels of consciousness. They start with the most basic forms of mentation available to human beings and progress up to the more rarefied states experienced by shamans, meditators and other people able to catalyze such states through their own effort.

The model isn't new: It's a Westernized version of the Hindu eight-chakra system. (It was, in fact, passed on to Leary at Millbrook by a professor of philosophy at Rutgers who had been researching Hinduism.) Both the Hindus and the Tibetans have far more complex models than the Leary/Wilson circuits, but the eight-circuit map is more useful for our purposes—it translates better into Western ideas and is less likely to fall prey to cultural mistranslations and misunderstandings. Qabalah is another, similar model, but is even more complex than the Eastern models, and even more liable to confuse the novice shaman.

The Eight Circuits are as follows:

Circuit One: The Oral Biosurvival Circuit.

This is the baseline consciousness of a human being: the pure "survival" mode of an infant looking for nourishment. Whether it finds nourishment or not determines whether the organism will later view the world as a safe place or not.

Circuit Two: The Anal Emotional-Territorial Circuit.

This is the circuit experienced by the "terrible toddler" who has begun walking and begins to learn lessons of boundaries, pecking orders, domination and submission. You can see the same behavioral patterns in a dog. This is where humans get their imprints about where they stand in the order of things.

Circuit Three: The Time-Binding Semantic Circuit.

This is the realm of numbers and written language, and is imprinted when somebody learns how to read and write, thereby accessing the "magical" power of binding time by representing reality in symbols. It is where we learn "rules" and "laws."

Circuit Four: The Moral Socio-Sexual Circuit.

This circuit is opened by puberty and/or the initial sexual experiences. This is where we imprint tribal ideas of right and wrong—as we are conditioned by society with subtle but incredibly powerful messages about who we should have sex with and under what conditions. This forms the basis for tribal morality and reproductive rules.

The four preceding circuits are the province of nearly everybody. They are the baseline for making a human being, and most live their existences within these four circuits alone. Accordingly, we see most of our major social and tribal battles fought in the second circuit (territorial fights between groups, up to the size of nations), the third circuit (wars fought over scriptural "truth"—mass murder over symbols and whose symbol set is the right one) and the fourth circuit (sexual freedom—for instance, the never-ending American culture battles over women's reproductive rights or the right of gay people to get married).

The next four circuits, as Leary and Wilson had it, are

increasingly rarefied and experienced by minority groups of forward thinkers.

Circuit Five: The Holistic Neurosomatic Circuit.

"I want to feel good." For instance: People who shop at health food stores, yoga addicts, people who go in for massages and other forms of body therapy, swingers, stoners, extreme sports fanatics and anybody else who seeks some form of "high" that lifts them out of the mundane rules and restrictions of the earlier circuits, even if temporarily.

Circuit Six: The Collective Neurogenetic Circuit.

The proverbial "breaking open the head." Mystical experience in which some kind of deep access to the "collective unconscious" is gained. Leary and Wilson were writing in the 60s and 70s and were largely talking about acid here, but acid is mostly shit these days and there are many other ways to open this circuit. Magical practice is a big one.

Circuit Seven: The Meta-Programming Circuit.

This is where you figure out how to change your reality, which practically speaking means that you start dropping all your old imprints that you picked up via nature or nurture and start re-imprinting yourself. One example: Sigil "magick." Neuro-linguistic programming has some techniques for this, but doesn't really go anywhere in particular. Religions re-imprint you, but largely to their designs. People who get here will usually talk about it by saying things like "I realized that I was just a story, that I wasn't real, and that I could change that story if I wanted." Often comes after the mystic ego-death experience of opening circuit six.

Circuit Eight: The Non-Local Quantum Circuit.

Massive brain events, near-death experiences, truly weird paranormal experiences. People with a religious background who get here will talk about it in terms like "I saw God," and whatever God they saw will usually be the one(s) they were imprinted with by their culture. It seems to occur with total overloads of the nervous system.

Hopefully this model (and it is JUST that—a model) is of use to you in your own meanderings up into higher states of mind. For more information, see *Prometheus Rising* by Robert Anton Wilson or *The 8-Circuit Brain* by Antero Alli.

(June 13, 2013)

The World is a War Between Competing Stories About You

On the Non-Existence of Self and the Dance of Reality

The core insight of the Tathagata, Gautama Buddha, was that there is no core self. There is nothing you can truly point to and say "this is me." The Buddha considered the self to exist only in relation to other beings or situations.

This historical insight, which the Buddha gained at his enlightenment some time between the 6th and 4th centuries BCE, stood in direct contrast to the Indian Vedantic schools which proclaimed that enlightenment consisted of grasping the innate, unchanging core of one's self, the Atman. But no such Atman exists, claimed the Buddha. There is no Self. Nothing perceiving, nothing changing, nothing born, nothing that dies—nothing, even, that can truly be said to reincarnate as a whole package from lifetime to lifetime. You may seek to discover yourself, but in fact, there's no "there there."

This singular insight prompted the four turnings of the Dharma and the immense diversity of Buddhist schools that flowered throughout Asia in a historical period running roughly parallel to the spread of Christianity throughout Europe. Both religions were founded upon a lone, revolutionary reformer figure—Buddha, the reformer of Hinduism, and Christ, the reformer of Judaism. Both directly espoused the nature of the world as unceasing suffering, and outlined a code of ethics and practice that individual human beings could follow to achieve states of freedom from that suffering, without need of an intermediary priesthood (the priesthood came later, and boy did it ever).

The insight that there is no intrinsic self lay at the core of the Buddhist rejection of violence. If reality is only a series of disjointed perceptions, how can we ever truly "know" another enough to necessitate we destroy them? We only see a behavior, interpreted through our own nervous system and specific moment in time. There's no "there there." Just perceptions, and interpretations.

Hollow Mirrors

The Buddhist memetic complex, which flowered from this initial insight, evolved into a potent driver for several major civilizations. It is an old insight, one which may be fruitfully compared and contrasted with the insights of competing religions, or even (very arguably) be superceded by later transmissions like *Liber AL vel Legis*.

But practically, experientially speaking, in the world of day-to-day living, this core insight holds true. Simply put: Whether or not your "true self" actually exists, it is at no time on stage in the day-to-day affairs of the world. What is on stage, what does compete in the marketplace, is a series of stories about you.

Consider the selves you enact during the day. There is a self for when you are alone, the self or role you play for your boss and co-workers if you have such relations, your lover(s) if you have them. For each person you meet in the street, for the cop who tickets you, for the person you buy groceries from.

Each and every person you meet, in fact, constructs a story about who you are based on your interactions, just as you do for them. This story will be a mixture of their perceptions of you, whether accurate or inaccurate, with their own past experience, chemistry, mood at the time, etc. It will not be based in any way on any kind of objective reality. The Buddhist view, then, is that reality is the sum total of these projections, a dependent arising of beings simultaneously projecting, and that *it is all bullshit*.

But practically speaking, these stories are your gods, even if fictional. Whether these gods co-operate, or are at vicious war with each other, will likely determine your happiness in this life.

The story your boss holds about who you are, for instance,

will determine your job security, upward mobility, and pay rate. Maddeningly for you, this story will not be based on any kind of intrinsic worth, your past history or your real ability. It will be based on things like how you dress, if you meet deadlines, and if you fill out your paperwork promptly. That is, the slice of your reality that directly intersects and affects your boss's reality. Nothing else is perceived even if you feel it internally. It is like this for all relations with other beings, even the most intimate ones, and it is these negotiations of reality and perception that maintain the illusion we call the social contract.

Dance the Mask

The great ascetics of our religious history, from whatever tradition, have sought to break from this social contract, realizing that it defines a perceived-as-false self that arises totally from negotiation with society. They have instead repaired to monasteries and lonely places to seek the reality of the self within themselves, far from the madding crowd. But as the Buddha discovered, and many have since, there's just no "there there." Perhaps it is within the bounds of the social contract that we perform the self, through the lens of others and inter-relation that we find that self. It is in the daily grind and frustration of the marketplace and relationships, far more humbling to the ego than isolation, that we enact our essence.

This is one of the great gifts not of Buddhism and the Eastern traditions, but of the Western way. To understand that all stories are untrue is one step, but to embrace the delight of the fiction, to "dance the mask and mask the dance," is even better than a dry religious enlightenment.

It's Magick.

(May 7, 2013)

The Chaos Matrix: Back in Thee Day

I recently went on a small nostalgia tweet spree about my chaos magic days on my Twitter:

> During the late 90s to mid 00s there was something called a "chaos magic scene" in America

> To this scene I gave my time and life. Now it is gone… nothing left but the recordings. Even those are faded

> I not longer have my clothes or my ideas about the world from that era. Everything is gone except my rage

> My rage that the world is not as it should be. That we can do better. That a better, more human, more humane future IS possible

> Those of us who remain here are like entrenched warriors, fighting a war that nobody told us ended

> Yet while others moved on I found I could not. Because I still believe one person can make a difference, however small. A group, even more.

> And as that t-shirt said… I Am Magical, M*therf*ker

Chaos magic, which people took a lot more seriously about ten years ago than they do now, can be boiled down to a few simple approaches to reality:

1. The world is infinite and magical in its wonder and complexity and

we will never understand it all. Therefore, everything in the world is just somebody's story about what the world is, and either it works for them or doesn't. The stories about reality that you've inherited probably keep you stuck in the same rut that everybody around you is stuck in, so if you want out, rewrite your story and see what happens.

2. There is no such thing as religious truth.

3. However, your brain and nervous system can be profitably rewired by the same tricks that religions have been using for thousands of years (ritual, trance, symbolism), so you might as well learn and apply them. Self-created symbolic representations of desire (sigils) plus sufficiently altered states of consciousness are a good place to start warping your mind.

Chaos magic has the same root impulse as every other gnostic or shamanic cult: Reject priesthood and inherited secrets and figure out the secrets of the universe yourself by actively getting out of your head and looking for them.

Chaos magic started in the 1970s in Leeds, England. It got popular in the 80s through industrial music and even more popular in the 90s through comic books. By the time I showed up there was an active and thriving scene that I had quite a bit of fun running around in until I largely grew out of the stylistic trappings. (By the time most chaos magicians hit 30 they are either dead, succumb to social pressure and become norms, or calcify and settle on whatever they decided was the "truth" about reality, and become acolytes of one religious system or another.)

For a little bit of archaeological fun, please see the Chaos Matrix, which was a crucial hub for all of us back in the early days of the Internet. This site may look laughably simplistic to cynical 21st century post-Eschaton minds, but I assure you that finding it and applying its content was like opening the gates of infinity back then, a total mind-torque that led to some utterly bizarre and transformative experiences for all concerned. (There is a ritual written by 18-year-old me somewhere on the site, bonus points if you can find it.) As far as the Chaos Matrix, this was 1995-98 we're talking about here. Long before *The Matrix, Supernatural* or the 10,000 commodified occult-themed shows and bands that the LA entertainment machine has pumped out since. Back then all we had was *Mondo 2000, The Invisibles* and Psychic TV. It was a scene consisting of a very few (and *truly strange*) people that seems disproportionately large in my mind, probably because my mind is permanently warped out of shape by those days.

Like a sand mandala, all of that has blown away in the wind now, but every grain of sand was a seed, planting strange weeds that grew irrevocably intertwined with the culture that we now live in. And we water them still…

(March 15, 2013)

The Fox

Once upon a time there was a boy who was born with wide eyes and wonder who looked at the world and saw how much potential it had. He saw an almost infinite world full of people with access to infinite consciousness, love, creativity and hope, and he knew that if they could just tap that consciousness they would not only be able to fix their differences and their problems and make their planet a place of love and beauty and joy and exploration and expression, but they would also be able to explore the very stars and bring that love to the whole universe.

He put all of his effort into learning as much as he could and expressing himself in the best way he could because he knew that even though right now these people spent all of their time hurting and killing each other for small scraps, abandoning the big picture in the process, they just hadn't had things explained to them right (yet). They just needed somebody to show them what was possible if they applied themselves in the right way, because he knew there was enough joy and love and energy in the universe for everybody if they were willing to work together and work towards the future.

As he got older he realized that, in fact, this was *not* what anybody wanted. They couldn't see those things, remember them or even conceive of wanting them, because they didn't want to. Then they decided to "educate" him. He realized that on this planet this meant learning how to stop focusing on these true things, and focus instead on how to count beans, believe in silly fairy tales about made-up people who could "save" others (from what, he could never figure out), and build shells around themselves. This hurt him so much because he realized that he would have to believe these lies to survive. So he got very good at pretending. This wasted so much of his time and energy that he despaired that he might not be able to fulfill his mission. He believed that pretty soon he would be an adult, though, and he would be able to get on with it.

Unfortunately, he discovered that as an adult, the only thing that changed was that he was now expected to maintain this shell himself, instead of other people building it around him. So he broke it and ran.

Off he went into the wilderness, where he spent years looking for others like him. He knew that if they found each other and ganged up, they would not only be able to survive, but they would be able to change everything and make the world see true things again, which he knew was what would make everybody happy. Most of all he wanted to find a woman who was just like him, because then he knew they would be able to do anything.

Out in the woods he found a lot of werewolves, trolls, and other assorted creatures of the night who were out there not for any noble reason but simply because they were monsters. Many of them pretended to greater knowledge but they all lied; they only knew the art of being monsters, which was certainly different, and sometimes charming, but ultimately not good for anything except being a monster. But here also he learned to wear the mask of a monster because it felt good to be different and have friends who accepted you for being different, until one day he realized it wasn't a game, because he was becoming a *real* monster.

So he ran away from the monsters and he went further until he found the Light People who dwelled on a hill far from town. Here they weren't pretending to be monsters, they were pretending to be angels. They wore all white and talked with beautiful words and always assured themselves that they were the good people, better than the others. They had come up on the hill because they all knew the world was a bad place and that meant they must be good, so they wanted to be with the people just like them. That was OK, he knew the world could be a bad place too and all he wanted at this point was friends, because he knew the normal people would kill him because he didn't think like them, and he knew the monsters would kill him, and probably eat him too, just because they were monsters, and that's what monsters do.

So he wore this mask for a while too, but pretty soon he started to realize that the good people weren't good at all. They were just people who lied to themselves that they were good, and surrounded themselves with people who agreed that they would believe the lie that they were good if they returned the favor. And then, in fact, he realized that they were monsters too. In fact, they were even worse, because they were monsters that pretended not to be.

So he ran again, and by this time the normal people, monsters, and angels had all figured out he wasn't one of them, so they chased him, because they wanted to drink his blood, either to prove that there was nothing different from them, or because they were just vampire freaks, why, he still has no fucking clue.

Ultimately he found a cave and there he prayed and prayed to whatever truth was in the universe and after a long time something happened. He was different now. He was so hurt and disappointed by the world but he still wanted to help it with all his heart because that was what he had come to do. So slowly he began to put together plans.

And soon, he found that he had somehow gained a magic power from his quest. It was not magic in the common sense, of making illusions and fantasies that some might believe for a short while, though he could do that too. It was a much stronger magic—the magic of taking illusions away, and showing the truth.

This magic took the illusions from his eyes. Now he looked at the dwellings of the monsters and angels and normals, and he saw that they were on fire. They were actually on fire. And nobody could see it, because they believed in their own smaller magic, the magic of fantasies and illusions so much, because they enjoyed being monsters and angels and normals with all their hearts, wanted nothing different, and thought it would never end.

Fuck, man, he thought. *This is a real son of a bitch of a situation. I just thought we had to get these people thinking higher and better, but their goddamn houses are actually on fire, and they're going to die if they keep pretending otherwise. Not only that, they're choosing this dumb shit of their own free will, and there's no force in the universe capable of overriding that.*

So he made books of how he knew the world should be, and he came back and he threw them like bombs into the places he had been, hoping to change people's minds. Now he knew he was really nothing, so he pretended to be whatever he had to. He could pretend to be a monster to scare the angels, or an angel to scare the monsters, or a normal to scare the angels and the monsters. And he tried with all of his might to wake them up so they wouldn't die in the fire.

Some listened, but the rest decided they had to get rid of this weirdo who was buzzing in their ear like an annoying fly and interrupting their fun. And they sent monsters, angels and normal people alike to do the deed. They beat him, bashed him, stole his dreams and drank his blood, but ultimately he was too smart for them, and he crawled away and found a place to hide and grow strong again. By this point he trusted nobody, but he still wanted to help everybody.

So he did the unthinkable—he put the shell back on, and went back to live in the world of the normal people, in order to rest, in a place that was only burning a little bit. He learned to think like them and take on their addictions and the ways they lied to themselves, in order to understand them, and also because he knew he had to survive no matter what, and no matter how much the normals sucked, the monsters and angels were just downright tacky.

Then one day, much to his surprise, the people who ruled this world appeared to him. They also knew the world was on fire, and surprisingly enough, they wanted the same things as him. Of course, they wanted to use him and drink his blood too, but *fuck it*, he thought, *at least let's play with the big guns*. He was strong enough and scarred enough at this point to take a crucifixion and live.

So that's what he did. He told his dream to the biggest and most powerful and strongest kings of the world, and they listened. And in his own small way, he saved the world. He showed a way that everybody, everybody, normal, monster and angel alike, could get out of the fire.

And, of course, nobody cared. When he told them what he had done they laughed, or pretended not to hear, or shrugged it off, or tried to kill him again, or tried to power-trip on him because they saw how much power he had and they felt they had to prove they were bigger.

He was very, very lonely by this point.

One day, while wandering through the woods, he found a small fox.

This fox had been wandering in the woods as well, looking for the secrets in the woods and for its true tribe. It had also been hurt, at a very early age, younger than the boy, but it had not become bitter. It had very big eyes and very shiny fur and was extremely unlike any creature that the boy had ever seen in the woods before. With interest the boy decided to sit down and speak to the fox and he discovered that although they were very different there was a strange effect when they sat next to each other, that somehow their energies combined to make a perfectly fitting energy that he knew was a Magic energy.

So they began to go on adventures together.

Soon he had forgotten about much of his troubles and pain and loneliness, because though he knew he would always be independent and have to stand on his own, now he had the company of a hot-ass hyperdimensional fox who could touch his soul with love so deeply, who was so well suited to him energetically—and even if there were fires at least they could curl up by one in the light and warmth in each other's arms. And this was good.

He saw that this fox was very strong and cunning, because if he was some six foot tall unshaven all-black-wearing dude, and everybody had been trying to eat HIM, how much more would the denizens of the woods have been trying to eat this small fox who looked like an after-dinner mint? He saw that, like him, she had had to become very clever, and also to make friends with monsters and angels, predators, in order to survive.

But he also knew that he was now a man of True Power. He saw that this fox had been running frantically through the woods, like he had, trying to find love and magic, and had only found the monsters and the angels. And he knew their game, and that it was fuckin' whack. So he began to explain this to the fox.

But as he expressed his anger, the fox heard the voice of a monster herself. She now saw that this man had much bitterness and anger inside, and she was afraid of what would happen if it was directed at her. This scared her, even though all the man was trying to do was offer her the real thing, real love and magic, and show that he could protect her from the false kind, the monsters and angels, because even though he didn't want to discourage her in her enthusiasms, he was attached to her now, and wanted to protect her.

But this scared her even more, because those monsters and angels the man was poking at were the very things she had surrounded herself with to protect herself in the forest, and she still wasn't sure where this man was coming from, where he was going, or who he really was. She was also terrified of being judged, because he was so judgmental, though what she saw as the hand of judgment he saw as his hand trying to pull her free and lift her up, to separate her from the things tying her wings down. (Winged foxes are awesome.)

Because she was afraid, she began to pull away, because she had been hurt so many times before and could not have her safety in the forest threatened. He, too, had been hurt so many times before, and so, as they had discussed before, he tried to offer more and more of himself. But the fox began to show that it was about to run back to the monsters and angels, away from him, and this scared him, so he thought, fuck it, I'll just explain how I really feel.

At this point the fox went Full Rabid and bit the shit out of him.

No way, the fox was saying, you're not wrecking my whole world, you asshole.

So there the man sat, patiently, the magician in his circle, while the fox stayed as far away from him as possible, either hiding in its own cave or in the houses of the monsters and angels, so that the man could not destroy her world.

But, in fact, he was not destroying it. Could not. He was only trying to show her his Magic power, the one he had gained in the woods so long ago. For with a single wave of his hand he could strip the illusions from these safe places she ran to, these old places and attachments, and show her what they were in actuality: buildings on fire, full of burning people, and the hungry demons who lived there.

And from his circle, safe on high ground, he could but do one thing, which was show her his only possession.

A single white feather. The feather of Ma'at.

And wait.

For he knew he could not make that choice for her. And he also knew that he could not go with her into those burning buildings, for he would perish. He also knew he could not stretch his arms out of the circle to grab her, because she would bite his hands and run in terror because of her old wounds and fear.

And he also knew he loved her.

So he sat and waited.

And with the nib of his single feather, he scratched there in the dirt:

> **Now I know**
> **Why the Magus wore that look**
> **Decades of standing in the cold**
> **And pounding at the door**
> **Of the burning house**
> **Never answered.**
> **Now I know**
> **Because I'm starting to get the same goddamn stare.**

(Summer 2011)

Sutras for Satyrs

Hymn to Shiva

It's good to have a point
To reference yourself by
It's good to have a light
To see yourself by
It's good to have an infinity
To be finite by
It's good to have a friend
To get outstoned by
It's good to have a lover
To be outloved by
It's good to have a Lord
To be outdone by
And it's good to have a fire
To throw yourself in & burn yourself to a crisp until there's nothing left of you but the little bits of bone they dig from the ashes and throw in the river to be washed away in the shit.

(2010)

She (To Nuit at the Expense of Lilith)

As long as your happiness is predicated on hers
You shall be miserable.
As long as your purity is predicated on hers
You shall be abased.
As long as she is the mark of your success
You shall fail.
As long as your aim is her

You shall miss.
Oh man born of woman
Your lot is misery
But your home is the stars
In the endless acceptance
Of Her embrace.

(2010)

The Voyeur (For Mark Zuckerberg)

What must it feel like?
Most your age accumulate pornography
If they have not yet learned of love
But you had to stash the world under your bed
You had to know our secret thoughts
And read our every desire
And sell them to the highest bidder
A new kind of pervert for a new world
The voyeur of cultures
Hunched masturbating to lives you will never live
And emotions you will never feel
How hollow must a man be
To have to fill himself with the lives of others
Not one or two but the stalker of millions.
It's such a shame though
They're on the other side of the glass
And you're outside looking in
Still.

(2010)

Hungry Ghosts

Hungry Ghosts
Burn in the hell
Created by their lust of power
And their need for control.
By seeing others as tools
They renounce their souls
And burn in their own attachments.
In the world they see a mirror
And seek to ensnare it
Entangle it in words
Cut it down to size
And only make themselves smaller
Burning in the fire of their own fear.
All fear is fear of death
And death will take no offering
There is no power
There is no control
And those ghosts who seek such imaginary things
Will be hungry forever.

(2005)

You Want to Watch What You Say

You want to WATCH what you SAY
There's always the right thing and the right time
And the moment when everything's the wrong thing
To SAY

And if I say the right words
Will you sleep with me
Will you be in love with me
Will you give me your mon-ey

And if I say the wrong words
Will you run from me
Screaming crying in the pews
With the hen with the black face of a man
And Christ

And if I say the right words
Will you take my fear from me
Will you rain your grace on me

And if I say the wrong words
Will you take my joy from me

You want to WATCH what you SAY

You want to WATCH what they SAY

When they don't think you're listening
When they don't think you're there
I'm never here

I'm never here
Sitting like a ghost in the corner
Listening to everything you say
Listening to the words you say
Filling up space
Clever boy
Quiet boy
Ghost boy

I can listen all day

All day

Every day

Same day every day

WATCH WHAT YOU SAY

(2006)

An Interview With Jason Louv

This interview was conducted by the very personable Vincent S. Baeza for his online zine.

Jason Louv is from San Diego, CA, and has had his energies directed in several realms. A jack of all trades and a feral spirit who lives as a pathway guider to new possibilities of being, he spent an apprenticeship under Genesis Breyer P-Orridge and compiled together *Generation Hex* with kindred spirits. The book was revolutionary for the dream believers and a teenager like myself who refused to let his spirit be lost in the middle, who felt like there were silent screams going unanswered for contact. Contact was made and the spell was cast 23 fold. For a down and out youth in search of something that I could not define or name, I always felt there was a little something more to this planet than the materialism and force-fed misinformation that only polluted the discovery of one's true self or that made you feel ashamed for even questioning anything and/or everything in the first place. In a place where all knowledge is free, things traveling fast with the Internet and things losing permanence, I felt like everything had been done before and everything was useless. I was so wrong. It came to me right after experimentation with psychedelics and a rune reading by a witch when I was at a crossroads in my life. After the three Norns spread reading, moving to a new city to try my life out, I felt safe and protected thanks to *Generation Hex*. The book inspired my divorce from vampiric people and a dive into the unchartered territory known as yourself, which is the greatest entry one can take in his/her life. The book inspired my first sigil and made me feel comfortable knowing there were others like me who had an intrinsic sense of suchness that life was something to dabble with in all extremes, and to break limitations of what societal chains I felt captive to.

You grew up in Southern California in San Diego with that big crazy military base and the jockery of beach culture. What inspired your disconnection from your surroundings and embarking on your unchartered journey into discovering yourself?

San Diego is a very conservative town but I was probably more depressed about it as a teenager than I should have been. People are generally very nice, and it's a really beautiful place. It's supposedly built on a shaktipith, which is an old Hindu story—the goddess Shakti was torn apart and scattered across the world, like Isis, and wherever one of her body parts fell it created a holy site. San Diego is very laid back but also can be incredibly extreme in contrast. It's a major drug town—it's right next to Tijuana, which is a bit hectic right now with all the cartel killings. It's also produced people like Diamanda Galas, Boyd Rice, Tom Waits, Frank Zappa. People can react to the sunshine overdose by becoming as intense as possible. I spent high school reading J. G. Ballard and William Burroughs and getting lit cigarettes and various solid objects chucked at me from passing pickup trucks, but also being inspired by teachers and mentors. I worked in a bookstore and did a lot of reading and went through all the counterculture freak classics, and of course the Internet was just rolling out to the public so I had that to explore with, and my mind was just warped to shit by the time I left.

I spent a lot of time in nature and I think being very connected that way. If I was disconnected, it was from being taken out of the unstructured world of nature, imagination and self-directed study and boxed into the school system, and like all creative and smart kids I went apeshit because I couldn't take the tedium. But even there I had some great teachers who inspired me. I think my angst has worn off by now!

In general I was pretty shy, bookish and awkward, so self-discovery was a compelling option because I hadn't discovered other people yet. I was bored and spending all my free time reading Colin Wilson, Robert Anton Wilson, H. P. Lovecraft, Hakim Bey, *The*

Invisibles, Mondo 2000, the chaos magicians, everything I could find on consciousness expansion and anarchy and magic and that whole world of fringe ideas we know and love. I was reading the books and I was using the books and figuring out how to get the thing to work. At the time I felt like I was the only one in the world who had ever been exposed to any of that stuff and connected the dots and of course that's not the case, far from it. I did *Generation Hex* to connect to the others. Now there is no "other," it's everywhere. Like, witch house–what was that about? There's *Generation Hex* for you.

What was the compilation process like for Generation Hex? How did this idea come into being and what was the editing process like? With such heavy material printed in an easy to understand way was that a method you wanted to maintain with the final result of the book?

I pitched *Generation Hex* when I was 21 because it seemed like a good idea at the time. It was just one of those things that has to happen. It was right after 9/11, a few months after we'd invaded Iraq, it seemed like every single utopian promise we'd been sold by the 90s chaos culture was evaporating before our eyes, and there was just this overwhelming sense of "You HAVE to do this right now. You can pass on it, but if you do, somebody else is just gonna end up doing the same idea, and it won't be as good as if you do it." Which is not meant to sound arrogant, it's just one of those time and place things. It was also the only "niche" that I could conceivably write about, where my inexperience would work for me instead of against me, because I'd be writing about my peers. Of course I didn't know if I actually had any peers at the time! But through many strange avenues, I found I did, and the book happened. It was kind of a beacon. And I got the attention I wanted, both positive and negative!

The editing process was that essentially I just told the publisher, "OK, I'll do this book, and it'll be great," without having any clue whatsoever how I was actually going to pull it off, and then went off to live in London for a year and threw myself into every conceivable venue of magical and shamanic experience I could, gathering contributors, doing balls-to-the-wall Hermetic and chaos practice, losing my shit, and at the end of it all somehow riding the coincidence train to Kathmandu and undergoing shamanic training up in the mountains. And then I came back to New York and pieced my brains and my notes back together and that was the book. It was a really weird time. When you dare the universe like that, it can get life-or-death serious pretty quick. Things start happening really fast, and it can be hard to regain your balance. (But you do.)

That all seems like it happened 10,000 years ago now. Sometimes I look at my records from that time and think "what the hell were you on about?" You'd have to be pretty naïve to do something like that, but I'm glad I did because it essentially forced a very quick learning experience. The comedown was brutal. I feel like I've been through endless reincarnations, dis/illusions and careers since. I stopped writing about magic because it's kind of like writing about hammers. If you know how to use a hammer, and you have a hammer, use it.

What age did you start writing?

JL: 3

Of all your various experiences on different lands, turfs and planes which moments stick out to you the most?

JL: As far as moments, not sure. (Insert tacky "be here now" joke here now.) Spending time with friends is good. Whenever something truly magical, truly occult that can't be explained by any recourse to science or psychology whatsoever happens, it really knocks you on your ass and shows you how small you are, but what a loving and magical place the universe is in the ultimate summation.

Do you feel like you created a hole in the fabric of life to create a new youth culture altogether? Once I found your book my life literally took on its own course. I was born in 1987 and in 2006 everything stopped making sense and started to make sense in ways only I could understand or try to understand for each situations unique circumstances. I was seeing my totem animals, snakes, and owls in the desert. I even had Huggin and Munin fly over a rune reader's house in Sedona as a gust of wind shot through the room and the clouds shot lightning as the three staves were laid out. I knew I tapped into something, and the only way that I felt balanced was to learn more and to keep looking…not for answers but for inspiration. I can't even feel like words or anything can do justice to the level of realness my experiences had and I feel like so much is owed to Generation Hex.

JL: Thanks!

Magic is part of the fabric of life. It's the "stream less taken" and you can dip in if you dare. It never ends and it's certainly not the easy way to do life, but it's there alright. People all over the world have been doing it since before the start of recorded history. It's the wellspring of everything, and it's a lot simpler than people often think.

Of all the places you've been what felt the most special?

JL: Kathmandu is my favorite place in the world. It's a Tantric empire, like a living DMT trip that hasn't ended for 2,000 years. That's my best way to describe it. It's inhabited by Hindus, Tibetan Buddhists and the old Jhankri and Bon shamans, and their gods and practices blend into each other and become interchangeable. Genesis described the city as a devotional computer, just endless statues and temples that people are constantly circumambulating, leaving offerings at, etc. as they go about their daily tasks. There's nothing that's not a shrine or holy in some way. There's a lot of Westerners, especially Germans, who went there in the sixties and never left, because you can just be in a magical, devotional space 100% of the time without having to slip back into the limited and often dehumanizing Western mindset.

Some of the places in India—the burning ghats at Varanasi, you ever lose track of reality, go there. You'll see it in technicolor. Chandrashila at 13,000 feet up in the Himalayas, which is the highest temple in the world, where Ram meditated for the strength to fight the Ramayana war. The old alchemists' quarter in Prague. The inside of a sensory deprivation tank. The taco truck in the Vons parking lot on Alvarado by Sunset Blvd in Los Angeles is pretty awesome.

Generation Hex to the Psychick Bible. Did you feel like you were giving out the rescue manual for youth ready to drop out into place they needed to be spiritually, mentally, emotionally?

JL: *Generation Hex*, yes. But that was just the starter kit. There are no guarantees in magic and there's no "there" to drop out to—it's a confrontation with reality, not an escape from it. You forge your own way and hopefully stand on your results, and hope that you learn to at least see some semblance of "where you need to be" before the trial and error process kills you! Magic can certainly "heal" you spiritually, mentally and emotionally, or it can be psychotoxic as fuck and damage you in places you didn't know you had. I've had both. All actions have reactions; be mindful. You may well lose everything before you learn to surrender.

Drugs, cults, predators, bad trips, ego trips, manipulation, secrets, lies, paranoia, madness, delusions, alienation, meaningless subculture bullshit, your own bullshit, accumulating side-effects, paradox backlash… the monsters that haunt this path are many. Dealing with them wisely constitutes a major facet of the Art.

Ultraculture Journal was a continuation of *Generation Hex* and was an attempt to provide a look at more accomplished magicians and complete the process of showing what the magical path is like. It was also a record of my personal comedown in a lot of ways—when you wake up one morning and realize that 99% of what you're doing is childish nonsense and you've been acting like a clown in public, and cold, hard reality is staring you down with a knife in its teeth, a stack of unpaid bills in one hand and a Google trail from hell in the other. That's when the real education begins, I suspect. Adapt or die.

Thee Psychick Bible was a totally different story. That was a crucial piece of history that I was given the responsibility of properly presenting, so that wasn't really subject to my own story and spin. That's the work of one of the pre-eminent magical "orders" of the 20th century, going back to 1981 and before, work which has had colossal resonance in our culture, whether or not that's widely recognized yet. That book hits on a LOT of levels, and it's a minor miracle it was even published given its, er, ontological weight. It's certainly a template showing that it can be done, that it can be done with groups, and what that can look like.

What was the strangest thing that happened to you today?

JL: This interview!

If you could have anything happen in the 9 worlds of Yggdrasil what would they be?

JL: For all beings in all worlds to be happy and free.

(April 2012)

VII
INHUMAN
RESOURCES

Letter to a Student on the Day of Enrollment in the Academy

Dear Student,

We commend you for your decision to enroll in our de-educational program at our Academy. We recognize that you have a choice when seeking alternative education, and are sure we will live up to your expectations.

Choosing to remove yourself from the normal course of human life is no small matter. Though we celebrate your clear passion to learn, your acumen in finding our school and your exemplary performance on your entrance exams, we remind you that the illusory nature of the world is maintained wholly by, and for, the best interests of those who dwell in it, yourself included. Upon graduation from the Academy, you will be required to return to, and make your own way in, the world. With degree in hand, however, we are confident that you will more easily find your way to a successful life and will be able to compete with the best in today's marketplace.

Your classes will begin on Monday. Please find enclosed a short prospectus of the work you will be expected to complete in preparation for obtaining a degree. While other institutions you may have been involved with during the time you have so far elapsed on this planet—schools, family, peer groups, government, religions, media—have been established in order to educate you, at the Academy we are concerned with your de-education and the reversal of that which you have learned and experienced up to this point. We are licensed (by the highest authorities) to use a wide array of the most modern and scientifically advanced methods currently extant in order to achieve this.

(Please also find attached a waiver form clearing us of any legal responsibility for your physical, emotional or karmic welfare during your time at our school. You will be required to sign and bring this form with you on your first day of class.)

During their de-education and de-testing, students will be required to pursue proficiency in identifying, and demonstrating the illusory nature of, thirty-six principles or veils which separate them from the infinite.

Initial study and experimentation will be conducted upon the constitution of matter and the physical world. In your worldly, exoteric education you will have hopefully gained at least a passing knowledge of physics and be aware of the superstring or M-theory that the universe is composed, at base, of vibrations of tiny, supersymmetric strings. However, at our Academy you will be introduced to the five esoteric principles—earth, water, air, fire and space—which exist behind the vibration of matter and from which all matter is constituted and patterned. Through practical, hands-on classroom experimentation with the manipulation of these principles via meditation and ritual, students will soon be able to demonstrate the illusory and arbitrarily malleable nature of matter to their, and their instructors', full satisfaction.

The next stage of the work will be conducted within the student's perceptual and mental faculties themselves, in which the false identification with a further eighteen veils of illusion dwelling therein will be removed from each student. The first five—smelling, tasting, seeing, touching and hearing—constitute each student's perceptions, and instructors are well-trained to practically demonstrate the extreme limitations of the senses in relaying any legitimate data whatsoever. Directly thereafter, the five subtle elements of smell, taste, sight, texture and sound themselves will be demonstrated as illusions, in and of themselves. Once the false identification with perceptions and perceivables is removed, so will each student's false identification with their actions. Here the student's powers of speech, grasping, moving, speaking and procreation will be shown to have no agency or origination whatsoever in anything approximating the student's true self and to be, at this stage, a distraction from that true self.

We warn in advance that during this stage the student will likely experience extreme disorientation and agitation as the faculties of perception and action they previously identified as belonging to them and constituting them as individuals are disproved as being anything but a flickering picture show projected on the movie screen of the mind. We remind you, however, that we are certified professionals and you need have no fear, for we will quickly proceed to assist you in the reversal of the next underlying principles. These are the mind's constructed image of the "world," the mind's constructed image of the "self," and the entire illusory proceedings of the vast drama your mind constructs for you from your unreal perceptions of unreal things.

Having completed the lessons of the external departments and gone completely inward, the student will soon see that the "world" is an interplay between the false belief that anything exists separately from the self and the false belief that the self exists as separate from anything. Lessons will immediately commence on identifying, and decommissioning, the function of consciousness that maintains the sense of a limited, rather than an infinite and immortal, self.

Before considering removing this function of consciousness, students are asked to take note that it is maintained for the exact same reason that moviegoers pretend not to know if the hero will or will not defuse the bomb and get the girl in the end, even if everybody knows deep down that that's what happens every time.

There are five forces of limitation that maintain the illusion of the "self." These are the illusions of limited ability, limited understanding, limited willpower, the illusion of linear time and the illusion of singular locality.

Beyond this veil of limitation dwell the three functions of divinity—the power to create, the awareness of creation and the will to create itself—and divinity itself, that is, the interplay of unlimited consciousness and unlimited creation, both of which themselves emanate from the Absolute.

We refer to this as the Principal's Office, and it is here that we will completely turn off the mind itself.

Having gained a better and more comprehensive grasp of the workings of the universe, students are of course free—even encouraged—to reconstitute the thirty-six veils of illusion we will have at this point trained them to identify and remove, and return to their worldly vocation along with the gift of identification with true reality.

Particularly motivated students, of course, will be pleased to know that completion of our program will open wholly new higher education opportunities and career options previously unavailable or even previously hidden to them. Our careers department will be more than pleased to assist you in finding a new track should you choose.

Please make sure you've enjoyed a good night's rest before reporting to your first class on Monday. Should you be successful in your studies, and with a bit of luck, it may be the last sleep you ever get.

Fiat Lux,

_____ _____, Ph. D.
Vice Chancellor, Admissions

(2007)

Conjurations in the Element of Flesh

What are the critical disciplines by which 21st century humanity will initiate itself? How will those who wish to move from reality's spectator seats to the middle of the ring do so?

How has humanity done so in the past?

The ancients represented the hall of initiation into the Mysteries as being flanked by two columns—one black, the other white. The tradition survives in Freemasonry, ceremonial magick and the High Priestess card of the Tarot, where Isis as initiatrix into the Mysteries sits between the pillars, reconciling them.

For the ancients, the black pillar represented, among other things, the path of ego calcination; the white, the path of ego dissolution. These more abstract principles, or "ways to do life," if you will, have ended up in the common parlance as "white and black magic" and have become divorced from their original meaning and taken on new and largely inappropriate baggage.

Restored to their original symbolic association, however, the Pillars of the Temple of Solomon can offer critical suggestions about the modes of transcendence that 21st century humanity is beginning to explore.

For the young psychonaut, I draw clear the lines:

The Left-Hand Path: The Transhuman

Transhumanism is the augmentation, and therefore reinforcement, of the self. It is the current edge of the "project of Western civilization" that is concerned, and always has been concerned, with the extension of the individual will into physical, manifest reality. It is the directed use of technology to amplify the human experience—and technology can easily mean nonphysical means or techniques as well.

Here I place the increasing inseparability of humans and advanced communication technology; actual augmentation of the body with wetware, body modification, nanotech, etc., but also body change techniques like hatha yoga, martial arts, plastic surgery; the work of Wilhelm Reich; energy medicine, EFT/EMDR; the contributions of the Human Potential Movement and the increasingly clever and byzantine supplement industry. We can add modern and ancient brain-change techniques like Neuro-Linguistic Programming, the Leary/Wilson Eight Circuit Model, Brion Gysin's Dreamachine, radionics, tantra, chaos magick and the rest of the never-ending occult and New Age corpus. All of these and more can be used to change, warp, clean out, amp up, empower, manicure and otherwise "make cooler" the thing you call "I."

Access to these technologies is increasingly wide-spread and I believe their use and refinement will likely produce some admirable customizations of the human experience as well as increasingly grotesque ego distortions as once-normal human beings mutate themselves into what might only be described as "creatures" comprised of a multiplicity of shattered and exaggerated ego shards rather than anything resembling a healthy, grounded, integrated identity.

The Right-Hand Path: The Transpersonal

If transhumanity can be seen as a continuing quest for dominance over the physical body and physical world, the transpersonal offers a much more direct (if perhaps even more dangerous) path—that of breaking down the barriers which separate the small-s self from the wider world itself. This is what might more vaguely be called the "spiritual path"—the path of the dissolution of the ego by uniting it with something larger than itself.

Under the heading of transpersonal we must place the many branches of mysticism: Gnosticism, Sufism, Qabalah, Advaita Vedanta, Mahayana Buddhism, the higher Yogas, true Tantra, shamanism, depth psychology and the activities that stem from the accelerated empathy that these practices can produce: namely activism, human rights work, ecology work, directed work on the problems of the human race and other such forms of "doing the world's dishes."

Leaving questions of actual higher spiritual perception or "cosmic consciousness" aside for the moment, and grounding the spiritual directly into the material world, I believe we can find the highest expression of the transpersonal path in the growing field of ecopsychology: a psychological model which proposes, broadly, that individual problems are in fact manifestations of the problems of the world itself, and that it becomes impossible to talk about healing a patient without healing the world they live in. Self and world are ultimately indistinguishable. There was never a separation to begin with.

Between the Gates

It's easy to see how these two paths may overlap and blur at their higher reaches. Push the self to the limits of its expansion, for instance, and you may well break it in the process, allowing the "greater reality" to flood in. Similarly, the depth insights that arise from transpersonal work can and should become more greatly actualized in the physical world through the strengthening and empowerment of the "individual" who experiences them—there comes a time when you may have to lift your scarecrow-like, malnourished body from the meditation mat, do some pushups, put on a suit and start communicating what you've learned within the marketplace.

You can also see how these two paths can be intensely antagonistic.

Have no illusions about it: transhumanism arises from the same dominator impulse that gave us empires, Satanic mills, nuclear and biological warfare, technological slavery, the rape and degradation of the physical world, and so on. To the expanded awareness of the transpersonal, the products of Western culture and the calcified, soulless ego-worship of the transhumanists can feel as comfortable as splinters under fingernails.

Alternately, it's questionable how much effect the insights of mystics actually produce—whether their "higher visions" are actually accurate new views into the human equation or just so much hallucinatory navel gazing. The most lasting contributions of the walkers of the transpersonal way are inner insights that, once expressed, can produce massive shifts in how cultures think—but these insights get turned into bureaucratic dominator religions overnight as soon as the original mystic is (all too often) conveniently disposed of... *Godfather*-style.

What Are We Left With?

Two paths. The black: Change the self as something separate from the world. The white: Delete the self and erase all separation from the world. Both provide a "beyond human" experience.

Followed exclusively, the transpersonal results in ineffectuality; take the transhuman alone, and end up a soulless machine in a world of soulless machines.

Or step between the pillars, and find something new—with no promises—for those who pass through these pillars step through and onto a yet-unlit road where only few have passed before, and where none has yet seen the destination.

Step mindfully.

(December 18, 2011)

An Oneironaut's Guide to Lucid Dreams

Dreams: Cool-ass movies you can watch for free with no download times and which often star you and often have porn. They can even tell the future (maybe), help resolve the past and give you insight into the present. What's not to love about these flickery little bastards? Next time you're complaining about life, just remember this: your brain, clever fucker that it is, has automatically provided for a good solid few hours every day where you get to be the star of the show, unicorns are real, you can fly, you get to have any kind of sex you want, and also Rodney Dangerfield is trying to kill you with a machete for stealing the plans to the replica of the Empire State Building he's constructing from light and candy in his garage. Wait, forget that last one. That's, uh, personal.

A lot of people complain they don't remember their dreams. That can be fixed. A lot of people claim their dreams are boring. That can be fixed, too. In fact, turns out that dreaming is a skill you can build just like any other with a little persistence and some simple techniques. With a little practice, you can activate Lucid Dream Mode and have conscious control while dreaming.

So if you're ready to throw out the TV and the YouTubes and get into some real deep inner territory, like *balls deep*, read on:

1. *Write your dreams down every morning.*

This is the most important thing in this list. If you don't do anything else, do this. Get a journal, stick it by the bed with a pen, and write down all the crazy shit you remember from your dreams the instant you wake up. Don't stall; if you switch gears even a bit to check your e-mail or take a shower, you're going to lose most, if not all, of what you dreamt. The more you do this, the more you'll remember from your dreams. This is basically the lock and key that opens up your dreamspace. The more detail you record, the more detail you'll remember the next night, and the more you'll start to gain control of what you're dreaming.

2. *Set your intention.*

Tell yourself what you want to dream about before you go to sleep. Visualize the type of dream you want to have. Ask yourself a question. Pick one thing, and stick to it; maybe write it in your dream journal and then see how you net out in the morning. Coupled with the practice of dream journalling, this will help you gain more and more control over the dream state, allowing you access to new capacities for problem solving and satisfaction.

3. *Dream-Induced Lucid Dreaming (DILD).*

This is, simply put, a dream in which you remember that you're dreaming. This is harder than it sounds, but can be done. The key is reality checking. Throughout the day, you want to constantly check if you're in a dream or not (a la the Dream Tokens from *Inception*). There are a lot of ways to do this. Try setting your phone to go off every hour, and every time it beeps, ask yourself "Am I dreaming?" Now try doing something you'd only be able to do in a dream, like flying or walking through a wall. If you can, holy shit: You're in a dream, you are now aware that you're in a dream, and you should now be able to do whatever the f*ck you wanna do in that dream. If you can't, you're still awake, but the idea is that if you do this enough while awake, eventually it'll become so ingrained into your consciousness that you'll do it while you're dreaming, and successfully go lucid.

4. *Wake-Induced Lucid Dreaming (WILD).*

This is a more direct technique that tends to be favored by lucid dream researchers. It's weird as shit. As one passes out of wakefulness and into sleep, one drifts into a state where what's known as hypnagognic imagery flashes before your eyes. It also happens in the morning when you're just waking up. In the weird in-between state between wakefulness and sleep, you start getting hypervivid dream imagery while still conscious. When WILDing, you focus on that imagery and drift into it directly, keeping the mind awake by an act of will while the body falls asleep. This works best when taking a nap during the day, or after waking up in the middle of the night, and it works best when lying on your back. Reaching total sexual exhaustion with or without a partner is also immensely helpful. WILDs are fast, frantic and often potently meaningful, like a DMT trip, but you're likely to only retain a fraction of what happens. This is where your journal comes in handy.

(Bonus: Salvador Dalí developed his own approach to what might now be called a WILD called the paranoiac-critical method. His version: Sit in a comfy lean-back chair and pass into sleep. In your right hand, hold a rock, which is positioned directly over a steel plate on the floor. At the moment you pass out, your hand will relax and the rock will hit the plate. Now immediately write down whatever you just saw.)

5. *Wake Back to Bed (WBTB).*

Get yourself up after you complete a sleep cycle in the middle of the night. Tough, but possible (low doses of melatonin can help to clearly regulate and demarcate your sleep cycles), especially if you don't have to be anywhere early the next morning. Get up and putz around for an hour. Drink some water. Look at the stars. Meditate or do some other deep shit that lets you stay awake without totally switching into normal consciousness. Now go back to bed. This is the primary time to initiate a WILD or DILD.

6. *Oneirogens.*

These are "dream psychedelics" that create a more fertile ground for lucid dreams. First and foremost, you want some melatonin, which isn't an oneirogen *per se*, but which will help put you in a more regulated, deeper sleep, allowing greater periods of REM. You can combine this with GABA and Valerian for more restful sleep overall. (Protip: If you're in the US, Costco's brand of Melatonin comes with GABA and Valerian already in it and is super cheap for big quantities.) Now, if you want to get into some real territory, go on Amazon or elsewhere and get hold of a Galantamine and Choline combo. There are a lot of oneirogens, but I have it that this is the favored compound of lucid dream researchers. Galantamine is a memory-booster that is currently being tried out with Alzheimer's patients; Choline activates it (and helps with sleep and cognition in general—by the way, Alpha GPC is the best form of Choline you can get). To use this Dream-DMT, you need to do a successful WBTB (you can't just take it before bed). Stay up for an hour and then scarf 400-800 mg of Galantamine/Choline, and go right into a WILD. Now enjoy your exit from this reality. You can also try taking Piracetam, a nootropic which is conveniently also potentiated by Choline, for overall dream clarity and recall. However, let me underline that without a steady practice of the above techniques, without the developed ability to recall and journal your dreams, and especially without the discipline and will it takes to successfully execute a WBTB, this stuff is going to be useless to you. You can't just take it and go to bed; without interrupting your sleep schedule it'll all wear off before you get to the part of the night you'll be able to recall details of your REM cycles from.

7. *Dream Yoga.*

If you want to get even more serious, the Tibetans have a whole arsenal of techniques for fucking with dreams. Check out *Tibetan Yogas of Dream and Sleep* for an introduction, or *Between the Gates* by Mark Stavish for a slightly more Westernized version.

Don't forget to set intentions (use sigils if you like) and record everything—Happy Travels!

(November 2, 2013)

The Wizard Way of Bro Science

About six months before turning thirty, I had one of those moments where you realize "damn, I gotta get my shit together."

Devastated from a cycle of working twenty-hour days for months, all of that time spent at the computer—like some freakish latter-day Jeremy Bentham—I was unable to properly climb the stairs without getting completely winded. I'd spent almost eight months unable to get out of bed. You know how it is: You feel like your mind is a machine made for shifting the building blocks of matter around with the power of the Internets and you get to it to the exclusion of all else. Unfortunately, the price is steep.

And so I decided to embrace my antithesis. To meld with the Other. To transcend high school Manicheanism and unify all opposites.

I decided to become a Bro. I decided to join the gym and get jacked. It had to be done. And, so entering upon the Path of the Bro, through that door that had been locked and barred for me all my life by my own blind prejudice and delusive belief in a mind/body split, I found it to be not only well-lit and maintained by all manner of helpful and cheery Bros but also to be a path of human development more demanding, more continually life-affirming and potentially even more satisfying than many of the higher consciousness change techniques I had immersed myself in while in my twenties.

Enough with the endless RSS feeds, the "I just had Red Bull to eat today," the Assangemode... Here was my new grimoire: Bodybuilding.com! Here was my new god: Zyzz! (More on this later.)

Cracking the Bro Code

To enter the path, I began with a few months of severing my bad habits. I switched to only pure unprocessed food and cut the chemicals out of my diet. Then I humbled myself before the Pylons of Brodom. I joined the gym, signed up for about thirty personal training sessions, and got the basics down. For the first three weeks, I couldn't even do the simplest exercises without having to sit down about three times a session feeling like I was going to pass out. There I sat, with a girl who weighed about a hundred pounds smirking at my out-of-shape ass. I did about a month of this, interspersed with daily hour-long cardio sessions to shock my system back into realizing it existed and that I would be needing it. Soon I wasn't near-fainting or feeling like a scarecrow. I felt… damn… I felt *fucking excellent*.

From there I shifted into bodybuilding. I calculated how many calories I was burning a day, and then maxed out my macronutrients to the point where I was consuming more than I was burning — in my case about 3,500 calories a day. Daunting, especially as a vegetarian—but with a few trips to Costco and Trader Joe's, I actually found that my new diet could be cheaper and easier than what I'd been getting before. A cup of Trader Joe's instant steel-cut oats with two tablespoons of honey? Costs about forty to fifty cents and gives you 800 calories of slow-burning carbs and protein with no fat, and cuts out your heart disease risk to boot. A can of kidney beans from Costco when bought in bulk? About a dollar, and another 850 calories of carbs, protein and no fat. Dig it. Throw in a good low-fat protein powder, some veggies and fruit, and eight glasses of water a day and you're good to go, and don't even have to cook your meals or deal with looking around for places to eat every day. Hacked!

Then I hit the weights. After four months of working out four to five times a week for an hour each, favoring compound exercises and free weights, I'd started to bulk up and look healthy. Now, I felt, I could see the path for the first time. I'd only taken a few steps on it. I was still just barely past the starting line. But I was on the path.

There I was, an out-of-place geek in the place I'd been trying to avoid with all my willpower since I talked my junior high school into letting me out of gym class so that I could sit in the library reading H. P. Lovecraft and Frank Herbert. A latecomer to the party, but a sincere one.

And there, all around me, were all the freaky people. Bros, juicers and lugheads of all ages. Beast-women who looked like they could savage you in three seconds and take your carotid artery as a prize. Ungodly Hot Girls and their professional killer boyfriends. Friendly personal trainers. New Year's resolution cardio warriors. And they were all kind of cool, I realized as soon as I got over my initial disorientation. They were all there to push their personal limits in a supportive environment, one big congregation in the Flesh Temple. What could be better?

After my initial four months, the Bros signaled that their conscious hive mind had noticed my continual presence, dedication and growth with a simple gesture: While doing concentration curls one day while that show *The Big Bang* played silently on the gym TVs, a huge powerlifter on my right said, simply, "Only nerds like this show, huh?"

Wait, I realized. Waaaaiit… he just said that like he was talking about people who aren't me.

It was like the proverbial Diamond Bullet to the Forehead.

Some Considerations on Bro Transhumanism

Once you start really getting into this stuff, you find yourself in a maze of data that you'd need a Master's in exercise physiology and the chemistry knowledge of the average Pfizer grunt to comprehend. What to eat. When to eat. How to manipulate anabolic and catabolic states. Bulking and cutting. Endless supplements to sort through. Sleep habits. And then we get into the realm of Bro Science, a mix of legitimate physiology knowledge and superstition that produces dubious body hacks like:

"Drink a ton of dextrose with your post-workout protein and creatine shake to spike your insulin and help your muscles absorb it."

"If you do tons of squats and deadlifts it will release extra testosterone that will help your arms grow."

Or even oddities like the infamous GOMAD diet—GOMAD

standing for Gallon of Milk a Day, which has you doing heavy compound lifting while carrying around crates of whole milk to chug all day long.

How much of it is real and how much isn't? It's anybody's guess. To find out, you're going to have to do your own testing, and you're going to have to machete through the overgrown thicket of online bodybuilder sites populated largely by teenagers looking to turn themselves into Hulk Hogan by prom.

After researching supplements for a while, I settled on the basics: high quality whey protein with a dextrose chaser, slow-burning casein protein to drink before bed to absorb while sleeping, a weightlifter-oriented multivitamin, DHA and EPA-inclusive flax oil, and creatine (a nitrogenous organic acid which naturally occurs in muscle and which you get from eating meat; if you supplement with it, it tends to put on muscle mass pretty quick by adding water weight. Opinions are divided on it, but I decided to cycle it since I'm a vegetarian and not getting it in my diet).

There's all kinds of crazy gear beyond that: BCAAs (branch-chain amino acids) to boost muscle growth (if your protein's good it'll have enough BCAAs anyway); L-Glutamine to aid recovery (should also be in your protein if it's good); ZMA (Zinc Magnesium Aspartate) to aid sleep and recovery; pre-workout Nitric Oxide boosters; Beta Alanine; HMA; thermogenics; various weird creatine modifications; waxy maize, glycomaize, maltrodextrin and other instant carbs; and on and on. Most of this stuff is overpriced and dubious. (Pro-tip: Never go to GNC to buy supplements. Those guys make commission and will run sales game on you to try to get you to buy obscenely priced placebo supplements full of fake-sounding chemicals that might as well be powdered unicorn horn. For my money, the best deals on supplements are all on Amazon. I mostly buy the stuff put out by Optimum Nutrition; they make top-reviewed, reliable gear.)

Beyond that, of course, there's steroids and human growth hormone. That stuff fucks you up and you can spot the dudes on it pretty easily. Example: Changing in the locker room, I watched a jacked guy with bloodshot eyes and a beady-sweaty forehead maniacally staring at himself in the mirror while slowly and precisely pulling every hair out of his chin with a pair of tweezers. An hour later, after my workout, he was still at it. Hmmm… in retrospect, that might have been crystal. But you get the idea.

The more I found my way into the strange world of bodybuilding, the more I was exposed to the online bodybuilding subculture, a dedicated pod of transhumanists if I've ever seen one, who devote daily physical and mental effort to pushing the limits of the human form, consistently obsessing over how they can overcome the barriers of time, genetics and aging to reach a physical perfection that they may have been told was impossible for them to aspire to every day of their lives until they decided to ignore all that and go for it.

The Bros have been at this for a long time, steadily working out the physical hacks it takes to turn a normal Joe into one of those guys from *300*. These guys, and girls, obsessively pursue the transcendence of the flesh through the flesh, like the reverse of Indian fakirs. It is a religion, a path through and beyond the confines of human, a path to an inhuman pinnacle of godly aesthetic glory that will look really good with a spray tan.

And if bodybuilding is a religion, it has a god: Zyzz, a personality so prominent and crucial that he deserves his own section.

How Do I Unlock Zyzzmode Brah?

Aziz Sergeyevich Shavershian, or Zyzz to his countless fans, was an aesthetically-oriented Australian Russian bodybuilder who went from a stick-bundle teenager to a shredded orange perfection of the male form in the short space of four years, and then proceeded to go shirtless to a lot of clubs and Australian music festivals with his Aesthetics Crew bros and pick up girls in quantities that mere mortals can only dream of, becoming a national celebrity in the process. Along with his brother Said Shavershian (a.k.a. Chestbrah), he also spent a lot of time on 4chan's /fit/ forum, where he was revered as the aspirational archetype by every single weightlifter on that board. Last August, at the age of 22, shortly after Chestbrah was arrested for possession of anabolic steroids, Zyzz collapsed and died in a sauna in Bangkok. His death has been attributed to an undiagnosed congenital heart defect.

Already a hero of the subculture, Zyzz has now ascended to the status of a minor god, a benevolent force that looks down over the striving /fit/izens and encourages them to push out just one more rep, so that the girls will be 'mirin and the other bros will be jelly, his trademarked spiked hair and mirrored aviator sunglasses surrounding a glowing, magnanimous smile.

For the younger generation, Zyzz is a symbol of human aspiration; for concerned parents and sundry authority figures, he is a symbol of the growing dangers of steroid abuse and of social pressure on teenage boys to meet appearance standards that can be just as unrealistic and damaging as the expectations on teenage girls, often leading to eating disorders (manorexia) and body dysmorphic disorder. But the revelation that Zyzz was "bicycling" (Zyzz and Chestbrah's slang for cycling anabolic steroids) has seemingly done little to tarnish his posthumous reputation. (One poster I just saw on /fit/ has this to say about Zyzz: "R.I.P. Bro you died for our sins. Every scoop of whey is in your name.")

He is, perhaps, an evolutionary marker, one of those oft-cited "outliers" who point a way forward for self-willed human change.

Eat Right, Sleep Well, Train Hard

Am I an inhuman jacked monster yet? No, I'm just a mere beginner, still figuring it all out. But in a few months I've deeply shifted my personality profile, listening to hard dance music (?!?) instead of the same old eighties post-punk records, and rearranged my mental outlook from seeing life as something that is happening to me and instead into something I'm aggressively surmounting through self-discipline, a mindset that has spilled over into and improved every other area of my life, even if I hit the bed so tired I'm almost unable to move every night. In a world of vagueness and open-ended tasks, racking steel at the gym gives me the satisfaction of a win every day, something that I can say I did right and did for myself.

Tripping hard and straight into the dense matter of the physical world is a weird ride, brah. But it's a great one.

And I know that maybe, just maybe, somewhere up there… Zyzz is smiling on me.

(February 15, 2012)

How to Make an Orgone Accumulator Blanket

Orgone, so its proponents claim, is the energy of life, expressed in the human body in concentrated form by orgasm. Its existence was postulated in the 1930s by Wilhelm Reich, Sigmund Freud's most brilliant student, who believed this life force circulated through the human body as well as nature and the universe itself. It wasn't too far off from the idea of the life force or "vril" that had previously been popular in German romanticism and occult circles.

Reich not only stated that he had found and was able to quantify this force, but also that he had built devices—orgone accumulators—for harnessing it, claiming to be able to cure both the roots of neurosis and a wide array of physical ailments... even to be able to affect the weather.

Were any of these theories scientifically validated? Nope. Even Einstein, who showed initial interest, threw Reich's theories out. For the orgone theory and others, Reich was blackballed from the psychoanalytic community, kicked out of half the countries of Europe, and finally imprisoned by the FDA in the United States. The FDA also burnt nearly all of his books and destroyed his lab equipment. But because Reich was so effectively shut down by the FDA, research stopped—his theories are so bizarre that they were largely laughed out of the room instead of being subjected to rigorous testing.

Luckily, building your own orgone accumulator—at least the most basic form, an orgone blanket—can be done for about $20 worth of materials and a few hours, at most, of effort. Here's how to do it:

1. Get enough 100% organic wool (100%—no synthetics. This is important) to make three 2'x 2'squares. One website recommends using Israeli surplus blankets off of Amazon. I had good results just going to the fabric district in LA and getting them to cut sized squares for me.

2. Also get a bunch of packages of very fine (000 or 0000 grade) steel wool. It's cheap, so buy a bunch. One or possibly two of these will likely do the trick.

3. Get some cotton (organic, not synthetic!) thread and a needle. That's all you need.

Drop one wool square on the floor. Unroll the steel wool bales onto the wool so it's completely covered. Put the second square of wool on top of that. Now make another steel wool layer. Now put the third square of wool on top, and sew the whole thing together along the edges so the steel wool is held inside.

There, done. According to Reich, the alternation of organic and inorganic material will generate orgone. So is this any different from a tin-foil hat? Well, William Burroughs, Norman Mailer, Saul Bellow, Sean Connery and many other luminaries were into it… but that's neither here nor there. Now you can try your own tests.

(My experience with the blanket is that it produces a subtle but persistent feeling of relaxation and well-being—it also tends to knock me out. Reich claimed orgone treatment might be able to accelerate healing of wounds and even help treat cancer. The FDA completely rejected these statements; your mileage may vary. Reich also built full-size accumulator boxes, orgone shooters and even anti-aircraft-gun sized "cloudbusters" that he claimed could be used to control the weather and shoot down UFOs—yes, the beams of orgasm energy promised at the top of the article. More involved instructions on making accumulators can be found in James DeMeo's *Orgone Accumulator Handbook*.)

(November 5, 2013)

Brion Gysin's Dream Machine: Build Your Own Portal to Inner Visions

The Dream Machine is a device for altering the brainwave frequency of the user and putting it into an alpha state, at which point it begins generating waking, sober hallucinations and internal "movies" on demand.

The machine is simple: it's a rotating cylinder with slats in the sides and a light placed inside, that creates a flicker pattern as it spins. The user of the Dream Machine sits in front of it with eyes closed, and allows the precisely-calibrated flicker pattern to play over their face, creating a strobe effect in the darkness behind their eyelids. After a short period of adjustment, the user begins to experience eidetic imagery, in the same way that one does while passing over the threshold between wakefulness and sleep.

This remarkable and overlooked object was invented in the late 1950s by artistic Renaissance man Brion Gysin and the electronics technician Ian Sommerville. Gysin was expelled from the Surrealist Group by André Breton at the age of 19; with the Dream Machine, he surpassed their previous techniques for image generation. (An example of a prior method is Salvador Dalí's Paranoiac-Critical exercise, in which the artist would fall asleep in an armchair while holding a rock in his hand and, upon his fingers relaxing and the rock crashing to the ground and waking him, would immediately record what he had just seen.) The Dream Machine allowed for a convenient and immediate way to get at eidetic imagery without having to go to sleep or take chemicals.

Gysin had been inspired by both childhood and adult experiences with the effects of flicker, by historical accounts of its use (Nostradamus was alleged to have received his visions by closing his eyes, facing towards the sun and flickering his fingers in front of his eyes) as well as by research into medical reports of its effects. At the infamous Beat Hotel in Paris where he lived with Sommerville and Burroughs (along with Allen Ginsberg, Peter Orlovsky, Gregory Corso, the crime writer Derek Raymond and others) he constructed the first prototype. (The same 78rpm record player version for which DIY instructions are freely available on the net.) It quickly became a source of fascination for the Beats.

Burroughs wrote about Dream Machines extensively in his novels, where he depicted them as a weapon for the freedom of consciousness in the eternal war against Control. The author spoke highly of his friends' invention, saying: "Subjects report dazzling lights of unearthly brilliance and color... Elaborate geometric constructions of incredible intricacy build up from multidimensional mosaic into living fireballs like the mandalas of Eastern mysticism or resolve momentarily into apparently individual images and powerfully dramatic scenes like brightly colored dreams."

The machine was officially unveiled in 1962, at the Louvre's Museé des Arts Decoratifs, to a fascinated public and press—but Gysin, unsatisfied with a small art audience, dreamed of mass production. Along with the cut-up method of text composition he had honed with Burroughs, Gysin considered the Dream Machine his magical message to the world.

He turned first to business magnate Helena Rubinstein, who was taken with the device and exhibited it in her shop windows, but then refused to pay for it. Next Gysin tried the Philips Corporation—a representative of the company, while visiting Gysin at the Beat Hotel, slipped on dogshit in the hall; the deal was cancelled. Later, Colombia Records wanted to market the Dream Machine as a lamp. Meeting with Colombia executives in 1965, Gysin (ever the magician) told them that vinyl records would soon be obsolete, replaced with optical discs that were read with a ray of light. He was not well received.

Gysin died in 1986, the cause of the Dream Machine having been taken up by his protégé Genesis P-Orridge and the loose occult and media subversion network the Temple ov Psychick Youth. TOPY both propagandized the Dream Machine and distributed information on how to make your own, using Gysin's original plans. It's not hard: All one needs is a large sheet of cardboard, an X-Acto blade to cut the slats out, a light bulb on a cord and a spare turntable. There are also Web pages and programs that generate the same flicker effect. You can even get a free Dream Machine iPhone app. (Your mileage may vary.)

Since the 90s, the Dream Machine has become a kind of elitist status symbol, often found in the possession of West Coast media types and young celebrities. Kurt Cobain bought one shortly before his death. David Bowie, Iggy Pop and Paul McCartney all used it. Other aficionados include Marilyn Manson, Floria Sigismondi, Bruce Labruce, Nick Zinner of the Yeah Yeah Yeahs, Beck and DJ Spooky. You can get your own fully crafted machine online; of course, you can also build your own or download the app. With so many ways to experience it, perhaps now the Dream Machine will finally get the mass attention Gysin always believed it deserved as a simple, drug-free path to altered states of consciousness.

(September 9, 2012)

Commandeering the Inner Space Shuttle

I recently began a series of experiments with the sensory deprivation tank as developed by John C. Lilly, M.D., a device that most have heard of but few have tried. (Yes, that's the one from the 1980 movie *Altered States*.) It took me a decade and a half of self-directed experimentation on consciousness to finally get around to using one. Luckily, when I was ready, I found that there was a facility five minutes from my workplace. I booked the time. I got in.

The sensory deprivation tank is exactly that—a large, soundproof, lightproof tank filled with shallow, warm, buoyant water, all designed to completely shut off all sensory input.

The tank itself is heated to exactly 93.0°, a temperature that feels warm without being intrusive, so that your body quickly tunes it out. The water—just shallow enough to lie in—is saturated with Epsom salt, which means that you float effortlessly on the surface. It also means any cuts or scratches that you may have gotten before going in will start viciously burning; for this Vaseline is recommended to cover over them and keep out the salt.

The inside of the tank is remarkably spacious—big enough to sit up in, even stand up while crouching. (The model I used was the Samadhi, the original developed by Lilly. There are other versions; tanks in Europe, apparently, are often much smaller and pod-like, offering very little room to move about in, limiting the size and weight of the occupant.) The inside of the tank is about three and a half feet wide; consequently, I spent a lot of time sliding from one side to the next until I figured out how to stabilize myself. (Hint: Stick your arms out and hold the sides until the water calms down, then hold yourself completely still and breathe slow and deep enough that you don't disturb the water. Breathing slow, of course, will also help stabilize your body and mind faster.)

One's experience in the tank, as I was told, is highly susceptible to suggestion. For this reason, the owners of the venue I visited told me they're very careful about not telling people anything but the basics when they get in, in order not to pre-load their trip.

I found I had some of my own pre-loading to get rid of after sliding into the comforting darkness of the tank. Foremost in my mind were the experiences of the tank's founder himself, Dr. John Lilly: born in 1915, Lilly was raised on a rigid scientific track, developing the tank in the early 1950s while studying neurophysiology for the US Public Health Service Commissioned Officers Corps—work allegedly connected with the CIA MK-ULTRA program, though he broke with the US government almost immediately thereafter. His own experiences were nothing short of revelatory. He later went on to do research trying to communicate with dolphins while on LSD, became involved in SETI, and continued using the tank until his death a few weeks after 9/11.

Lilly reported some mind-stretching tank visions in his books. At one point he believed he had come into contact with extraterrestrials, or "Earth Coincidence Control Organization (ECCO)," as he called them. He also spoke forebodingly of a potential period in the future where "Solid State Intelligence (SSI)," an entity that he believed was composed of the entirety of electronics on earth, would take over and dispense with human life. (Facebook anyone?) But then again, Lilly wasn't just going in cold: he extensively experimented first with using LSD in the tank, then with Ketamine, both substances he had easy access to as a member of the medical establishment.

These are the images I had swirling in my mind as I climbed into the tank; not surprisingly, nothing happened as long as I continued expecting fireworks on-demand. It wasn't until I consciously let go and decided to see what the tank had to offer on its own terms that I started to get something. And at least for me, what I experienced wasn't "psychedelic" at all—far from a mental experience, what I discovered was a drop into a deeply physical, embodied state; once this had happened, the boundaries of the body, tank and space itself just seemed to fall away. Thereafter I seemed to enter into a primal infinity, from which perspective I could comfortably see not just my rational mind but the entire mental bandwidth of Western culture as a tiny, almost inconsequential pinprick in a vast field of mystery. Not "the light," not "the void" or other shorthands for the unthinkable… simply an endless mystery.

I've tried innumerable meditation techniques over the last decade and a half: I've learned to sit inhumanly still for hours, slow my breath down to one inhale/exhale per minute, learned the original kundalini yoga of the Himalayan adepts up at 13,000 feet in India, studied a bit of Zen and Tibetan forms of meditation like Samatha or "calm abiding." But no matter how you twist, prime or calm yourself, the same problem always remains: the body just won't go away. Even if you've "mastered" your awareness of the physical and can sit like a rock with little to no breath, you're still going to have awareness of the body, and it will continually remind you it exists. Which gives you two options: suppress it as much as you can, or work with it.

But with the tank, the body is just so free of external sensation, and so contented with its literally womb-like surroundings, that it just kind of *blips out*.

Well, let me rephrase that. First, it fidgets insufferably. Adjusting to the tank can be so initially frustrating that the center I visited gives the first hour for free. Once you "get it," though, your body remembers the right position and will enter that state rapidly every time you get into the tank from then on.

After the initial learning curve I ended up in place more relaxed, more contented, more free, more expanded than I have after years of meditation—in a few minutes. So much of the discipline of yoga and classic meditation manuals like the *Hatha Yoga Pradpika* is concerned with "turning the body off" with proper physical postures; a sensory deprivation tank does it almost immediately. The classic instructions for yoga all seem to continue to apply to the tank experience—stilling the body and breath, offering the in-breath into the out-breath, and so on—but one is immediately put into an ideal state physical state, the kind it presumably takes years of yoga practice to get to, if it is even reachable at all without the tank.

For that alone, I'm a new convert. Take away all the spiritual woo, the promises of inner experiences, and at the very base level you have a tool for relaxing more deeply than perhaps previously thought possible, identifying and then releasing muscle tension you weren't even aware was there. You feel it. And then you let it go, bit by bit. And then you float. The applications for health alone, when so many physical problems are caused by chronically holding tension, are obvious. Of course, as the physical tension goes, so does the mental tension. I found myself getting insights into, and letting go, of long-standing mental cramps, deep unsolved indecisions or confusions, that I'd forgotten were even there, as they had been embedded into the background noise of the mind for so long.

Of course, that was just the beginning. Beyond the relaxation of the body, I observed a secondary effect: the body enters what I can describe only as an orgasmic field. Here we enter into the domain of Wilhelm Reich's orgonomy or even of mysticism but, put simply, the message was that nearly all mental and physical tension is the individual attempting to suppress its natural orgasmic state. By orgasmic I don't specifically mean orgasmic release through sexual contact—I mean that when the body's energy becomes unlocked, it itself, becomes all-over orgasmic. One releases into infinite "bliss," the body-as-orgasm melting into the universe-as-orgasm.

Lilly experienced something similar, writing in his autobiography *The Scientist* (in third person) that "The tank experiences gave him new access to bodily pleasure which he found difficult to integrate with his rather… Calvinistic conscience. His conflicts with sexual expression, sexual transactions, took up a good deal of his time. The resting body accumulated positive energies that were expressible sexually to an almost intolerable level. He began to recognize the intrinsic nature of sexual drives. His parallel studies in neurophysiology revealed the sources of the sexual energy within the central nervous system. He began to see that these sources existed in himself, in his own brain."

The next level was the seeming heightening of "psychic" phenomena such as telepathic communication (with people who could be dozens of miles away) and the intrusion of "energies" or imagery from the collective unconscious, or simply the individual unconscious depending on how much one gives credence to the idea of transpersonal mind. As these phenomena are entirely subjective, unverifiable and largely deeply individualized to those who experience them, I here pass over details of any specific content, leaving this to individual experience.

The usual tank session is an hour. One returns to "normal" consciousness immediately and seamlessly after exiting the tank. There is no hangover or disorientation. I found rush hour traffic while leaving the facility slightly more aggravating after the peaceful tank experience, but beyond that there were no noticeable side effects. More importantly, one feels as if one has just awoken from a deeply satisfying and relaxing sleep, even if one didn't sleep in the tank, and even, as I experienced, if floating after a long and hectic working day.

It seems that, when separated from outside stimulus and given free reign, the bodymind knows exactly what it needs to do to restore health and equilibrium to itself, and goes about doing it, quickly and precisely.

For these reasons—and more I'm sure I've yet to discover—I recommend the tank to all.

It's a technology that has largely fallen by the wayside, though it's recently been making a comeback thanks in part to the highly enthusiastic publicity the comedian Joe Rogan has given it. I suspect that it probably has more to offer us now than it did when Lilly invented it. Silence is a rare commodity in our overstimulated world.

We owe it to ourselves to give ourselves back to ourselves.

(January 4, 2012)

On the 8 Limbs of Yoga

Yoga is an ancient spiritual technology, with a precise series of steps and methodologies—and it doesn't have much to do with the yoga currently in vogue. Yoga means Union in Sanskrit—Union With God.

In one sense, a yoga is a technique. The yoga which is commonly and popularly practiced is technically called hatha yoga—the yoga of the body. It is an excellent technique for keeping the body flexible and healthy… but real yoga is the yoga of the soul, not the body. It is the technology of harnessing the mind and training it to rest steadily in the Divine. What we commonly think of as "meditation" is in fact much closer to the classical meaning of yoga.

Patanjali, who composed the *Yoga Sutras* during the second century BCE, laid down a scientific framework for following the essential steps and stages of Union. These are the eight limbs of yoga, and together comprise what is perhaps the most elegant and precise system of spiritual development known to man. They are a series of practices which exist outside of the framework of ideology—yoga is not a religion or belief system. Rather, it is a series of practices and techniques which can be applied within the framework of any belief system (or without one) to accelerate the soul's progress to the Divine.

The eight limbs of yoga are as follows, and are meant to be followed successively, building upon each other, each increasingly focusing the yogi's life and practice, and aiding the path to single-pointed focus on God:

1. Yama.

Universal morality; rather, living a life free of impurities. Classically, Yama consists of having compassion for all life, truthfulness, non-stealing, proper focus of sexual energy, and getting over the need for constantly trying to get more money, wealth, stuff, status, and so on.

2. *Niyama.*

Proper personal habits aimed at living a pure life, including keeping a clean body and mind, being content and peaceful with one's lot in life, self-discipline in how one uses one's time and energy, introspection into one's own self, and a holding of the importance of the Divine as central to one's life.

These two form the basis of the yogi's lifestyle. They are concerned with living a balanced and non-disturbed life – keeping a clean house, as it were—in order to form a good foundation for meditation, clear from the mental disturbances that come with a chaotic, undisciplined and unfocused life. The next two form the physical requirements of spiritual practice.

3. *Asana.*

This is the posture of the body—but doesn't necessarily mean the pretzel-bending antics of popular yoga. At its most basic, Asana simply means finding a position which facilitates meditation, and which you can hold still in for long periods of time. If you can't do this, the physical fitness routines of hatha yoga can help, but the goal isn't to touch your toes to your head. The goal is to be able to sit for long periods of time in still silence, without fidgeting or otherwise allowing the body to get in the way of one's meditation.

4. *Pranayama.*

Pranayama means the way of breath. It's the regulation of the nervous system by using the breath. As with Asana, there are many complicated forms of Pranayama; however, at its most simple, Pranayama is simply a slow, steady regulation of breathing, through the nostrils. Breath is directly linked to the mind. Steady and still your breath, and you will steady and still your mind.

The next four form the purely internal requirements of meditation.

5. Pratyahara.

Pratyahara is the withdrawal of the senses. With a calm life and environment, a stilled body, and regulated breathing, the yogi's (five plus) senses will slowly begin to withdraw from the environment. This is "going within," turning the senses (and therefore the mind) away from the outside world. Instead of focusing on something "out there," the mind begins to focus on itself.

6. Dharana.

Dharana means concentration, and is what most people commonly think of as "meditation." With the senses turned inward, and the stimulus of the outside world (the conditions of the yogi's external life, the body, the breath, and the senses themselves) stilled, the yogi begins to focus the mind on one thing, and one thing only: the Divine. This process is called concentration, but it is not until the mind becomes single-pointedly focused that the yogi can truly be said to be in meditation.

7. Dhyana.

Dhyana means devotion, and this is true meditation—when the mind comes to rest in single-pointed focus upon its beloved, the Divine itself.

8. Samadhi.

The Holy Grail of Yoga, Samadhi is the erasing of the difference between the Divine and the soul which observes it, between the observer and the observed, subject and object. From meditating only on the Divine, the soul now merges with it.

This exceedingly amusing party trick can be studied in *The Yoga Sutras of Patanjali*, the classical manual on Yoga—but true practice takes the commitment of one's life to the path, daily discipline, and a qualified teacher or Guru, one who has trod the path to its completion.

May all beings in all worlds attain to happiness.

(April 7, 2011)

3 Books to Take With You On a Psychedelic Voyage

Psychedelics are a perennially popular tool for young seekers—and they're a double-edged sword. They're responsible for everything from the birth of the Apple computer (Steve Jobs was an acid-head in college) to the discovery of DNA (Francis Crick had a vision of the double helix while on LSD) to a whole lot of acid burn-outs and casualties. What's the dividing line? There are a lot of variables at work here: the two biggest being the individual user's chemical makeup and the chemical purity of whatever they're taking. Another is set and setting, meaning the mindset you're in, place you're in and people you're around. And while we know a lot more about these things as a culture now than we did in the 1960s, thanks to a lot of scholarly, academic and scientific work that's been done on psychedelics—not to mention the Internet—people are also doing all kinds of crazy f*kd up research chemicals, using them casually to party and generally being nihilistic and irresponsible. After all, we live in the age of krokodil, do we not?

Psychedelics are sacred. Done right, they can catalyze deep spiritual seeking and provide a glimpse of the "other side." Done wrong, they can mash your shit up but good. You cannot, as Bill Hicks once said, "take mushrooms and go to Astro World" and expect to have a good time. However, if you do your reading and exercise some respect and restraint, you just might. Here's three excellent places to start, which range from "trip guide" (*The Psychedelic Experience*) to "general education on consciousness expansion" (*Prometheus Rising*) to "how to integrate psychedelic experiences into your day-to-day life without becoming a total space case" (*The Bhagavad Gita*).

1. *The Psychedelic Experience: A Manual Based on the Tibetan Book of the Dead* by Timothy Leary, Ralph Metzner and Richard Alpert (aka Ram Dass).

This is the classic manual of psychedelic experience. It's an interpretation of the *Bardo Thödol* or "Tibetan Book of the Dead" in light of the LSD experience. The entire first wave of LSD users largely had this book—written by acid evangelist Tim Leary along with psychologist Ralph Metzner and Harvard professor Richard Alpert (who would later become the Hindu spiritual teacher Ram Dass) as their only trip guide.

The original Bardo Thödol, it should be noted, has nothing to do with psychedelics. It's a Tantric (magical) text of the Nyingma school of Tibetan Buddhism, the oldest school of Buddhism in Tibet, with the least bureaucratic overhead and the most retention of the pre-Buddhist indigenous shamanism of Bön. It's a funerary text meant to be read over the body of the dying or dead, which is meant to guide their soul through the intermediary "bardo" or dimension between this world and the next and allow them to attain liberation by letting go of all of the illusions and delusions of their life... more or less.

Leary, Alpert and Metzner, however, repurposed the text for LSD, guiding the user to let go of the hang-ups and complexes that inevitably become enflamed during the psychedelic experience and attain to the "clear light."

2. *Prometheus Rising* by Robert Anton Wilson.

This book has created more free-thinkers, mutants and freaks than any other I can think of outside of *Cosmic Trigger*, RAW's autobiographical account of his adventures in mysticism, magick and consciousness alteration. *Prometheus Rising*, however, is a comprehensive manual of beginner's exercises not just in psychedelics but in all kinds of brain-change techniques drawn from Eastern mysticism, Western occultism, Gurdjieff, General Semantics, Buckminster Fuller and all kinds of other sources. It's truly the "rainy day" guide to psyching yourself out into truly bizarre mental states. The eight-circuit model of consciousness, which Wilson developed with Leary as an alternative interpretation of the Hindu chakra system (much as Leary, Metzner and Alpert had re-interpreted the Bardo Thödol for druggies), remains one of the best beginner's models for mapping different states of consciousness.

3. *The Bhagavad Gita.*

One of the most popular Hindu texts for Westerners, the *Bhagavad Gita* consists of a dialogue between the god Krishna and the Panadava prince Arjuna, as Arjuna prepares to go to war in the *Mahabharata* epic. A deep exposition of how one's spiritual quest should intermesh with one's work and duties in the world, it's also a text on yoga and how to overcome the (to radically oversimplify here) negative thoughts that constantly besiege an untrained mind. It's the easiest Hindu text to understand, and was another cornerstone of the psychedelic movement in the 1960s.

(January 1, 2014)

10 Ways to Protect Yourself From NLP Mind Control

Neuro-Linguistic Programming (NLP) is a method for controlling people's minds that was invented by Richard Bandler and John Grinder in the 1970s, became popular in the psychoanalytic, occult and New Age worlds in the 1980s, and in advertising, marketing and politics in the 1990s and 2000s. It's become so interwoven with how people are communicated to and marketed at that its use is largely invisible. It's also somewhat of a pernicious, devilish force in the world—nearly everybody in the business of influencing people has studied at least some of its techniques. Masters of it are notorious for having a Rasputin-like ability to trick people in incredible ways—most of all themselves.

After explaining a bit about what NLP is and where it came from, I'm going to break down 10 ways to inoculate yourself against its use. You'll likely be spotting it left, right and center in the media with a few tips on what to look for. Full disclosure: During my 20s, I spent years studying New Age, magical and religious systems for changing consciousness. One of them was NLP. I've been on both ends of the spectrum: I've had people ruthlessly use NLP to attempt to control me, and I've also trained in it and even used it in the advertising world. Despite early fascination, by 2008 or so I had largely come to the conclusion that it's next to useless—a way of manipulating language that greatly overestimates its own effectiveness as a discipline, really doesn't achieve much in the way of any kind of lasting change, and contains no real core of respect for people or even true understanding of how people work.

After throwing it to the wayside, however, I became convinced that understanding NLP is crucial simply so that people can resist its use. It's kind of like the whole PUA thing that was popular in the mid-00s—a group of a few techniques that worked for a few unscrupulous people until the public figured out what was going on and rejected it, like the body identifying and rejecting foreign material.

What is NLP, and where did it come from?

"Neuro-linguistic programming" is a marketing term for a "science" that two Californians—Richard Bandler and John Grinder—came up with in the 1970s. Bandler was a stoner student at UC Santa Cruz (just like I later was in the 00s), then a mecca for psychedelics, hippies and radical thinking (now a mecca for Silicon Valley hopefuls). Grinder was at the time an associate professor in linguistics at the university (he had previously served as a Captain in the US Special Forces and in the intelligence community, *ahem* not that this, you know, is important… aheh…). Together, they worked at modeling the techniques of Fritz Perls (founder of Gestalt therapy), family therapist Virginia Satir and, most importantly, the preternaturally gifted hypnotherapist Milton Erickson. Bandler and Grinder sought to reject much of what they saw as the ineffectiveness of talk therapy and cut straight to the heart of what techniques actually worked to produce behavioral change. Inspired by the computer revolution—Bandler was a computer science major—they also sought to develop a psychological programming language for human beings.

What they came up with was a kind of evolution of hypnotherapy—while classical hypnosis depends on techniques for putting patients into suggestive trances (even to the point of losing consciousness on command), NLP is much less heavy-handed: it's a technique of layering subtle meaning into spoken or written language so that you can implant suggestions into a person's unconscious mind without them knowing what you're doing.

Though mainstream therapists rejected NLP as pseudoscientific nonsense (it has been officially peer reviewed and discredited as an intervention technique—lots more on that here), it nonetheless caught on. It was still the 1970s, and the Human Potential Movement was in full swing—and NLP was the new darling. Immediately building a publishing, speaking and training empire, by 1980 Bandler had made over $800,000 from his creation—he was even being called on to train corporate leaders, the army and the CIA. Self-help gurus like Tony Robbins used NLP techniques to become millionaires in the 1980s (Robbins now has an estimated net worth of $480 million). By the middle of the decade, NLP was such big business that lawsuits and wars had erupted over who had the rights to teach it, or even to use the term "NLP."

But by that time, Bandler had bigger problems than copyright disputes: he was on trial for the alleged murder of prostitute Corine Christensen in November 1986. The prosecution claimed that Bandler had shot Christensen, 34, point-blank in the face with a .357 Magnum in a drug deal gone bad. According to the press at the time, Bandler had discovered an even better way to get people to like him than NLP—cocaine—and become embroiled in a far darker game, even, than mind control. A much-recommended investigation into the case published by *Mother Jones* in 1989 opens with these chilling lines:

In the morning Corine Christensen last snorted cocaine, she found herself, straw in hand, looking down the barrel of a .357 Magnum revolver. When the gun exploded, momentarily piercing the autumn stillness, it sent a single bullet on a diagonal path through her left nostril and into her brain.

Christensen slumped over her round oak dining table, bleeding onto its glass top, a loose-leaf notebook, and a slip of yellow memo paper on which she had scrawled, in red ink, DON'T KILL US ALL. Choking, she spit blood onto a wine goblet, a tequila bottle, and the shirt of the man who would be accused of her murder, then slid sideways off the chair and fell on her back. Within minutes she lay still.

As Christensen lay dying, two men left her rented town house in a working-class section of Santa Cruz, California. One was her former boyfriend, James Marino, an admitted cocaine dealer and convicted burglar. The other, Richard

Bandler, was known internationally as the cofounder of Neuro-Linguistic Programming (NLP), a controversial approach to psychology and communication. About 12 hours later, on the evening of November 3, 1986, Richard Bandler was arrested and charged with the murder.

Bandler's defense was, simply, that Marino had killed Christensen, not him. Many at the time alleged he used NLP techniques on the stand to escape conviction. Yet Bandler was also alleged to actually use a gun in NLP sessions in order to produce dramatic psychological changes in clients—a technique that was later mirrored by Hollywood in the movie *Fight Club*, in which Brad Pitt's character pulls a gun on a gas station attendant and threatens to kill him if he doesn't pursue his dreams in life. That was, many said, Bandler's MO.

Whatever the truth of the matter, Bandler was indeed let off, and the story was quickly buried—I've never spoken to a student of NLP who's ever heard of the murder case, I'll note, and I've spoken to *a lot*. The case hardly impeded the growing popularity of NLP, however, which was now big business, working its way not only into the toolkit of psychotherapists but also into nearly every corner of the political and advertising worlds, having grown far beyond the single personage of Richard Bandler, though he continued (and continues) to command outrageous prices for NLP trainings throughout the world.

Today, the techniques of NLP and Ericksonian-style hypnotic writing can be readily seen in the world of Internet marketing, online get-rich-quick schemes and scams. Their most prominent public usage has likely been by Barack Obama, whose 2008 "Change" campaign was a masterpiece of Ericksonian permissive hypnosis. The celebrity hypnotist and illusionist Derren Brown also demonstrates NLP techniques in his routine.

How exactly does this thing work?

NLP is taught in a pyramid structure, with the more advanced techniques reserved for multi-thousand-dollar seminars. To oversimplify an overcomplicated subject, it more or less works like this: first, the user (or "NLPer," as NLP people often refer to themselves—and I should note here that the large majority of NLP people, especially those who are primarily therapists, are likely well-meaning) of NLP pays very, very close attention to the person they're working with. By watching subtle cues like eye movement, skin flush, pupil dilation and nervous tics, a skilled NLP person can quickly determine:

a) What side of the brain a person is predominantly using;

b) What sense (sight, smell, etc.) is most predominant in their brain;

c) How their brain stores and utilizes information (ALL of this can be gleaned from eye movements);

d) When they're lying or making information up.

After this initial round of information gathering, the "NLPer" begins to slowly and subtly mimic the client, taking on not only their body language but also their speech mannerisms, and will begin speaking with language patterns designed to target the client's primary sense.

For instance, a person predominantly focused on sight will be spoken to in language using visual metaphors—"Do you see what I'm saying?" "Look at it this way"—while a person for which hearing is the dominant sense will be spoken to in auditory language—"Hear me out," "I'm listening to you closely."

By mirroring body language and linguistic patterns, the NLPer is attempting to achieve one very specific response: rapport. Rapport is the mental and physiological state that a human enters when they let their social guard down, and it is generally achieved when a person comes to the conclusion that the person they're talking to is just like them. See how that works, broadly? An NLP person essentially carefully fakes the social cues that cause a person to drop their guard and enter a state of openness and suggestibility.

Once rapport is achieved, the NLPer will then begin subtly leading the interaction. Having mirrored the other person, they can now make subtle changes to actually influence the other person's behavior. Combined with subtle language patterns, leading questions and a whole slew of other techniques, a skilled NLPer can at this point steer the other person wherever they like, as long as the other person isn't aware of what's happening and thinks everything is arising organically, or has given consent. That means it's actually fairly hard to use NLP to get people to act out-of-character, but it can be used for engineering responses within a person's normal range of behavior—like donating to a cause, making a decision they were putting off, or going home with you for the night if they might have considered it anyway.

From this point, the NLPer will seek to do two things—elicit and anchor. Eliciting happens when an NLPer uses leading and language to engineer an emotional state—for instance, hunger. Once a state has been elicited, the NLPer can then anchor it with a physical cue—for instance, touching your shoulder. In theory, if done right, the NLPer can then call up the hungry state any time they touch your shoulder in the same way. It's conditioning, plain and simple.

How can I make sure nobody pulls this horseshit on me?

I've had all kinds of people attempt to "NLP" me into submission, including multiple people I've worked for over extended periods of time, and even people I've been in relationships with. Consequently, I've developed a pretty keen immune response to it. I've also studied its mechanics very closely, largely to resist the nonsense of said people. Here's a few key methods I've picked up.

1. Be extremely wary of people copying your body language.

If you're talking to somebody who may be into NLP, and you notice that they're sitting in exactly the same way as you, or mirroring the way you have your hands, test them by making a few movements and seeing if they do the same thing. Skilled NLPers will be better at masking this than newer ones, but newer ones will always immediately copy the same movement. This is a good time to call people on their shit.

2. *Move your eyes in random and unpredictable patterns.*

This is freaking hilarious to do to troll NLPers. Especially in the initial stages of rapport induction, an NLP user will be paying incredibly close attention to your eyes. You may think it's because they're intensely interested in what you're saying. They are, but not because they actually care about your thoughts: They're watching your eye movements to see how you store and access information. In a few minutes, they'll not only be able to tell when you're lying or making something up, they'll also be able to figure out what parts of your brain you're using when you're speaking, which can then lead them to be so clued in to what you're thinking that they almost come across as having some kind of psychic insight into your innermost thoughts. A clever hack for this is just to randomly dart your eyes around—look up to the right, to the left, side to side, down… make it seem natural, but do it randomly and with no pattern. This will drive an NLP person *utterly nuts,* because you'll be throwing off their calibration.

3. *Do not let anybody touch you.*

This is pretty obvious and kind of goes without saying in general. But let's say you're having a conversation with somebody you know is into NLP, and you find yourself in a heightened emotional state—maybe you start laughing really hard, or get really angry, or something similar—and the person you're talking to touches you while you're in that state. They might, for instance, tap you on the shoulder. What just happened? They anchored you so that later, if they want to put you back into the state you were just in, they can (or so the wayward logic of NLP dictates) touch you in the same place. Just be like, o*h hell no you did not.*

4. Be wary of vague language.

One of the primary techniques that NLP took from Milton Erickson is the use of vague language to induce hypnotic trance. Erickson found that the more vague language is, the more it leads people into trance, because there is less that a person is liable to disagree with or react to. Alternately, more specific language will take a person out of trance. (Note Obama's use of this specific technique in the "Change" campaign, a word so vague that anybody could read anything into it.)

5. Be wary of permissive language.

"Feel free to relax." "You're welcome to test drive this car if you like." "You can enjoy this as much as you like." Watch the f*k out for this. This was a major insight of pre-NLP hypnotists like Erickson: the best way to get somebody to do something, including going into a trance, is by allowing them to give you permission to do so. Because of this, skilled hypnotists will NEVER command you outright to do something—i.e. "Go into a trance." They WILL say things like "Feel free to become as relaxed as you like."

6. Be wary of gibberish.

Nonsense phrases like "As you release this feeling more and more you will find yourself moving into present alignment with the sound of your success more and more." This kind of gibberish is the bread and butter of the pacing-and-leading phase of NLP; the hypnotist isn't actually saying anything, they're just trying to program your internal emotional states and move you towards where they want you to go. ALWAYS say "Can you be more specific about that" or "Can you explain exactly what you mean?" This does two things: it interrupts this whole technique, and it also forces the conversation into specific language, breaking the trance-inducing use of vague language we discussed in #4.

7. *Read between the lines.*

NLP people will consistently use language with hidden or layered meanings. For instance "Diet, nutrition and sleep with me are the most important things, don't you think?" On the surface, if you heard this sentence quickly, it would seem like an obvious statement that you would probably agree with without much thought. Yes, of course diet, nutrition and sleep are important things, sure, and this person's really into being healthy, that's great. But what's the layered-in message? "Diet, nutrition and *sleep with me* are the most important things, don't you think?" Yep, and you just unconsciously agreed to it. Skilled NLPers can be incredibly subtle with this.

8. *Watch your attention.*

Be very careful about zoning out around NLP people—it's an invitation to leap in with an unconscious cue. Here's an example: An NLP user who was attempting to get me to write for his blog for free noticed I appeared not to be paying attention and was looking into the distance, and then started using the technique listed in #7 by talking about how he never has to pay for anything because media outlets send him review copies of books and albums for free. "Everything for free," he began hissing at me. "I get *everything. For. Free.*" Obvious, no?

9. *Don't agree to anything.*

If you find yourself being led to make a quick decision on something, and feel you're being steered, leave the situation. Wait 24 hours before making any decisions, especially financial ones. Do NOT let yourself get swept up into making an emotional decision in the spur of the moment. Sales people are armed with NLP techniques specifically for engineering impulse buys. Don't do it. Leave, and use your rational mind.

10. *Trust your intuition.*

And the foremost and primary rule: If your gut tells you somebody is fucking with you, or you feel uneasy around them, trust it. NLP people almost always seem "off," dodgy, or like used car salesmen. Flee, or request they show you the respect of not applying NLP techniques when interacting with you.

Hopefully this short guide will be of assistance to you in resisting this annoying and pernicious modern form of black magic. Take it with you on your phone or a printout next time you're at a used car sales lot, getting signed up for a gym membership, or watching a politician speak on TV. You'll easily find yourself surprised how you allow yourself to notice more and more NLP techniques… more and more… don't you think?

(January 16, 2014)

9 NSA-Defying Tools for Anonymous Browsing

NSA spying was the breakout story of 2013. The revelation of constant monitoring of all electronic communications not just in the United States, but across the entire world, will have shockwaves that last until the end of Western democracy. We are standing too close to this event to see it clearly; it's too big. We may not see the ramifications for decades.

But in the meantime, there are some tools we can use to keep our online communications secure. They're not without their downsides, but they're there to use for anonymous browsing and conducting day-to-day affairs. These tools may not be 100% NSA-proof—nobody quite knows what the NSA is capable of—but they're a start.

1. Tor.

Tor (short for The Onion Router) is a free software package that allows anonymous browsing with Firefox. Its use is mandatory for accessing the so-called "Deep Web." Tor conceals its users' identities by directing traffic through over three thousand relays, all of which are maintained by volunteers. Tor is a double-edged sword: although it's a tool that can enable whistleblowing (WikiLeaks conducts business in the Deep Web, and even Edward Snowden used Tor to leak his PRISM documents to Glenn Greenwald), it's also a tool that's favored by everybody from drug dealers to child pornographers to jihadis, making Tor a flashpoint in the current civil ethics debate America is having over anonymity. Though Tor certainly does provide anonymity, it's also a beast to use: Web sites load glacially, so it's not a tool for casual browsing. Users also voice concern that even if what you're doing while on Tor can't be seen, the fact that you're using it at all can be seen, and may immediately raise suspicion. It's also only truly safe if you use it behind multiple proxies.

2. *Pirate Browser.*

For those who don't want to jump into Tor, there's Pirate Browser, a browser package created by the infamous Pirate Bay torrent network, and which incorporates Tor. As a bonus, Pirate Browser will circumvent content filters if you have them in your country.

3. *VPNs (Virtual Private Networks).*

VPNs are private groups of computers networked together and nested within a public network. Accessing such a private network can render your data encrypted and secure—you can also access one, and its security, even if you're on an untrusted public net connection (Starbucks, let's say). They're favored by people who want to use BitTorrent anonymously, for instance. VPNs can offer a considerable level of protection, and their use is expected to become much more widespread as concern about net surveillance grows.

4. *HTTPS Everywhere.*

Developed by the Electronic Frontier Foundation, "HTTPS Everywhere" is a Firefox add-on that forces your connection to major websites (like Facebook and Google) into a secure HTTPS connection instead of only HTTP. This immediately adds a modicum of online anonymity without having to go through Tor.

5. *Anonymous Search Engines.*

Services like Ixquick and DuckDuckGo allow for anonymous search, instead of going through untrustworthy Google or Bing.

6. Anonymous E-Mail.

Anonymous e-mail providers like HushMail and Safe-mail can provide secure, disposable e-mail addresses for sending information without interference.

7. Anonymous Chat.

To open an anonymized chat room, try the CryptoCat extension or the web-based ChatCrypt. Especially when combined with an anonymized browser, these programs will allow for chat that doesn't leave a record.

8. Burner Phones.

Burner Phones provide a 30 day disposable anonymous cell phone for $75. You get it for a month, and then you throw it away when it deactivates at the end of its use period.

9. Bitcoin.

As it's been the subject of just about every Internet commentator and "digital freedom activist's" tweets for the last, uh, forever, you may be a bit tired of hearing about Bitcoin—but let's include it anyway. Bitcoin is an anonymous, open source, P2P online currency that can be transferred over the Internet without having to go through a financial institution. This, obviously, scares the hell out of a lot of people—not to mention its insanely fluctuating exchange rate and the fact that people often use it to buy drugs and conduct other illegal transactions online.

The above resources can bring the Internet and your communications back under your control, somewhat—a major step towards regaining some of the freedoms that have been infringed upon by the NSA, DEA and others. But their use is only a patch on a broken system: in a sane world, normal, law-abiding citizens wouldn't have to use shady technologies just to talk without fear of government surveillance. But here we are, so use these technologies wisely. And like law-abiding citizens, please.

(September 13, 2013)

How to Be Your Own Media Gatekeeper

There is no information age.

It doesn't exist. There is only the Age of Noise. Because although we now appear to have an infinite ability to see everything that's going on in the world at once, from photos of the world from space to the fact that our friends are indecisive about what to eat tonight, we have no ability to filter that information and sort for what matters. We have no reliable media gatekeeper.

We used to pay people to filter information for us: these were called professional journalists, writers and artists, whose job it was to dive into the sea of information and come back up with pearls for us. But we don't pay those people anymore, because the media conglomerates that have consolidated into only a few massive holdings since the 1990s have realized that they don't have to.

They don't have to because their interest isn't providing real information or truth; their interest is in providing content that gets as many people as possible to look at it, in order to get the most advertising money possible, because that's how they get paid and can afford the salaries and insurance costs of the large staffs they need to do what they do. That's their daily reality. And so they're in the business of giving people what they want.

Since the 90s, the trend has increasingly been to cut out professionals and get people to generate their own content. That means reality television, YouTube, Facebook. No big budgets needed and far more profit gained. Since everybody is a star now, everybody is constantly generating more free content than we can ever consume. And so professional creatives have gone the way of the dinosaurs, as R. U. Sirius just pointed out in a great and painful article for *The Verge*, and instead of getting reporting on, say, Karen Silkwood blowing the whistle on nuclear power, or Gary Webb's expose of CIA drug trafficking, you're getting reporting about how LeeAnn Rimes is in a Twitter feud.

We have no more professional gatekeepers. We are scattered to the four winds, drowning in Facebook feeds or aggregation blogs. These mega-blogs, which we have mistakenly expected to replace major media outlets, are in the same position: largely beholden to the tastes of their audiences, and stuck having to keep people happy with unchallenging, crowd-pleasing content to drive traffic to their site advertisers so that they can eat.

So where does this leave the information-poor individual who hopefully wants to get their head over the waterline enough to start to see the things that actually matter?

It means you have to be your own media gatekeeper. Flat out. You can't outsource that job to somebody else anymore, because the corporate media, or the alternative media, or Blog X, Y or Z, are not going to comprehensively do that job for you the way you need it done. They're too beholden to economics, ratings and their own viewpoints and reality tunnels. And more and more, they're probably not able to do that job because they're not properly trained for that job, and I don't mean just bloggers, because these days very few people who work in the mainstream media have any journalistic training at all. Nobody can get the information you need for you. You've got to do it yourself.

Luckily, we've got tools that can help us do that. Here's a few beginning steps:

1. *Decide what matters.*

Faced with infinite information, you've got to decide up front what you're going to filter for, at least initially. You've got to restrict your data to some extent, which sounds counterintuitive, but is necessary. You don't need more information, you need more information about the things that matter. I suggest that the things that matter are, simply, information that can directly positively effect the welfare of you and your family, and information about the general welfare of the planet.

2. *Use Web tools to automate your info intake.*

Everybody on the Web is largely in the same position: grab info from a few news sources (like AP or Reuters) and then recycle it into blog content. They're using the same tools as you to get their info. So cut out the middleman. I recommend setting up Google Alerts, for a start, to give you info about the issues you actually care about instead of waiting for somebody else to. Beyond that, I highly recommend using an RSS aggregator like Bloglines to dump a lot of media outlets into an easy-to-digest feed. Work done upfront will pay off in time saved later. Reddit is also an excellent tool, as long as you stay off the dreaded, time-sucking front page and keep to subreddits pertinent to important topics.

3. *Expand outside of your demographic bubble.*

Whoever you are, you fit a demographic, which means that the media specifically tailors content that it knows you will like for the shows you watch and blogs you read, so advertisers can sell you products they've determined your demographic buys and use the language and images they know you will respond to, all in order to get you to make that purchase. Expand out of the box they've decided you fit in. Read blogs and consume media from sources outside of your demographic, and that definitely means outside of your political and religious persuasion. Otherwise you're blinkered not only to things that are going on around you, but also to parts of life you might be ignoring.

4. *Read a book.*

You still won't get nearly as good of an info download from months on the Internet as you will from reading a well-researched, info-dense book, a book which, never forget, can represent years or decades of professional research and experience rather than an afternoon spent dashing off a blog post to throw out into the netherworld. Don't stop reading, and reading better and more challenging books. The Web is really only a menu of culture; don't forget to eat the meal.

5. *Think critically.*

Understand what confirmation bias is, and always consider the source of an article. Who wrote this, and what's their agenda? What are they selling? Do they cite their own sources? Is this from a professional journalist/writer or from some wackadoo or salesman spouting off on the net? Here's a quick guide to spotting bad info. To dig deeper, get this excellent, comprehensive primer in critical thinking skills.

6. *Meditate.*

Sounds potentially hokey, but there is no better discipline for learning how to shut off what is pointless bullshit and go only for what actually matters than meditation, because in learning to control one's own thoughts internally, dealing with external noise becomes immensely easier.

Information is power. Know how to get it.

(November 7, 2013)

The Western Esoteric Tradition— The World's Most Misunderstood Spiritual Path

Despite my best efforts to the contrary, I get consistent requests to talk about "magick" or, as somebody with a lack of understanding might put it, "how to be a witch." This is something I've been reluctant to do for the last six or seven years, because it's a topic that's so easily misunderstood, and that so easily gives the wrong impression— immediately conjuring images of mouth breathers in black robes hanging out at the local mall's food court or New Agers trying to rip you off with nonsense woo claims.

But it's not like that. Underneath that giant layer of foolishness, misdirection and misunderstanding, Magick is, in my opinion, one of the great gems of Western culture. It's the tradition that some of the great geniuses of Western history—including the originators of science—were involved in: Francis Bacon, Daniel Dafoe, William Butler Yeats, Dr. John Dee, Giordiano Bruno, Pythagoras and many, many others, whether remembered by history or not.

"Magick" is the long-running sacred tradition of the West, in the same way that esoteric yoga or Tibetan Buddhism are sacred traditions in the East. Practically speaking, it's the path of enacting your spiritual growth ritually, in the day-to-day world, because that's what tends to be healthy for people in Western cultures.

Dropping out of life and sitting up on a mountain-top meditating for the rest of your life is, by-and-large, an Eastern path. It's an outgrowth of Asian culture and a path that can work remarkably well in the cultural context of Hinduism or Buddhism. But people living in America, the UK, Europe or other "Western" locales by and large do not live in a culture that supports that. (Just try it!) We live in a culture that forces action in the world, where the path to independence, self-reliance and happiness tends to rely on rolling up your sleeves and getting stuff done in the real world.

While the Western tradition incorporates a lot of meditation, it isn't a path that allows escape from reality. It's the path of directly confronting reality, the circumstances of your life, and using those circumstances as the raw material for your spiritual growth. Consider the legend of alchemy, in which the practitioner is spoken of as having the "magic" power of transmuting lead into gold—or even, in some versions, turning shit into gold. This is what it's about—taking lead, which represents mundane, boring existence, and turning it into gold. Taking the shit that you're given, and turning it into gold. Taking the raw matter of existence and making something incredible out of it.

The Western sacred tradition has been an underground tradition for most of the last two millennia because of persecution by the Church and other religious institutions (despite, ironically, the fact that many of its adherents were historically seeking direct communion with Christ, perhaps a threat to the priesthood's monopoly). It has snaked its way through our history and manifested under various names and at various times as Gnosticism, Catharism, witchcraft, alchemy, Qabalah, Enochian, Freemasonry, Rosicrucianism, the Golden Dawn, Thelema, Chaos and many other forms.

The Western tradition is often given the blanket name "Magick." This is unfortunate in some ways, because it conjures up fanciful ideas of "magic powers" (not the point), and immediately makes people associate the Mysterium Tremendum with the following things which are bullshit:

Tacky Satanic nonsense; New Agers trying to charge you $180 for a lavender-scented enema; people into magic mainly as a way to accumulate jewelry and flashy clothes to one-up other outsiders; people into magic to collect books or art (see reason above); people telling you "heyyy man you don't have to do it the hard way" despite never having done it the hard way; people using spirituality to advance a personal, cultural, financial or political agenda; religious or cult servitude; servitude to evil spirits; being into that one band that uses occult imagery; people who think they can "put spells" on other people; people who take a lot of *drugs and conclude that they are special; creepy swingers who lure impressionable undergraduates into their mildewy dens of suburban sin with the promise of "real power!!!1*

Magick has nothing to do with any of this.
It does have to do with:

Hard work, perseverance, study, discipline, self-sacrifice, years and years of painful trial-and-error learning, humility, constant adaptation and evolution, devotion to your own integrity, learning to let go.

There are no hard and fast rules on how to do that—and the details are different for every single individual. But there are guidelines and practices that help. So, "How to Be a Witch"? Broadly, you live a magical life by:

1. Disciplining your body, mind and spirit;

2. Figuring out what you're here for—your unique purpose for existing (note that this is a continuum, and evolves over time);

3. Using the discipline developed in Step 1 to accomplish Step 2, understanding that when you Do Your True Will, or engage in your reason for existing, life makes a whole lot more sense. It's not necessarily easier, but it's infused with meaning, a major accomplishment in a world where people drift through seas of endless meaninglessness.

A Practical Resource Guide to Magick

For more practical information, here's a resource guide to the Path composed of articles I've written:

1. I've written about the basic disciplines of magic here. Shows exactly how to break out of the conditioned social trance and begin the process of taking control.

A couple of books I've put together on the subject:

1. *Generation Hex.* A beginner's guide to the initial stages of magical training, in a 21st century context.

2. *Thee Psychick Bible.* The total archive of Thee Temple ov Psychick Youth, which contains the complete writing of Genesis P-Orridge and TOPY, the primary magic group active in the 1980s-90s.

Beyond that, I recommend three primary sourcebooks for exploring the Western esoteric tradition. These books contain a huge amount of material, organized in proper fashion, that thousands of other books fall far short of in terms of raw information.

1. Beginner Level: *Liber Null & Psychonaut*, **Peter J. Carroll.** The practices of ritual magic, stripped down and taken out of context. Good for picking up the very basics but take Carroll's reductionist editorializing with fifty times the salt one would reserve for Crowley.

2. Intermediate Level: *The Golden Dawn*, **Israel Regardie.** Contains the ritual corpus of the Golden Dawn, the 19th century Victorian magic group which counted many of the country's primary cultural movers among its members. This is a synthesis of most of what came before and the foundation of most of what came after.

3. Advanced Level: *The Mystical and Magical System of the A.'.A.'.*, **James A. Eshelman.** A condensation and organization of Aleister Crowley's system, which took the Golden Dawn material, added in Eastern mysticism and sex magick, and ratcheted the whole thing up to the tenth power. Alongside this you'll want copies of *Gems From the Equinox* and *Magick: Liber ABA* by Crowley.

(Bonus! For a look at the Eastern side of things, in a format accessible to Westerners: *Autobiography of a Yogi* by Paramahansa Yogananda.)

Good luck, stay out of trouble, and don't let nobody tell ya what to do, ya hear…

(July 24, 2013)

Start Your Own McMansion Empire

It's very likely that within a few years, there are going to be whole sections of America plastered with pre-bubble McMansions that never found occupants.

Therefore, why hang out in San Francisco or New York paying $3K for a shoebox apartment and the rest of your paycheck on an iPhone to Instagram your damn enchiladas when you and your friends could, with a little bit of that old-fashioned American settler spirit and some good old gumption, go start your own weirdo empire out in some abandoned suburb?

I can imagine, for instance, whole sectors of America occupied by die-hard Burners, trained by their forays to Black Rock City to brave the elements and practice sustainable, self-sufficient existence, creating their own version of the American suburban dream.

According to *Grist*, we're looking at 40 million (!) unoccupied McMansions:

Americans, especially generations X and Y, want shorter commutes, walkability and a car-free existence. Which means that around 40 million large-lot exurban McMansions, built primarily during the housing boom, might never find occupants.

Only 43 percent of Americans prefer big suburban homes, says Chris Nelson, head of the Metropolitan Research Center at the University of Utah. That mean demand for "large-lot" homes is currently 40 million short of the available stock — and not only that, but the U.S. is short 10 million attached homes and 30 million small homes, which are what people really want.

The 60s saw the rise of communes that mostly failed due to issues arising from lack of space, boundaries and resources: transplant that same spirit to some midwestern cul-de-sac with houses for all, and what might happen?

You can already buy foreclosed houses in the most devastated parts of America, like the outskirts of Detroit, for a few months' rent on an apartment in a major city. That's likely a condition that's only going to increase.

One unfairly snotty *Gawker* article nonetheless contains a key piece of info: students are already ganging up and splitting foreclosed McMansions instead of renting dorm rooms, and paying to the tune of $250 each in rent. And that's not even squatting—that's legitly paid-up ones in a college town in California.

So the smart ones cluster together (solidarity) and head for the subdivisions, plunking down $250 or $350 per person to rent out one of the many foreclosed-upon castles and enjoy Jacuzzis, chandeliers, and other luxuries. "I mean, I have it all!" says Merced senior Patricia Dugan—who's majoring in marketing, a practical field.

Millennials are increasingly rejecting the concept of ownership (not surprising for a generation raised with the Internet and downloading) and reclaiming blighted urban space. Thinking about those trends going forward, the potential of more economic downturn and this new data about unclaimed houses, I can see a whole new way of living coming. Don't mortgage your life for a chance at the American Dream: just move in to the one that's already there.

Think about it. That's all I'm saying. Just think about it.

(August 20, 2012)

5 Ways to Get Inner Peace

Inner peace is an elusive beast. Stalking it through the alleys of your mind can be a herculean task, and it is dogged on every side by how much energy you invest in the actions of the people around you. Luckily, it's not impossible. Here are five ways to let go of the things that ail you and regain your inner peace.

1. Understand that the internet is full of assholes and fools that you cannot control. It's also full of a lot of wonderful people. But communication with those few people will inevitably be drowned out by the absolute narcissistic nonsense and vapid self-promotion spewed out of the keyboards of the many. The Internet will assault you every day with spew from the bowels of Hades, and there will always be something to outrage you. Unless you're a masochistic analyst of society's pathology such as myself, you're best off ignoring it. In twenty years a whole generation will look back over their youths and wonder where the time went. The answer will be social media.

2. Meditate and exercise. As much as you can. Start a meditation practice with five minutes a day and work up to thirty, consistently. Watch the stress steadily decrease. For exercise, try twenty minutes of walking, jogging or running a day, which doesn't require any fancy equipment or gym membership. Long walks are very good for de-stressing. Like with meditation, you get to the flow states around 45 minutes in.

3. Understand that you're going to die and it won't mean anything. Really. It's not a big deal. Being born means you have to die. Billions have died before you. Billions will die after you. Death isn't an issue. What's more important, according to all world religions, is your state of mind when you die, and that's dependent on how you live. So enjoy life, and don't get hung up about mortality.

4. Surround yourself with people who actually care about you instead of chasing after people that you want to like you. Everybody wants to be liked by the cool kids, but chances are that the cool kids are actually so narcissistic and paranoid about losing their status as the cool kids that they won't bother with you. Whoever that "cool kid" is in your life, forget them. Focus on the people who actually care about you. If they're in your life already, it's because they want to be.

5. Understand that you can't change people. Leave them be. They're totally embedded in their own stories. Trying to modify the behavior of other human beings is a colossal headache and the cause of international warfare. If you want the world to be a better place, start with yourself. If other people follow suit, awesome. If they don't, awesome. No attachment.

Improving your emotional health is a never-ending work, but the steps listed above are big ones. I hope they help.

(March 19, 2013)

Learning to Let Go

Modern life is rubbish.

We all want it all. To conquer the world with our ideas and do good and play all of our roles perfectly for all people. And get rich in the meantime.

But life is short. Ten years spent learning to walk and talk and what not to eat because it's poisonous, ten years spent dealing with becoming social and the opposite sex, ten years fitting in to the adult world, ten years maintaining it all and reproducing and then your body slowly starts to pull the plug while you raise the next generation to do it all over again. More or less. Salmon up a stream.

It's important to stop sometimes. To let the madness of our social obligations, nearly all of which are about what other people can get from us, to settle, and to listen to what's really going on.

What's really going on is this Thing. It's not the drama you assign to your ego, your personal myth. It's not some cosmic mythology of good vs. evil or whatever vs. whatever. It's not even time, this "be here now" moment. It's this Thing. This completely inscrutable, breathing, transforming, pulsating Thing called existence, driven by water, food, air, information. This process called life that we largely fritter away on momentary distractions, work, business, chasing money or sex or highs or religion or getting pointlessly riled up about one thing or another on the Internet.

Stop. Relax. Be with yourself. Don't be here now, either. Fuck Now. Now can fuck off. That slippery bastard always gets away from you anyway. Just be.

In this calm abiding all is known and all is present.

Give in. Just give in. You can't change the future. You can't make the past come back. You can't manifest a billion dollars with the Secret™®©. Let go of your clinging to illusions, to the Santas you have not yet ceased to believe in. Let go of your clinging to anything. All that craving.

And stop.

There is nothing but this breath. And one day even this breath will leave you. And where will today's mad thoughts of who said what on Facebook be then? Where will all the gold you have won or lost in this world be then? Where will all your daily dramas be then? Gone away.

Stop. Remember. And return.

(February 7, 2013)

The final and most terrible form of magic is Grey Magic: not grey as in "between black and white," or "alien," grey as in the art of dealing with reality as it is, the grey world. The one you tried with all your might to escape through magic in the first place. Hah! But of course it is in the Desert of the Real, not the Desert of Da'ath, that all power is given and expressed. Chew on that if you can and if you dare. Mi nnu mi basn mi shes mi bpyod mi sgom rang sar bzhag. Let go of past, present, future, don't try to understand, don't try to make anything happen. Stop. Thus is the terrible poison of Control itself taken and transmuted at the razor's edge...

Article Histories

"Hail to the Broken-Tusked Elephant Lord" first appeared on jasonlouv.wordpress.com

"The Upturned Rock of Western Civilization, and What I Found There" was written specifically for this volume.

"The Apocalypse is Cancelled" was originally released as an ebook through Ultraculture.org.

"The Two Great Lies" first appeared on ultraculture.org

"Soft-Sell Slavery" first appeared on ultraculture.org

"Meet the Planet-Murdering Sociopaths Bankrolling Climate Denial" first appeared on ultraculture.org

"Zbigniew Brzezinski vs. Global Awakening" first appeared on ultraculture.org

"We the People are Tired and Cold" first appeared on ultraculture.org

"From Fast Apocalypse to Slow Apocalypse" first appeared on ultraculture.org

"When the CIA Got Busted Selling Crack" first appeared on ultraculture.org

"The NSA Has Set Up Shop at the US Embassy in Mexico" first appeared on news.vice.com

"The Trans-Pacific Partnership Could 'Establish a War of All Against All'" first appeared on news.vice.com

"Slave Children Used by Major Corporations to Make Chocolate" first appeared on ultraculture.org

"The Dalai Lama Will Not Return to Lead Tibet" first appeared on boingboing.net

"Germany Condemns 'Illegal Killings,' Halts All Purchases of American Drones" first appeared on motherboard.vice.com

"Insanity: Female Inmates Forcibly Sterilized in California Prisons" first appeared on dangerousminds.net

"The Long Tail of America's Eugenics Problem" first appeared on motherboard.vice.com

"When Monsanto Had Its Own Disneyland Exhibit" first appeared on ultraculture.org

"Mexico Just Won a Major Victory Against Monsanto" first appeared on ultraculture.org

"Why Neil deGrasse Tyson is Dead Wrong About GMOs" first appeared on ultraculture.org

"Every Person on Earth is Polluted With Hundreds of Human-Made Toxins" first appeared on motherboard.vice.com

"Scientist Threatened and Stalked for Findings on Syngenta Herbicide" first appeared on ultraculture.org

"Thanks to Dredging and Coal, the Great Barrier Reef Is More Threatened Than Ever" first appeared on motherboard.vice.com

"How America Interrupted Wilhelm Reich's Orgasmic Utopia" first appeared on motherboard.vice.com

"Paramhansa Yogananda and the Legacy of India's Mission to Enlighten America" first appeared on boingboing.net

"Buckminster Fuller's Vision of Enough for Everyone" first appeared on ultraculture.org

"Colin Wilson, Grandfather of the Occult, 1931-2013" first appeared on ultraculture.org

"Judee Sill, the Rosicrucian Folk Singer That Time Forgot" first appeared on ultraculture.org and dangerousminds.net

"James Dallas Egbert III: The Dungeon Master" first appeared on dangerousminds.net and boingboing.net

"Robert Anton Wilson's Cosmic Trigger, and the Psychedelic Interstellar Future We Need" first appeared on boingboing.net

"It's Aleister Crowley's Birthday" first appeared on ultraculture.org

"The Beast in Berlin" first appeared on ultraculture.org

"For Lady Jaye Breyer P-Orridge" first appeared on ultraculture.org

"Chelsea Manning is Dying for Our Sins" first appeared on ultraculture.org

"California Screaming: Los Angeles' Culty Weirdness" first appeared on dangerousminds.net

"In Memoriam: Arthur Magazine, 2002-2011" first appeared on swoonmagazine.com

"Lost in the Filth Kaleidoscope" first appeared on humanityplus.org

"In the Valley of the Porn Witches" first appeared on motherboard.vice.com

"Lady Gaga and the Dead Planet Grotesque" first appeared on humanityplus.org

"Brooke Candy, 'Opulence,' and the Work of Integrating the Shadow" first appeared on ultraculture.org

"Die Antwoord's 'Pitbull Terrier' and Occult Social Control" first appeared on ultraculture.org

"Imagine! The Metropolis of Tomorrow!" first appeared on jasonlouv.wordpress.com

"I Am a Mechanical Man: Robocops and Robowars" first appeared on humanityplus.org

"Get Up Make Love: 21st Sentury Space Sexploration" first appeared on humanityplus.org

"Dementing Augmented Reality: How Future Activists Will Break People Out of Their Digital Trances" first appeared on acceler8or.com

"The Headset Revolution Will Be a Blizzard of Conflicting Realities—If it Happens, That Is" first appeared on boingboing.net

"Will Smart Drugs and Cybernetics Create a Superhuman Workforce?" first appeared on motherboard.vice.com

"Extraterrestrial Intelligence" first appeared on humanityplus.org

"Wal-Mart Mutants: Welcome to Aisle 23" first appeared on ultraculture.org

"There is No Singularity. Welcome to the Multiplicity." first appeared on ultraculture.org

"The Freedom of Imagination Act" first appeared in Swoon No. 6 and in The Fenris Wolf No. 5

"On Compassion" first appeared on ultraculture.org

"Conjurations in the Element of Flesh" first appeared on acceler8or.com

"An Oneironaut's Guide to Lucid Dreams" first appeared on ultraculture.org

"The Wizard Way of Bro Science" first appeared on acceler8or.com

"How to Make an Orgone Accumulator Blanket" first appeared on ultraculture.org

"Brion Gysin's Dream Machine: Build Your Own Portal to Inner Visions" first appeared on acceler8or.com

"Commandeering the Inner Space Shuttle" first appeared on acceler8or.com

"On the 8 Limbs of Yoga" first appeared on jasonlouv.wordpress.com

"3 Books to Take With You on a Psychedelic Voyage" first appeared on ultraculture.org

"10 Ways to Protect Yourself From NLP Mind Control" first appeared on ultraculture.org

"9 NSA-Defying Tools for Anonymous Browsing" first appeared on ultraculture.org

"How to Be Your Own Media Gatekeeper" first appeared on ultraculture.org

"The Western Esoteric Tradition—The World's Most Misunderstood Spiritual Path" first appeared on ultraculture.org

"Start Your Own McMansion Empire" first appeared on ultraculture.org

"5 Ways to Get Inner Peace" first appeared on ultraculture.org

"Learning to Let Go" first appeared on ultraculture.org

Also Available From Jason Louv and Ultraculture

MONSANTO VS. THE WORLD: The Monsanto Protection Act, GMOs and Our Genetically Modified Future
$4.49 Paperback • $2.99 Kindle • Available Now on Amazon

Monsanto—one of the largest agriculture and biotech companies in the world, and widely considered the most "evil" one, has given us GMOs, DDT, PCBs and even Agent Orange. But what is Monsanto truly doing to our diet—and why do many consider their business practices deeply abusive? Meticulously researched, *Monsanto vs. the World* puts to rest the myths, and shows the shocking reality.

QUEEN VALENTINE
$10.95 Paperback • $2.99 Kindle • Available Now on Amazon

Jason Louv's first novel, *Queen Valentine* delves into the occult underworld of New York City, depicting the war for the soul of humanity that seethes just under the city streets—a dark fantasy and social satire, *Queen Valentine* is a tour de force that led legendary comic book artist Brendan McCarthy to call Jason Louv "…a top tier talent who can really tell a story. A unique fusion of Alan Moore and Neil Gaiman."

ULTRACULTURE JOURNAL
$19.95 Paperback • $9.99 Kindle • Available Now on Amazon

On the acidic edge of Western and Eastern Magick: Ultraculture Journal is a collection of some of the world's best and most cutting edge occult writing, from luminaries like Genesis Breyer P-Orridge of Psychic TV and Throbbing Gristle, Jhonn Balance of Coil, Beat lgends Ira Cohen and Brion Gysin, and many, many more. At over 400 pages, it's an indispensible addition to the library of any explorer of the outer edges of consciousness.

CLASSES AT ULTRACULTURE UNIVERSITY • www.magick.me

Visit Magick.me—Ultraculture's online education portal, and a radical experiment in democratizing and teaching consciousness alteration and spiritual techniques online—to take video courses on meditation, mysticism and consciousness expansion from Jason Louv. Join the growing community and get involved!

ULTRACULTURE.ORG

@jasonlouv

Made in the USA
Las Vegas, NV
27 July 2023

75324869R00203